Tales of Elijah
the Prophet

Tales of Elijah
the Prophet

Retold by
Peninnah Schram

Foreword by Dov Noy

JASON ARONSON INC.
Northvale, New Jersey
London

Permission to use the drawing of Elijah by Zuni Maud has been granted by Ben Kaplan.

Library of Congress Cataloging-in-Publication Data

Schram, Peninnah.
    Tales of Elijah the Prophet / retold by Peninnah Schram.
      p. cm.
    Includes bibliographical references (p.) and index.
    ISBN 0-87668-580-7
    1. Elijah (Biblical prophet)—Legends. 2. Legends, Jewish.
  3. Jewish folk literature. I. Title.
    BS580.E4S36 1991
    296.6′—dc20   90-24914

Manufactured in the United States of America. Jason Aronson Inc. offers books and cassettes. For information and catalog write to Jason Aronson Inc., 230 Livingston Street, Northvale, New Jersey 07647.

To the six people in my life
who opened successive doors to teach and to tell—
to record and to write—
in them are sparks of Elijah

Alan J. Schwartz
Abraham Tauber ז"ל
Dr. David Mirsky ז"ל
Nathan Kolodney
Richard Borgersen
Arthur Kurzweil

Contents

Foreword

eninnah Schram's newest book, *Tales of Elijah the Prophet,* concentrates on a single "hero," unlike her previous collection (*Jewish Stories One Generation Tells Another,* 1987), whose subject matter was universal. However, because of the specific and unique role played by Elijah in the folk tradition of every Jewish ethnic group, and because the main source of selected folktales—the Israel Folktale Archives (IFA) at Haifa University—universally acclaimed as the world's storehouse of Jewish narrative lore, the present sample is characteristic of Jewish folklore in the past and present.

The legends selected, each because of its literary and ethical values, as well as the editor's Introduction and her annotations,. are indeed praiseworthy. Peninnah Schram poses the most important question in the Jewish folklore connected with the acting character of Elijah the Prophet. This "puzzle," as the problem is called (and rightly so) in the Introduction is: Why is Elijah so revered a character in every age and in every land where Jews have lived? This question can be expanded to: Why has Elijah become a favorite hero who overshadows other biblical and postbiblical heroes in the Jewish folk-tradition, heroes who undoubtedly play a more important role in Jewish thought and tradition (such as Abraham our Father, Moses our Teacher, King David, and others, among them many folklore protagonists like King Solomon, Maimonides, and chasidic rabbis)?

The conventional answers to the above questions, suggested also in the Introduction, connect Elijah, the living folk hero, with his biblical predecessor, the Israelite prophet of the ninth century B.C.E. Although there is no doubt that many of the narrative motifs in the Elijah stories in 1 Kings and in our collection are identical or similar, the main features of Elijah among us, in our time and space, in disguise, appearing unexpectedly and solving problems, rescuing Jewish individuals and communities in danger, punishing and rewarding human deeds, stressing social justice, all these and many other features, cannot be explained by biblical parallels or roots.

The same holds true with customs prevailing in the life-cycle and yearly cycle of almost every Jewish ethnic group, during the circumcision ceremony, the end of Shabbat, the Seder night, and on many other occasions. A clear biblical connection is hardly possible. Let us take, for example, the circumcision chair. Why is it an Elijah chair and not an Abraham chair? Was not Abraham the first man circumcised in the Torah? Was he not the first circumciser? Elijah the Prophet can, of course, be connected with some logic to the rite of circumcision, but is this connection stronger than that of Abraham our Patriarch?

Many Elijah narratives go back to Jewish customs whose origins in the realm of folk-belief are obscure; the biblical connections, often proposed by the participants in the rite, the performers of the custom, and the narrators and their audiences, have no scientific basis. Until this very day, the "practical" kabbalists solve problems, both halakhic and real, by seeking an Elijah Revelation (*giluy Eliyahu*), mostly in a dream, following forty days of taboos, compulsions, or magic practices. Visiting holy sites bearing the name of Elijah and telling stories there (in addition to prayer) are part of that tradition. Can the Elijah caves and synagogues in Alexandria, Damascus, and many other places be connected to a biblical context, as often claimed by the narrators in their etiological legends? These Elijah sites play an important role in Jewish folk-religion and in Jewish folk-medicine. Many of the IFA

Elijah folktales were collected in the Mount Carmel Elijah cave, revered and used by Jews, Moslems, Christians, and Druze of Haifa and northern Israel.

Not one Elijah tale of the approximately 600 Elijah stories at the IFA is set in biblical time and space. Not one of them is an "expanded biblical legend" with King Ahab or Queen Jezebel, Elijah's contemporaries, as its protagonist, expanding on the confrontation with the priests of Baal on Mount Carmel or the incidents with the woman at Zarephat, or the ravens feeding beside the Charith brook. Nor do we have among the "living" stories narratives about Elijah as the herald of the future redemption or as the precursor of the Messiah, motifs so well known from rabbinic literature and written sources.

There is, however, an inherent structural connection between Elijah the Prophet legends and those relating to the thirty-six Hidden Saints (*Lamedvovniks*) who imitate the deeds of their prototype, although not explicitly. The Hidden Saints tradition is another late Judaic folk-tradition—although the roots and the formulistic number are old, the intensity of the *Lamedvov* legends is late—and the thirty-six Elijah samples selected by Peninnah Schram may be connected to the Hidden (and therefore unexpected and unpromising) Hero motif.

Some scholars, who admit that the present mainstream of Elijah traditions does not originate in the Bible, claim an early postbiblical origin and a connection with Enoch in order to explain it. There is, indeed, a structural similarity between Enoch and Elijah, and it is mentioned by the sixteenth-century Safed kabbalist Rabbi Moses Cordovero. Their main similarity is that they were the only two biblical heroes to be carried from earthly life in an extraordinary way. They can therefore be regarded as human symbols of immortality. In the early postbiblical, pseudoepigraphical literature, the only outstanding protagonist is, however, Enoch. And no wonder. His advantages over Elijah are many: his is the seventh, and therefore the holiest, generation of the human race; his span of life in years corresponds to the number of days in the solar year; his extraordinary termination of life on earth is clearly connected, twice, with God, with whom he "walked" and who "took him." None of these three merits is mentioned in the case of Elijah.

The biblical Enoch played an important role in early Jewish

legend. He became the significant protagonist in the various spiritual sectarian circles and movements during the last centuries of the Second Temple period. His figure was used more and more in gnostic and sectarian speculations, and the early Christians, elaborating on the immortality of their Messiah (born as a human being) regarded Enoch as the prototype of Jesus.

This penetration of the Enoch figure into the speculative apocalyptic identifications in non-Jewish sects probably aroused the opposition of the Jewish sages and of normative Judaism. However, Enoch was rooted too much in the early Jewish legends and in the literary tradition of many Jewish circles (for example, the apocalyptic, Ethionic, and Slavonic Book of Enoch, the Book of Jubilees, the Testament of the Twelve Patriarchs, and the Dead Sea Scrolls).

There were only two ways to eliminate Enoch from the Jewish tradition: by playing down his role or by replacing him. The first trend is evident in the talmudic-midrashic anti-Enoch statements, stemming from the later normative tradition (the earlier one is preserved in pro-Enoch sayings). Accordingly, the miraculous translation of Enoch is denied, and his early removal from earth is explained by God's concern with Enoch's urge to sin and his potential fall (Genesis *Rabbah* 25:1).

The trend to replace Enoch with a more suitable hero could take only a single direction: Elijah the Prophet, his structural companion. So, for example, an early pro-Enoch legend (preserved in a late midrash, *Pirkey de-Rabbi Eliezer* 7:40) relates the tale of Enoch's miraculous rod with which Moses later performed the miracles in Egypt. This origin of Moses' rod had vanished in the later aggadah, but an "Elijah-rod" is still used among Afghani Jews and other Jewish communities to ease the pangs of birth and to overcome dangers and threats in times of tension and distress. However, this Enoch-Elijah theory still does not explain the substantial discrepancy between the Elijah figure in talmudic-midrashic literature and the same figure in the contemporary oral-legend tradition.

Circulating mainly in the kabbalistic oral tradition, the following solution to our "puzzle" may be the closest to the truth. It assumes an independent origin, not related generically to earlier literary sources. It is based on the importance of Hebrew letters and on the Hebrew language, especially theophoric names. Both elements are most significant in normative Judaism, but they are dominant in the kabbalistic tradition.

The biblical Hebrew name of Elijah (Eliyahu—אליהו) consists of five letters (alef, lamed, yod, heh, vav), which are the five letters of the two names of God: El (alef, lamed) and YHVH (yod, heh twice, vav). As the two divine names stand for justice (*din*—El) and mercy (*rachamim*—YHVH) and for other abstract ideas confronting and opposing each other, their combination into a single entity symbolizes the whole world of ideas. Accordingly, the name of Elijah endows him with multifaceted, all-embracing, and multidimensional merits that unite confronting and seemingly opposed values: leniency and strictness, love and hatred, zealotry and tolerance, and so on.

There are, of course, many Hebrew theophoric names in biblical and later usage, but most of them have only one of the two divine names as their component (for example, Joshua and Uziahu are derived from YHVH and Yetrahmeel and Eliakim from El). Elijah's name is exceptional and unique, containing two theophoric components—the two divine names. There is no other name of this kind in the Jewish tradition, and according to the belief of nomen-nomen (in Hebrew, כשמו כן הוא), the bearer of the name is like the name itself.

The literal translation of Elijah's name is "My God is YHVH," which gives the name a personal and religious character. This character is the common denominator in most of the Elijah legends. The prophet, who is very seldom a seer or fortune-teller in the literal sense and usage of the term, always acts by himself. He does not invoke divine help, he does not pray, and he behaves in a strange, unique, individual way. On the other hand, most of the stories belong in the realm of religious folktale, according to the universal classification system of the A. Aarne and S. Thompson *Type-Index* (Types 750–849). The same holds true with the motif-classification, according to Stith Thompson's universal *Motif-Index*. Most of the motifs belong to Chapter P there: Rewards and Punishment, the main motifs in the present collection.

I know that this collection of pearls will be widely read by young and old, Jews and non-Jews, scholars and laymen, students and performers. Since pearls are enhanced by becoming part of a necklace, so too should these stories be adapted for plays and expanded in prose and poetry. This wider public will not only enjoy the tales but will also benefit from the annotations to the individual tales. Here they can glimpse the scholarship connected with folk-narrative research within the framework of folkloristics.

Dov Noy
H. Grunwald Chair of Folklore
Director of the Folklore Research Center
Hebrew University, Jerusalem

Preface and
Acknowledgments

earching for stories of Elijah the Prophet is both a pleasure and an adventure, and it is as intriguing as the character of Elijah himself in all his various disguises. And although Elijah is so intricately connected with Passover, I found that there were hundreds of stories about him that were not necessarily concerned with themes for Passover alone. How to choose the stories for this collection? I used the same criterion as for my last book of stories, namely, I chose the stories I love best. These are the stories I need to listen to and retell so as to keep learning the wisdom they offer. And so by reading and retelling these stories, we open the door to Elijah and continue to draw from the well of wisdom from the ages.

I chose to retell thirty-six stories, using the Jewish symbolic number of twice eighteen, *chai,* which is the equivalent in Hebrew to "life." However, I added another story, my first remembered story—an Elijah story—at the end of the Introduction. And there I explain why this became such an important story in my life and why I am fascinated with Elijah as a folk hero.

Of course, I included in this collection stories that deal with Passover. Those five stories (17 to 21) are grouped together, but only by the character and reference to the holiday. As you will discover, these thirty-six stories (actually thirty-seven) vary greatly as to mood, characters, plots, locales, time, themes, and so on. There are stories that are fantastic, realistic, and humorous, some filled with riddles and questions, one with a lullaby. All teach lessons of behavior, especially hospitality and *tzedakah,* or other Jewish values and customs.

I begin this volume with a story from my book *Jewish Stories One Generation Tells Another,* as a connection to that book. While there are thirteen Elijah stories to be found there, I repeated only three in this book (plus the one in the Introduction). Why these stories? Because they are such strong, important folk stories that I tell them more frequently than many others. I felt that they needed to be included so that this Elijah collection would be more complete, if that is possible, in painting the portrait of Elijah and his role in Jewish life and tradition throughout the ages.

For this book, which I carried as a dream for years, to become a reality, I must acknowledge and thank several people. First of all, I thank my friend and editor, Arthur Kurzweil, vice president of Jason Aronson Inc., for his continuing extraordinary enthusiasm and encouragement for my writing these stories, editorial director Muriel Jorgensen, production editor Gloria Jordan, and copy editor William Drennan. Thanks also to Beatrice Silverman Weinreich, folklorist at YIVO Institute for Jewish Research, for her permission to use several stories from her unpublished master's thesis; to Chana Mlotek, music archivist of the YIVO Institute for Jewish Research and co-editor of a bi-weekly column on Yiddish poetry and song in the *Jewish Forward,* for adapting a melody for the lullaby; and Roslyn Bresnick-Perry for the English translation of the lullaby. I acknowledge with appreciation the always gracious help of the staff at Yeshiva University's Stern College Hedi Steinberg Library, especially Edith Lubetski, director; Sara Leah Gross; Rabbi Daniel Greenwald; and Rabbi Tzvi Flaum, Professor of Jewish Studies at Stern College, who answered many questions and found books and sources that I needed, always with patience and a smile. A heartfelt thanks to Professor Dov Noy of Hebrew University and founder of the Israel Folktale Archives, and Israel Folktale Archives coordinator Edna Cheichel, for their cooperation in helping me find the Elijah stories I was seeking and in answering many questions.

As always, I appreciate the encouragement and confidence my husband, Jerry Thaler, gives me when he listens to my stories. I am grateful for everyone's good counsel! In addition, there is a special thanks and gratitude I want to acknowledge—to the young woman who did a masterful job of translating from Hebrew to English the majority of these stories, Rebecca Schram Zafrany, my daughter. As a result of listening to and transcribing her translations I feel that her voice, along with mine, has become interwoven in the fabric of those stories. In a way, she is my co-reteller. This has given me great pleasure and joy.

Introduction

y earliest remembered story is an Elijah the Prophet tale that my father used to tell me when I was a young child, one I requested over and over as I sat on his lap in his oversized, cushioned, living-room chair. And each time he would say, "And Elijah whistled . . . ," a wish was granted in the story. That was a magical phrase that I continued to recall, even when the actual story receded from my active memory.

Only after years as a storyteller, a transmitter of the Jewish oral tradition, did I begin to see a recurrent character and theme in the stories I chose to tell and record. Very clearly I was telling a significant number of Elijah tales, more than of any other character, and tales dealing with the themes of hospitality *(hakhnosas orchim)*, of offering help to those in need, of families being reunited, and so on. Why? I asked myself.

In searching for the answer, I realized in a powerful and personal way the importance of metaphors and images, of stories and the storytellers in our lives. I discovered that my love for Elijah the Prophet and those themes that are most often found in his stories stem from that first recollected story. Furthermore, I understood that I needed to tell those stories, a form of my legacy, in order to continue learning the wisdom in those stories.

Apparently I am not alone. Elijah the Prophet, Eliyahu Hanavi, is not only the most beloved character in all of Jewish folklore, but also the most popular. He appears significantly more often in folktales than does any other character, far more even than Maimonides, King Solomon, King David, Shalom Shabazi, and Moses. Passover, then, cannot be the only or even the main time for telling stories of Elijah. Although most of us may associate Elijah primarily with this holiday, because of the participatory rituals of opening the door for Elijah and setting his cup of wine on the seder table, Elijah stories are told year round, throughout the world, by both Ashkenazi and Oriental-Sephardi Jews, under various circumstances and occasions.

Before turning to the types and themes of Elijah tales, Elijah himself must be introduced. Elijah the Tishbite was a prophet in the Kingdom of Israel in the ninth century (about 920–850 B.C.E.), during the reigns of Ahab and Ahaziah. His name, Eli-Jahu, literally means "YHWH is God." (Through these four Hebrew letters, YHWH, the Divine Name of God is never pronounced as written. The Divine Name is spoken of as the *tetragrammaton,* a Greek word that means "the name of four letters." *Elohim* is the more general Divine Name, which denotes God as the Creator and Moral Governor of the Universe.) Elijah's origins are clouded in mystery since there is no mention in the Bible of his father's name or his tribe. "His belonging to the tribe of Gad, the son of Leah [the Matriarch], is substantiated in the Aggadah historically and geographically by the fact that Gilead, the place where he originally lived, was situated in the district of the tribe of Gad. At the same time, the word *Gad* is interpreted as 'luck' in the world and also as 'destroyer' of the peoples oppressing the Israelites at the time of the redemption" (Wiener 1978). However, there are other interpretations that identify Elijah as a son of Rachel [the Matriarch] and thus belonging to the tribe of Benjamin. According to others he was a Levite. Elijah never married; there is no reference to his family in the Bible. His teacher is identified as Ahijah the Shilonite.

The role of a prophet is to listen to the voice of God and transmit God's message to the people. As a prophet, Elijah was a fiery, zealous preacher who fought against cults and alien religious influences—and against social injustice.

Well known by the way he walked and his manner of dress, King Ahaziah's envoys described Elijah as "a hairy man, and girt with a girdle of leather about his loins" (2 Kings 1:8). Elijah also wore a mantle, a cloak, that had supernatural powers. As he rose to heaven, he dropped the mantle, and, with its help, his disciple Elisha performed miracles, too (2 Kings 2:8,13).

Elijah the Prophet plays three main roles in Jewish life. On Shabbat HaGadol, the Great Sabbath, which comes just before Passover, the last verse of the special Haftarah section read in synagogue is, "Behold, I will send you Elijah the Prophet before the coming of the great and terrible day of the Lord" (Malachi 3:24). This passage highlights Elijah's dominant role as the one who will usher in the messianic era—he is the forerunner of the *Messiah*.

A second role is that of arbiter of Jewish law. There are several examples in the Talmud of legal disputes concerning, for example, money distribution. Whenever a just decision could not be determined, the rabbis agreed to put the entire sum into escrow until the coming of Elijah. Indeed, whenever there is a debate in the Talmud that remains unresolved, there you will find the word *taiku*. In his commentary at the end of Tractate *Eduyot* (8:7), Tosefot Yom Tov suggests that *taiku* is an acronym that means "Tishbi [Elijah] will resolve all of our questions and difficulties."

A third role that Elijah plays is that of mediator between parents and children. The Book of Malachi (3:24) describes Elijah as the one who will "turn the heart of fathers to the children, and the heart of children to their fathers." As the one who will reconcile families, the one who will settle legal arguments, and especially the one who will announce the imminent arrival of peace and harmony in the world, we all continue to search and hope for Elijah the Prophet to appear soon in our day.

How Elijah became so popular is often a bit of a puzzle for those who know the Elijah of the Bible. How was the stern biblical prophet transformed into a kindly folklore hero? Playing an important role in the Bible, in Aggadah, in mysticism, and in Chasidism, why is Elijah so revered in all the Jewish sources, in every age and in every land where Jews have lived? (See Foreword.)

In Jewish folklore, Elijah is quite different from the biblical character. He excels in his domain, the domain of miracles. Already a legendary figure in biblical and talmudic times because the Amoraim and Tannaim created and retold Elijah stories, Elijah appears and rescues the Jewish community and especially worthy individuals. He helps those in need, especially the poor and pious. He brings hope and reconciliation. He tests and heals. He sees who is unselfish, who offers hospitality, who gives charity, who learns humility, who deserves help. His chameleonlike disguises are marvelously clever and numerous: an old man, a poor man, a beggar, a student, a traveler, a doctor, an Arab, a robber, a drunkard, a matchmaker, a magician, a dwarf, a farmer, a merchant, a slave, a handsome horseman—always so as to heighten suspense and fantasy, to test people's behavior, to restore faith, and to bring about a happy resolution. Elijah remains as one of the people, in touch with their problems and needs; in other words, a true leader and inspiration. He is indeed a master of miracles.

Elijah, like Solomon, can understand the language of animals. He learns valuable information from them. After all, while a person may hide information from his business or marriage partner, animals see and hear all.

Most of all, Elijah cannot bear to see injustice and wants to set things right, often through his miracles. Elijah's miracles make him a sort of *deus ex machina* (as in Greek drama), always bringing about a happy ending.

Perhaps the main reason Elijah remains the most ubiquitous hero of all is because according to the Bible, he never died. His departure from the earth was both miraculous and marvelous. The Bible describes it this way: "And it came to pass, as they [Elijah and Elisha his disciple] still went on, and talked, that, behold, *there appeared* a chariot of fire, and horses of fire, and parted them both asunder; and Elijah went up by a whirlwind into heaven" (2 Kings 2:11).

Although Elijah could retain his earthly shape as a man of many disguises (and even once as a harlot), his spirit wanders everywhere and we feel his presence at the *brit,* at the seder, and at private moments when a mysterious stranger appears, often saving someone from trouble or performing other miracles. His name also appears on amulets. And so Elijah remains alive for us in a way that no other biblical figure does, from generation to generation. And we, in turn, tell his stories from generation to generation, keeping him alive in us. Elijah stories continue to give us that hope and optimism for justice and peace and harmony in our world.

Sometimes Elijah appears and then vanishes without revealing his true identity, although the main character in a story usually realizes who he is after the miracle occurs. Other times, Elijah introduces himself without having a disguised appearance. But when he does appear in the guise of an ordinary person, or as Elijah himself in his earthly form, and then reveals who he really is, it is an experience of *giluy Eliyahu,* which means "Elijah revealing himself" or "Elijah's revelation." Almost all such mystical experiences related to an encounter with Elijah are generally called *giluy Eliyahu.* From the time of the teachers of Talmud and especially from medieval times, this term enters the discussion regarding Elijah's influence and inspiration. This mystical experience manifests itself through a dialogue with Elijah, often in a dream. Elijah appears and teaches the secrets of the Torah, *sitrei Torah,* or reveals solutions to a difficult problem. In this way, Elijah is the divine guide who inspires understanding and enlightenment by allowing the deserving person to experience *giluy Eliyah.* See, for example, "The Emissary of Elijah the Prophet," "Elijah's Partnership," and "The Modest Scholar." (For further discussion on *giluy Eliyahu,* see Wiener [1978].)

There is a great deal of mystery concerning Elijah as a person, for even the names of his parents are not mentioned in the Bible. Some attribute Elijah's miraculous deeds as well as his live ascent into Heaven to the fact that he had been an angel even before his "earthly career."

> When God was about to create man, Elijah said to Him: "Master of the world! If it be pleasing in Thine eyes, I will descend to earth, and make myself serviceable to the sons of men." Then God changed his angel name, and later, under Ahab, He permitted him to abide among men on earth, that he might convert the world to the belief that "the Lord is God." His mission fulfilled, God took him again into heaven, and said to him: "Be thou the guardian spirit of My children forever, and spread the belief in Me abroad in the whole world." [Ginzberg, vol. 4, pp. 201–202]

As a legendary figure in folktales, Elijah's appearances and disappearances create a continual mystery and fascination for the storyteller/listener. Elijah sometimes appears in a dream; he often studies with a poor student in the woods or during the night—there is always mystery. In some of these stories, appearance and reality are sometimes transposed, adding another dimension of mystery. Through this deceptive guise, Elijah teaches that we cannot, and indeed must not, judge from external appearances. Two of the most striking examples of this lesson are in "Elijah's Mysterious Ways" and "Beroka and Elijah the Prophet."

Elijah stories are found in the Bible, in both the Babylonian and Jerusalem Talmuds, in medieval, kabbalistic, and Chasidic collections, in Yiddish chapbook literature, and generally in the folklore of the Jewish people. As do all folktales, these, too, contain the collective spirit and composite portrait of the Jewish people. In these stories, Elijah is the hero who serves as intermediary between heaven and earth, helper, teacher, guide, miracle maker. Elijah is rarely the sole hero in the story, but rather aids the protagonist to reach his or her goals.

In talmudic–midrashic literature, Elijah is usually referred to by his name alone. However, in folklore he is almost always called Elijah the Prophet. Often the words "may he be remembered for good" or "whom it is always good to mention" or "of blessed memory" are added to his name as a form of eulogy and blessing. As a folklore hero and angel, Elijah can traverse the world with four strokes of his wings (*Berakhot* 4b). As a result, he can be anywhere in the world very quickly indeed. This is very comforting to know.

In the Bible and Talmud, Elijah deals with individuals who are identified by name, such as Rabbi Joshua ben Levi, Akiva, and Rachel. In folktales, the characters are usually anonymous—everyman and everywoman.

We are all familiar with Elijah visiting every house during the seder when we open the door to welcome him with the traditional *Barukh haba, rebbe* ("Blessed be he that comes, my teacher"). But since Elijah can be everywhere and anywhere, why do we need to open the door and call out a welcome? Why can't he just come in on his own, through the window or keyhole? The rabbis say that we must also do some work on our own to bring redemption. We must welcome Elijah in as a sign that we are willing to help bring the Messiah. And is there a child who has not carefully watched Elijah's cup to see if the level of the wine has not gone down, even a drop, as a sign that Elijah has been there and has taken a sip?

Although not visible to human eyes, Elijah is present at every *brit*. This was Elijah's reward from God for his defense of the observance of Abraham's covenant during the days of persecution of the pious by the wicked Jezebel. Thus, during the *brit* there is the chair of Elijah as a reminder of Elijah the godfather and protector of children, a custom observed by Jews for over 2,000 years. When a baby is about to undergo circumcision, there is the customary greeting *Barukh haba,* which is also extended to the welcome guest Elijah.

Moreover, Elijah is also present at births, weddings, and other life events, all of the especially vulnerable times when the demons and the Angel of Death threaten life itself. Elijah serves as the adviser of how people should behave to ward off the evil spirits or to conceive a child, as in the tales, ''The Bride's Wisdom'' and ''A Blessing in Disguise.''

Most of the Elijah stories are religious tales with an intended message or moral that needs to be learned and integrated into one's life. These tales often have as their main purpose the teaching of values and faith in God; they embody a *musar haskl,* an ethical lesson. However, these tales go beyond mere moralizing. As a matter of fact, many motifs that can also be found in secular folktales are blended into these pious tales. These narratives serve to entertain and inspire. They not only bring hope, but also give people a perspective of ''This, too, shall pass.'' The tales allow people to express their wishes and prayers through words, no doubt to be able to bear the persecutions better or relieve tensions from blood libel accusations; to help endure poverty or whatever other problems and crises are encountered in life, times when people need a good, compassionate angel.

The best way to understand what has already been discussed about Elijah and his roles in Jewish life is to tell a story. ''When Will the Messiah Come?'' is a folk legend written in Aramaic, the language of the people. The source is *Sanhedrin* 98a. An extremely popular tale in the folk imagination, it was told by Jews everywhere from generation to generation to illustrate the people's longing and yearning for redemption, and to affirm that just as we wait for the Messiah, so too he waits for us. It is a reciprocal partnership between the Jewish people and God in bringing about the Days of the Messiah.

* * *

When Will the Messiah Come?

Rabbi Joshua ben Levi met Elijah the Prophet, his teacher and friend, standing near the entrance of the cave of Rabbi Shimon ben Yohai. They greeted each other and Rabbi Joshua asked, "When will the Messiah really come?"

Elijah replied, "Why not go and ask him yourself."

"And where can I find him to ask him?" asked Rabbi Joshua.

"He is sitting near the entrance of the town." Elijah answered.

"And how will I recognize him?" asked Rabbi Joshua.

And Elijah answered this way: "The Messiah sits among the poor people and the beggars who are suffering from various diseases and illnesses. Everyone of them takes off and then ties up all their wounds at the same time. The Messiah, on the other hand, takes off the bandages one by one, wipes the wound and then ties it up with bandages before he goes on to the next. He does not treat all the sores at one time because the Messiah says, 'If I will be asked to bring redemption, in this way I will not be delayed.' "

Rabbi Joshua arrived at the gate and found such a man tending his wounds. He approached and said, "*Shalom Aleikha,* my rabbi and my teacher."

The Messiah answered, "*Shalom aleikha,* ben Levi."

"And when will you come?" asked Rabbi Joshua.

"Tell the people I will arrive *today,*" replied the Messiah.

When Rabbi Joshua returned to Elijah, Elijah asked, "What did the Messiah say to you?"

"He greeted me with '*Shalom aleikha,* ben Levi,' " Rabbi Joshua answered.

"By this welcome and blessing he has promised that you and your father will have a place in the World-to-Come because he called you by your name and by the name of your father at the time he blessed you with *shalom.*"

"But the Messiah lied when he said, 'I will come *today.*' He has not come," protested Rabbi Joshua.

Elijah answered, "Thus he said to you, '*Today, if you hear his voice,*' He too is waiting to be called."

* * *

As a supernatural figure, Elijah has also been credited with creating the mystical teachings of kabbalah. He revealed mysteries and secrets of the Torah to Rabbi Shimon ben Yohai and his son Rabbi Eliezer, and then, 1,000 years later, to the Nazarite Rabbi Jacob, then to his disciple Abraham ben David. He instructed them, and others, in the secret lore taught in the heavenly academy. Elijah was able to reveal the birth of Rabbi Isaac Luria, the great kabbalist, as well as the birth of Rabbi Israel Baal Shem Tov, the founder of the chasidic movement, to the fathers of these great leaders. (See Endnote to story, "The Jewels of *Mitzvah*," regarding Elijah's revelation of the birth of Rashi.)

Elijah stories have had an influence on Christian and Muslim lore, where one can also find stories with such a hero/saint. The Arabs identified Elijah with Khadir. According to folklorist Beatrice Silverman Weinreich, there are at least three Elijah tales in *The Arabian Nights* (Weinreich 1957), (where, in addition, there are many rabbinical stories, perhaps 200). Here Elijah becomes an "angel," or *gadi* (judge), or an unnamed "messenger of God." In Christian stories, Elijah sometimes becomes changed into St. Peter, St. Nicholas, Jesus, or an angel.

Since Jewish stories often were heard by non-Jewish merchants or customers at inns or coffeehouses, many of these orally told stories became transformed into Christian or Arabic tales. The story "A Beggar's Blessing," from the Midrash, has been collected as a German Jewish story. But it is a tale that became a popular and universal favorite in many nations across Europe. This same fluid folklore process took place in reverse as well. In addition to Hebrew and Jewish dialects (Yiddish, Ladino, Judeo–Arabic, etc.), Jews knew the languages of the marketplace and of other countries, wherever they traveled. They heard other people's tales and changed them into "Jewish" versions. This borrowing, with the attendant changing of characters, settings, and other details while retaining the theme and lesson (if they were consistent with Jewish values) is a process that is part of our oral tradition. It often gives rise to the variants and parallel versions that folklorists trace and classify, as well as to simultaneous versions of certain themes that are told in the far corners of the world. In exploring the subject of cross-cultural influence in her monograph on Yiddish folktales about the Prophet Elijah, Weinreich points out that "the Jewish factor in the origin and development of Christian saint legends . . . along with the influences of Slavic and Teutonic pagan mythology and of Buddhistic literature, may well have been underestimated" (Weinreich 1965, p. 231).

Classifying the folktales in which Elijah appears is a complex task, as there are so many of them scattered around the world. From a study of the first 1,000 folktales collected in the Israel Folktale Archives (IFA), folklorist Dov Noy found that 36 contained Elijah as a character, the most of any of the 94 Jewish historical or legendary heroes appearing in the stories. Of more than 17,000 stories in the IFA today, there are 575 Elijah tales. In her important study, Weinreich analyzed and classified sixty-one Elijah tales according to tale type and other criteria. She found that some of the tales are short and one-episode simple tales, whereas many others are long and contain several interweaving themes that combine the pious tale with the secular fairytale. There are also some tales that use the frame structure of the Arabic tale, incorporating a story within a story, such as "The Wine of Paradise," "The Jewels of Mitzvah," and "A Tale Retold at a Feast."

Elijah is part of our days, every day. In addition to the Passover seder and the *brit,* Elijah is remembered at the end of the three daily prayer services so as to keep alive his memory as a herald of the Messiah. After each meal, at the end of the grace *(birkat hamazon),* this prayer is said: "May the Merciful One send us Elijah the Prophet—remembered for good—that he may bring us good tidings, salvation, and consolation." At the end of Shabbat, after Havdalah, the song "Eliyahu HaNavi" is sung as a way to segue from the sacred Shabbat into the secular time of the week. After Havdalah, telling Elijah stories is considered to be a harbinger of good luck, a *segulah.* At the end of the Shabbat, it is said, Elijah sits under the Tree of Life recording the rewards for those who celebrate the Shabbat. Furthermore, there are numerous songs in our Jewish tradition about Elijah the Prophet and proverbs as well.

The songs can be found in music anthologies and recordings.

One proverbial saying is: "The Prophet Elijah's blessing is in this." May his blessing find its way into this book!

* * *

Elijah and the Three Wishes

When Elijah the Prophet wanted to see how the people were behaving in a certain town, he would disguise himself as a beggar and walk around its streets. He would observe how the people were acting toward one another in the shops, in the parks, in the marketplace, in the synagogue. As he walked, he would blink his eyes, nod his head, shrug his shoulders, stroke his long white beard, or tap his walking stick as though he were recording what he saw, adding that message to the already bulging sack he carried over his shoulder. He often smiled to himself, too, while humming a melody as he walked from place to place.

One day, he noticed a small cottage. "This place needs a great many repairs," he observed. "A new roof, better window shutters, a gate. Yet here are some beautiful flowers growing in the tiny front yard. Hollyhocks, poppies, a mandrake plant. I like that!" Weary from traveling, and hungry, too, Elijah decided to stop at this house to rest a while. He knocked on the door.

In this cottage there lived a poor man and his wife. The man came to the door. When Elijah asked him for some water to drink, the man invited him in. Seeing how hungry and tired this traveler was, the couple asked him to stay and share their meal.

"Come and eat with us," said the good wife. "Eating with a guest makes the meal feel like a banquet, even though we cannot offer you more than the little we have."

"Come," said her husband. "We will gladly share whatever we have." The couple offered him what they had prepared for their dinner. There was a small piece of herring and a thick slice of black bread, and some water to drink. The meal was hardly enough even for the two of them.

When the stranger had eaten and was refreshed, he turned to the couple and said, "Because of your kindness to me, I will grant you any three wishes."

At first not believing what he had heard, the poor man just stood there quietly. Then he began to think, "Let me test him to see if what this bedraggled traveler says is true. There is some mystery about him. Maybe God has answered our prayers to help us out of our hard times."

After a few minutes, the poor man replied, "This house needs so much repair and it is so tiny that I don't have room enough for my books. I would like to have a large house, like a palace.''

Elijah whistled, and instantly a mansion appeared where the cottage had stood.

At that moment, the woman, looking down at her clothes and quickly taking off her old apron, exclaimed, "Oh, we should have beautiful clothes, with shining, glittering jewels," gesturing wildly as she pointed to her hair, ears, neck, and wrists. "We look so plain in this wonderful house," she explained.

Again Elijah whistled, and the couple was instantly dressed in clothes of velvet and satin, with magnificent diamond, pearl, and emerald jewelry covering the wife's head, ears, neck, and wrists.

"Gold!" they both shouted together with great excitement for their third wish.

Elijah whistled for the third time, and sacks of gold appeared. A moment later, Elijah disappeared.

Several years went by, and Elijah wanted to see how the good couple had fared. When Elijah appeared at the gate of their mansion, again disguised as a beggar, he looked around first. He saw heavy shutters on the windows and high fences around the house. While there was a great deal of land around the house, nowhere were there any flowers. As he stood looking through the gate, the servants, seeing this stranger through the watchman's door near the gate of the yard, would not let him stand there.

"I would like to see the master of the house," demanded Elijah. The servants laughed and brought the dogs closer to the gate, signaling the beggar to leave. The master of the house himself came to the door to see what the commotion was. Since he did not recognize the beggar, he shouted orders for the beggar to leave or be chased away.

Disappointed and saddened by what he had seen, Elijah whistled once and the gold disappeared.

He gave another whistle, and the beautiful clothes and jewels vanished.

Then Elijah gave a third whistle, and the mansion instantly turned back into the small cottage that had once before stood in that place.

In the same moment, the couple realized how selfish they had become. They understood then how poor they had been, even when they had all the riches in the world.

1

Elijah's Mysterious Ways

n a certain town, there lived a God-fearing and good man, Reb Shmuel ben Yosef. He trusted God and accepted whatever happened to him and to his family—most of the time. Sometimes, though, he was puzzled by the things that happened to his people.

"Why should such a good woman as our neighbor Sarah is— why should she suffer the death of her only child, while others who do not practice *tzedakah* or fulfill *mitzvot*—why do they enjoy large families?" he would ask of God, not to speak ill of people, Heaven forbid, but only out of a sense of confusion.

Once, he saw a wealthy family become poor. "How cruel that this family will be without all the things they are accustomed to," he thought. "Why did God do this?"

Other things troubled Reb Shmuel as well. Day after day, as he looked around, he would ask again and again, "Why?" and "How?" And he began to ask more and more often.

"*Ribono shel Olam*, Creator of the Universe," he would call out, "help me understand your ways. I know your miracles are every-where. But I am beginning to see only the despair, and I am perplexed by what I see. If only I could meet Elijah the Prophet.

3

Maybe then I could begin to understand and see once again your daily miracles.''

Reb Shmuel fasted and prayed that he might see Elijah.

One day, as he was walking in an open field, a stranger approached him and said, "I am Elijah. What would you ask of me?''

Reb Shmuel answered, "I need to see the wonders that you perform in the world, for my world is dark, and I do not understand much of what goes on around me.''

And Elijah said, "When you see what I do, you will certainly not understand my actions. Then I will have to explain them to you, which will take time. . . .''

"No, no, I promise I will not take up your time or ask you to trouble yourself with me,'' Reb Shmuel assured him. "I will just come along with you to observe—to witness your miracles. That is all.''

"Very well,'' said Elijah, "but remember—if you ask for any explanations, I shall leave at once.''

Reb Shmuel had no choice but to agree to this condition.

He began to walk with Elijah until they came to a small cottage where there lived a poor man and his wife. The couple had very little and owned only one cow, but they received the strangers with a warm welcome. Placing whatever food they had on the table, they invited the two men to sit and eat. All evening, they discussed some points of law, and the hosts were delighted to have such learned men in their home.

In the morning, as they were about to leave, Elijah gave a signal and the cow, this couple's *only* cow, suddenly died.

As Reb Shmuel and Elijah continued on their way, Reb Shmuel muttered to himself in anger, "This is some repayment for kindness! That these kind people, who welcomed us so graciously to their home, should be so repaid!'' Unable to hold back his deepening confusion, he turned to Elijah and pleaded, "Why? *Why* did you cause their cow to die?''

Elijah kept walking as he replied, "Have you forgotten what I asked of you? You must not ask for an explanation no matter what I do—or else I will leave.''

Reb Shmuel wanted to argue and ask, "But where are your miracles that save lives or help the poor?'' Instead, he said nothing more and continued to walk behind Elijah.

That evening, they came to the mansion of a wealthy man. They knocked on the door. The master of the house sent his servant to bring the two men to the place where the servants slept. But since they were offered no food, not even a piece of bread, they went to bed hungry. In the morning, as they were leaving, Elijah noticed a tree near the house that had been uprooted by a storm. Elijah passed by the tree, nodded, and the tree was returned to its former position, with its roots deeper in the ground than before.

When Reb Shmuel saw this, he was even more puzzled. He thought, "To restore his tree! Why should a stingy man receive such a reward from Elijah?" But he said nothing to Elijah. He hoped he would understand in some way, perhaps by some sign or word from Elijah.

All day long they walked, until they came to a synagogue in another town. When they entered, they found that the seats were made of gold and silver. The people sat in their seats, but no one rushed to welcome them or to give either one his seat, and not even one person invited them to his home for dinner, as was customary when strangers came to a town. "Such men can get along well enough with bread and water. There is no need to invite them to our homes," said one of the members of the synagogue to the others around him.

Since no one asked them home for dinner, Elijah and Reb Shmuel remained in the synagogue all night, sleeping on the hard benches in the back. The next morning, as Elijah stood by the door, he said to all the people, "May God make you *all* leaders."

Again Reb Shmuel did not know what to make of all this.

The next evening, they stopped at a small community where everyone was extremely poor. But the people welcomed the two travelers and asked them to stay with them. Everyone began to bring food to the synagogue, and soon there was a wonderful feast with plenty of wine and food. When they left in the morning, Elijah said to the people, "May God bless you with only *one* leader."

Reb Shmuel waited until they were on the road, and then he turned to Elijah and cried out, "No more! No more! I cannot continue to see such injustices done. Forgive me, but even though I know you will leave me, *please tell me* what you have been doing. I do not understand any of this. It appears to me that you are doing the opposite of what the people deserve." And Reb Shmuel wept.

Elijah replied, "My friend, listen carefully. Do you remember the poor couple whose cow died? The wife was destined to die that very day, so I pleaded with God to accept the cow's death in place of the woman's.

"When we were at the home of the greedy rich man, I straightened the tree that had fallen over. Had I not done that, the man would have found the hidden treasure that lies in the ground under the tree's roots.

"When I wished the wealthy but selfish people in the synagogue to have many leaders, that may have sounded like a good thing. But it was a curse, because any group that has too many leaders cannot agree on anything and can never make any decisions.

"Therefore, when I wished for the poor but hospitable community to have only one leader, that was a blessing, for it is said, 'It is better to have one wise man rule a city than a group of fools.' "

Before Elijah departed, he said to Reb Shmuel, "I want to give you some advice that will be useful to you, my friend. Whenever you see a wicked person who is prospering, keep in mind that his wickedness will ultimately work against him. And if you see a righteous person enduring hardships, remember that that person is being saved from something worse. Do not doubt these things any longer. One cannot always understand God's ways."

Elijah departed. And Reb Shmuel returned to his home, seeing once again the wonders and miracles in the world.

And so may we all.

2

The Life-giving Flower

Once, a long time ago in a small town, there was a great rabbi whom everyone respected and loved. He had a special gift, a blessing in his hand, when he wrote an amulet or talisman for any woman who couldn't have a child. When he gave that amulet to a woman, she would become pregnant and give birth. But he himself did not have any children. His wife would plead, "Write the amulet for me, too, the way you do for the other women."

"No, we will have a child if God wills it. Only He can give us a child."

And the woman wept.

One day she was walking in the woods when she came to a well. She sat down next to the well and started to weep and weep and weep. All of a sudden, someone came out of the well. It was Elijah the Prophet. And he said to the rabbi's wife, "Good woman, why are you crying?"

"Leave me alone, please. I have my own problems," she answered.

"Tell me your troubles, and I will perhaps be able to help you," he said gently.

"If God hasn't helped me yet, how can you help me?" she answered.

"Well, why not tell me anyway?" he persisted.

"I will. You see, my husband is a great rabbi. He writes amulets for all the women who don't have children, and they have children right away. But my husband won't write an amulet for me." And she began to cry once more.

"Is that all? Why, listen. Go to your husband and ask him to make a choice of whether he wants a son or a daughter. If he wants a son, an eagle will come when the boy is 13 years old and take him away. If he wants a daughter, she will die on her wedding night. Return to tell me what he has decided."

The woman returned home and approached her husband and told him what the old man had related to her in the woods. After some time, he said to her, "It's a pity that a daughter we raise should die. We would also suffer, along with her husband. So therefore choose only a son. No matter what punishment will come to him, it will pass."

The woman went back to the well in the woods and waited.

Suddenly Elijah the Prophet came from the well and asked, "Good woman, what did your husband choose?"

"He chooses a son," she answered.

"God will give you a son. Return home and very soon you will be expecting a child."

The woman went home and told the husband what the old man said. Then she went to the *mikveh,* immersed herself, and purified herself. All was in order. After two days, the woman became pregnant. Everyone in the town was very happy for the good couple, and they waited for the birth.

When the rabbi's wife gave birth to a son, there was a great celebration. Everybody in the town was happy, especially the rabbi. The child grew up healthy. The parents kept the child always in the house or near them, to protect him. The father taught him Torah at home. The child studied Torah and he was a *talmud chakham,* like his father.

Soon the boy reached the age of *bar mitzvah,* 13 years old.

One day, there was a fierce argument outside. The servant woman went up to the roof to see what the commotion was. The boy went with her as he, too, was curious to know what was happening. But the servant was not paying attention to the boy, and when she went back to the house, he remained on the roof.

Suddenly a huge eagle swooped down to the roof and picked the boy up. The eagle flew until it came to the palace of the king of Spain. There, the eagle dropped the boy into the flower garden of the palace. In the very spot where he fell, there suddenly grew a flower, a magnificent flower, unlike any that grew anywhere in the world.

A servant of the princess witnessed all this, and she ran to the princess to tell her what she had seen. "My princess, my princess, put your hands on me and have pity on me, for what I tell you is the truth."

"What has happened?" asked the princess kindly.

"Somebody fell into your garden, dropped there by an eagle!" cried the servant girl. "Believe me, I am not lying. Come and see."

The princess went out to the garden.

When she saw the boy, she asked, "Where are you from? From above the earth or under the earth?"

"From above the earth," the boy replied.

"Good! Then come." And the king's daughter brought the boy into the house.

"Wait! Wait!" shouted the boy. He quickly ran back to the garden, picked the unusual flower, and put it into his pocket.

That night, at the dinner in the palace, the princess offered him some food and drink. But whatever she offered him, he refused. "No, thank you. I don't want anything."

The king looked closely at the boy, and said to the princess, "I believe this boy may be a Jew and therefore he will not eat our food." The king had taken a liking to the boy, so he brought a Jewish woman to the palace to cook his meals. He even ordered a new set of dishes for the boy and gave him his own room. "Please come live with us," the king said to him. And the boy accepted this invitation.

In the evenings, the angels visited the boy in his room and taught him more and more Torah.

Early one morning, the servant girl woke up to begin her work. She woke up earlier than usual, and as she walked by the boy's room, she saw that the door was closed, but she heard voices from inside.

She ran to the princess and woke her. "Come quickly. The boy is not alone in his room. I have heard a lot of voices coming from there."

The two of them approached the boy's room, and they both heard the voices. Just as soon as the princess knocked on the door, the voices stopped and the angels disappeared.

When the rabbi's son, now a young man, opened the door, she asked, "I have heard voices in your room. What is the meaning of this? Who is here with you?"

"No one is here, Princess. I am studying, but each chapter I learn in a different voice. Then I change to another voice when I am not studying. I hope I did not disturb you," answered the young man.

"Please tell me what you are studying," asked the princess. "I see that your writing is different from ours."

"Princess, this is Hebrew writing of the Jews," he answered. And to each of her questions, he explained more and more about the Torah and its laws. He spoke about God and the wonders of the world. And she listened well.

And so it became her custom to visit the young man at midnight and discuss the Torah portion as the angels had taught it to him the night before. And night after night, the princess listened, and all the while asked still more questions.

All this time, for time was passing, the princess began to feel a great love for this young man and so, too, for the Torah and the Jewish ways.

One day, she told her father, "Father, I would like to marry this young man."

"But daughter, this young man is a Jew and we are Christian. He will not marry you." Then after some thought, he said, "Why don't you ask him?"

The princess approached the young man and said, "I would like to marry you because I love you."

The young man loved her in his heart, too, but this is how he answered: "If you will find it in your heart to become a Jew and keep our traditions sacred, then I will marry you. But it is not easy to keep all our ways of living and eating." He tried to persuade her to forget this matter.

But she insisted, saying, "I wish to become a Jew. The love of Torah is in my heart. I will devote my life to Torah—and to you."

The young man replied, "Then if you wish to become a Jew with your whole soul, this is what you must do. Tomorrow night, come here to the lake. Bring with you new clothes. First you will remove all the clothes you are wearing, and then immerse yourself, your entire body, three times, in the cool, fresh water of the lake. After that you will put on the new clothes. We will be married on the following day."

The princess happily agreed, and on the next night she did all that was according to Jewish law. With joy in her heart she recited the blessing after her immersion in the lake water, as she had been taught to do by the young man. He stood nearby all the while as a witness.

When she had dressed, the young man said, "Now you are a Jew. Like a new person, then, you must have a new name. Your name will be Sarah."

And so they were married, the king's daughter and the rabbi's son.

Every day the young man taught her the Hebrew alphabet, and the many prayers and blessings. They studied Torah together and everything she would need to know so she could live as a Jew. The young couple found that they were united by the bonds of love.

One evening, when they were sitting together, his wife said to him, "My husband, I never before asked you about that flower that you picked on the day you arrived at the palace."

"In a dream, I heard a voice explaining that this flower had magical powers. If you put it next to a dead person's nose, as long as his blood is still vital, that person will be revived and live," he explained. Then he added, "Hide this flower and guard it carefully, my wife."

The wife took the flower and, with great care, put it in a safe place.

A short time later, a son was born to this couple. Soon after, another son was born.

One day, as the rabbi's son was walking in the garden, an eagle swooped down and picked him up and flew with him higher and higher. And where do you think the eagle brought him? It brought him to the roof of his parents' house. The people in the house heard the noise of something being dropped on the roof. The rabbi and his wife went up to the roof and there they saw with great joy that it was their son, returned as mysteriously as he had left them. The rabbi thanked God and cried from happiness.

In the town, they held a great celebration in his honor, and everyone was invited to this party.

A few days passed, and the son became ill. All this time, he had not told his parents anything about what had happened to him and where he had been. The father sat near his son and finally asked, "My son, life must have been difficult for you all this time. What is wrong? What is lacking?"

"Father," answered the son, "I want to tell you everything." And he told his father about the eagle and all that had happened since he was 13 years old. "Father, I have a good wife and two wonderful children. And how I miss them, Father."

The rabbi stood up and said to his wife, "Prepare a basket of food for the road. I will bring my son's wife and their two children here." He saddled the mule, took the basket, and also his son's wedding ring, and set out on the journey.

The rabbi traveled for five days, until he got to the town that his son had told him about. He heard the king's messenger proclaim, "Whoever can cure the king's daughter will be greatly rewarded with half the kingdom. But whoever claims he can cure her and does not succeed will be executed."

As soon as he heard this, the rabbi ran to the palace and asked to be brought before the king. "Your Highness, I am a doctor and I am willing to cure your daughter."

"Many have tried before you, including physicians, priests, witches, and magicians. But they have all failed," the king warned, "and their heads were cut off. Are you willing to take this risk?"

"Yes, Your Highness. I will succeed," answered the rabbi-doctor, and he was led to the room where the princess was lying.

"Send everyone away, for I must be alone with the patient to determine what her illness is and the cure for it," ordered the rabbi-doctor.

The king and queen agreed, and all the people left the rabbi-doctor alone with the princess.

The rabbi went into the bedroom and presented himself to the princess and said, "My daughter, I am your father-in-law. You are married to my son. Look at this ring. Do you know it?"

At first the princess did not open her eyes. Finally, after he had repeated these same words gently three times, the princess looked at the ring—for a long time. Then she said, almost in a whisper, "Yes, it is the ring that belongs to my husband. Where is he?"

"I will take you to your husband," spoke the rabbi. "He is with us at home. Just as he was brought here by an eagle, so he was returned to us. If you are willing, here is what you must do. Ask the servant to bring you some turmeric and rub some on your face. The yellow color will make you look pale and sickly. Then tell your father you must go to the country for some air."

The princess agreed, and together they went to see the king. "Father, I now feel better, but according to this good doctor, I should have some country air for a few days. Then I will be even healthier." And the king agreed.

"As I promised, I will give you half my kingdom," the king added.

"No, I do not wish anything for myself, Your Highness. I am only happy that the princess is well again," the rabbi-doctor told him.

In the palace, they prepared a basket of food for the journey. The princess then prepared her sons, packed up her husband's books and a few more things, and they all set out.

When they arrived at the rabbi's house, they heard crying. People wept, telling them that the rabbi's son had died.

The rabbi, the princess, and the two children went into the house. The princess quickly said to the rabbi, "Allow me to enter my husband's room alone with our sons."

"But your sons will be scared," objected the rabbi. Finally he agreed.

They quickly went into the room and she saw that her husband was dead. Without waiting for the door to close, she took the flower from her pocket, placed it next to her husband's nose, and said, "My husband, my love, wake up, for your children are here, your wife is here. We have come to you. Wake up and see us." And as she watched and waited and hoped, she called out, "Blessed is the Lord God who listens to our prayers."

The aroma of the flower began to seep into his nostrils. All of a sudden, he began to move and his eyes opened. He immediately recognized his family. They embraced one another as they wept tears of joy.

Great was their happiness from that time until this day.

3

Welcome to Clothes

 nce it happened at a wedding feast that Elijah arrived dressed like a beggar. Seeing him at the door, the father of the bride ordered him to leave—and quickly— or else he would have the servants throw him out.

A while later, a handsome man, wearing a well-tailored suit, an elegant sable hat and carrying a cane with a golden handle, arrived at this same wedding. The guests all stood up, out of respect for this gentleman. They all greeted him with *Sholom aleikhem,* and the father of the bride said to him, "Please do us the honor of sitting at the head table with the bride and groom." And they all vied to serve him the finest wine and the best of foods.

As the guest sat there being served one course after another of the choicest foods, he took each plate and shoved its contents into his pockets—the meat into his right pocket, the potato pudding into the left, the fish into his upper pocket, the carrots into his inner vest pocket. And when he had finished stuffing the food into the pockets, he poured the fine red wine over it all.

The guests stood there amazed, with their mouths and eyes wide open, not understanding what this strange behavior meant.

They certainly had never seen such a ritual before. Finally, with great curiosity, one of them asked him for an explanation.

Then the guest explained, "When I came to the door to celebrate the wedding with you but dressed as a beggar, you practically threw me out. Then when I came dressed in such elegant clothes, you suddenly rushed over to me to show *me,* a stranger in your community, such *koved.* But what you were doing was really showing this respect and honor only *because* of my clothes. As a person, I had not changed from the beggar who first appeared here. *I* remain the same. But since you showed such respect for my *clothes,* then why should not the clothes be fed the feast?"

With that explanation, Elijah laughed, and when the company at the wedding feast looked again at the chair, Elijah was no longer there. But there was something lying across the seat of the armchair—the gold-handled cane.

4

Beroka
and Elijah the Prophet

Once, as Rabbi Beroka was walking in the crowded marketplace, Elijah, who it is always good to mention, appeared and began to walk along with him. Curious to know certain secrets that only Elijah could know, the rabbi asked, "Tell me, for I want very much to hear, is there anyone in this busy marketplace who will deserve to live in Paradise?"

Elijah looked around and continued walking, remaining silent. As they came to the edge of the marketplace, Elijah saw a man walking. He wore no fringes and had black scandals on his feet, like a heathen. "That man," answered Elijah, nodding in his direction, "*that* one will enjoy a life in the World to Come."

Hearing this, the rabbi was astounded, but then he asked permission of Elijah to approach the man. "Excuse me," he said, and introducing himself, he continued, "I need to ask you a question. What is your business?"

The man answered, "I am a jailer."

"A jailer?" Beroka did not understand. "Well, do you do anything out of the ordinary? Something other jailers don't bother doing?" persisted the rabbi, still wondering why this man, not even a religious-looking man, should be deserving of Paradise.

"Oh, yes," replied the jailer, "I maintain morality in the prison. I keep the men and women separate and guard them all night long in case one of the men should try to rape a woman prisoner."

"But why do you dress like a heathen and not like a Jew? After all, a Jew does not wear black scandals," said the rabbi.

"I wear black on my feet so that when I go to the royal palace, they will not recognize me as a Jew. In that way, I can hear if there are any plots that threaten the Jews and bring the news to the Jewish leaders."

Hearing this, the rabbi bade him farewell, saying, "Go in peace, my friend," and continued walking with Elijah.

But Elijah had another surprise in mind for Rabbi Beroka. Walking toward them were two jesters. "Those two will also inherit a place in Paradise," said Elijah, pointing to them.

The rabbi quickly ran over to the jesters and began to talk with them, too. "What do jesters do?" asked the puzzled rabbi.

"What jesters have always done," they answered.

Then the first jester spoke, "When we hear that someone is ill or suffering . . ."

And the second jester continued, "Or when someone is in mourning or distress. . . ."

Then the first one continued, "Or when two people have been quarreling. . . ."

Then they both spoke together again, saying, "We go to their homes and try to bring consolation to them. We sigh with them, we listen. We talk and remain silent, all the time trying to bring some joy back to the mourner's dark life. We tell stories and sing songs, until we see that there is harmony in the mourner's soul and gladness in the mourner's heart. We are peacemakers, for we remember what Hillel said, 'Love peace, and pursue peace.' "

Turning once again to speak to Elijah, Rabbi Beroka found that Elijah was no longer by his side in the marketplace. But a warmth filled his heart as a broad, understanding smile spread over his face. "What deserving companions they will be in Paradise," the rabbi said softly to himself. But Elijah was there, listening, and smiling, too.

5

The Wine of Paradise

 ne day, at a wedding of a young bride and groom, the guests were feasting and drinking wine and drinking a *l'chaim* to the young couple. The wine was sweet and tasted like the wine of Paradise.

After the meal, the guests recited the blessing the *birkat hamazon*. When the grace was concluded and the special seven blessings, the *sheva berakhot*, were recited at the wedding meal, the leader took a full glass of wine and mixed it with another wine glass that was not so full, and then he poured an equal amount of the combined wines into a third glass. After that he gave one glass of the combined wines to the *kallah*, one to the *chatan*, and took one for himself and recited the seventh blessing over the wine. Everyone shouted *Mazel tov!* and began to sing with great joy.

But the taste of the wine lingered, and the wedding guests wanted more of it. The owner of the inn where the wedding was taking place, who was also the father of the groom, got up from his place and said, "I regret to tell you that the wine you are asking for is finished."

"Where can we go to buy more?" called out one of the guests.

"My friends, such a wine is not sold anywhere. It is not possible

27

to find it in the shops. If my words puzzle you, then allow me to tell you the story of this miraculous wine.'' And the father of the bridegroom told this story.

When I was a young man, I was a *mohel* and my wife was midwife. While she performed the mitzvah of bringing children into this world, I performed the mitzvah of bringing them into the covenant with God and the Jewish people. I earned very little from this work. Often I would have to go miles away because there were fewer *mohels* than midwives. So my wife earned most of the money for our family. However, I would always accept the mitzvah of circumcision. After all, the baby boy had to become a Jew.

Once, *erev* Yom Kippur, a man arrived at my house to tell me that his son had been born just eight days before, and he begged me to come with him to his village, which was several hours' walk from my house. How could I leave and go with him? How could I perform the *brit* and be able to return in time for the meal? After all, this was just before the most holy of days. And yet, how could I *not* go? And so I decided there was no question. I would accompany this man and perform the *brit*.

We started out, walking as quickly as we could. I had hoped that perhaps he could hire a cart and a horse. But the man had not a single coin in his pocket. And after some time, I had to walk slower, but that peasant walked even faster and he was soon out of sight. I kept going, knowing the name of the village.

When I reached the house, the new mother was lying in bed, very weak. The father was nowhere to be found. A real peasant. And there I was with no one to help me. Normally, a *brit* is a simple task, which I did with joy and thankfulness in my heart. But to perform a *brit* without someone holding the baby is difficult, if not impossible. And I was filled with terror at the thought that I would have to do this alone. I looked around outside for someone to come to my aid. There was no one around. The house was far from other houses and the time was short, as I had to return in time for *Kol Nidre*. And also, if I did not come back in time for the meal, I would have to fast both days. Such thoughts went through my head. Perhaps I should perform the *brit* on my own. But then I thought, "No, I must not endanger the life of a child." Then I decided, "I'll leave the child without circumcising him." But then I answered myself, "No, this is the eighth day. He must have a *brit*."

As I stood there thinking one thing, then another, I saw in the distance a man, wearing high boots and with a sack on his back, coming toward this house. I ran out to him and pleaded with him to come help me. The old man turned aside and said, "I must hurry to collect alms. This is *erev* Yom Kippur and the people are generous, hoping to atone for their sins before the holy day begins. I cannot chance to lose so much money." And he was about to leave.

I ran after him and said, "I'll give you whatever you might hope to collect from the villagers. Just please help me and hold the baby. Please come and be *sandak*."

The old man stopped and said, "Why, I would collect a gold piece."

"Then that's what I will give you," I promised frantically.

At first he didn't believe me, but I finally persuaded him. He followed me into the house, sat on Elijah's Chair, and held the baby on his lap. And this is how I performed the *brit*.

After this, I washed and returned home, reciting the Afternoon Prayers on my way. I arrived home just in time for the meal before the fast. At the end of the meal, I saw the man through the window. I ran to get the gold coin, hoping my wife would not notice and question me. We did not have so much money that I could be so generous. But I had promised. The man took the gold coin, but then insisted, "I would like to have a glass of wine."

"The sun is about to set. We must hurry to the synagogue. Perhaps you will come and join us tomorrow night instead," I suggested.

But the old man insisted on drinking the glass of wine at that moment and no other. What could I do? So I invited him in and placed a glass of wine on the table. Then he insisted that I, too, drink a glass of wine with him. But no matter how much I argued that I needed to leave and had no time for wine, that I could not drink wine before the fast, he just sat there calmly insisting that we both drink a glass of wine. "Why do you not honor my request to drink a glass of wine with me?" he kept repeating.

My patience was at an end but I saw no other way to make him leave, so I drank a glass of wine, and we wished each other a good year filled with life and peace.

Then he asked me, while he sat there smiling, "Do you have more wine in the barrel?"

"Only a little bit more," I answered.

At that moment he blessed me and said, pointing to the wine barrel, "May your wine barrel continually be filled with sweet wine until the last blessing at the wedding of your youngest child."

Then he vanished.

Then the father of the bridegroom concluded his story and said, "The promise that that man made that day has been fulfilled, with the help of God. And who could he have been except Elijah the Prophet, may his name be remembered for good! Today we have shared in the *simchah* of the wedding of my youngest child. Until now there has been sweet wine in the barrel all these many years. Now the wine is finished."

6

The Synagogue
of Elijah the Prophet

t the edge of the town of Yazad, in the ancient neighborhood of Parsim, there stands the Synagogue of Elijah the Prophet. Why was this synagogue built in this alien place, a good day's walk from the Jewish neighborhood?

People of the city of Yazad tell the story that once, the owner of a weaving business was deep in debt, almost bankrupt, so the weaver decided to run away from the city. One morning when the light of dawn had not yet appeared, the weaver left his wife and children still asleep at home and went on his way. He traveled all day and all through the darkness of evening and came to an abandoned ruin. The weaver decided to sleep in the ruin and to continue his journey the next morning before dawn. Although he was very tired, he could not fall asleep. Thoughts about the fate of his wife and children troubled him. After all, he hadn't even told them about his leaving. Who knew where they would get their food? He began to worry about how their hunger would bother them, no doubt in the same way that hunger was bothering him now—since the morning he left, he had not put any food into his mouth.

During the time that the weaver was deep in his thoughts, an old man entered the ruin. He was using a cane, and his white beard was very long. He put down the sack he was carrying and asked, "What are you doing in this ruin?"

"I am here to pray," the weaver answered quickly.

"But why didn't you pray on the road?" asked the old man.

"I didn't want to have my prayers interrupted by any passer-by," the weaver replied.

"You could have prayed a short prayer," replied the old man. And looking more closely at the weaver, he asked in a gentle voice, "Why did you come to this ruin, which is far from your home? What is troubling you, dear friend?"

And the weaver began to talk with the old man. During the conversation, he told the old man about his situation.

The old man asked him, "Are there any threads left on your loom?"

The weaver answered, "Yes, there are still some threads left on the loom."

The old man said to the weaver, "Go back tomorrow to your workshop. Hide the machine in the back so no one from the outside will be able to see it, and then continue to work. *HaKodosh Barukhu* will send a blessing for all that you will do."

The next day the weaver got up when darkness was still on the land. The ruin was empty. Not one other living soul was there. But in his memory of the discussion with the old man from the night before, the weaver realized that it must have been Elijah the Prophet who had come to him in a dream to bless him.

The weaver started back in the direction of Yazad. On the way he met a goatherd, who gave him some milk to drink. Although he was very hungry, the milk was enough to satisfy his hunger and give him strength.

Then suddenly a miracle occurred. The road seemed to lift him up, as if it were a flying carpet. Although the sun hadn't yet risen to the middle of the sky, the weaver found himself in front of his weaving business.

The weaver went into the workshop. In a corner he found a large piece of cloth, which he hung up in front of the machine to hide it from the customers, should anyone enter. Then he began to weave. He worked and he worked, and the threads—threads of every color—never ended. With great happiness, the weaver continued to work all through the night.

The next morning, the weaver heard a knock on the door of the workshop and the sound of his wife's voice. She was scolding him because he hadn't returned home for two nights.

"Husband, did you at least bring home a few slices of dry bread to satisfy the hunger of the little ones? Were you even worried about us while you went on a journey for two nights?"

The weaver got up from the loom, his knees a bit wobbly, and opened the door for his wife.

In answer to her questions, he replied, "Dear wife, I had no money and lots of debts and I didn't have any money to buy food to feed the children. I couldn't repay my debts. I was afraid to be seen in the street. That's why I stayed alone in the workshop, hoping and waiting for some help, perhaps from Heaven."

And the woman became angrier when she heard her husband's answer. "How could you lie to your wife?" She raised her voice to him. "Because even in the middle of the street, I heard the sound of the loom."

"Yes, I turned on the loom so that people who loaned me money would not think that I didn't have any money to buy thread for weaving."

The bitter wife was not convinced by what her husband said. With great anger, she went forward, pushed aside the great piece of cloth that had been used as a curtain, and there, before the couple's eyes, was a long piece of cloth that the weaver had just had enough time to weave during this last day. But now the cloth was even longer, as if someone else had been there to finish the weaving. When the weaver saw the magnificent cloth, he began to dance with happiness. Then after reciting a prayer of thanksgiving, he went back to the loom to continue his work.

But the blessing had passed and was no more. Because the loom had been seen by someone else, the spools became empty and the loom stopped weaving.

The weaver took his merchandise to the market, and with the money that he made from selling the cloth, he was able to repay all his debts. He continued to work and became very rich.

Then one day he decided to rebuild the ruin where Elijah was revealed to him. He built in its place a synagogue. And that's how the miracle that happened to him in this place became known.

Since then, the people of the community of Yazad travel during Chol HaMoed Pesach and Sukkot to pray in this place. Any person who has troubles comes to pray in this synagogue and to request an answer from Elijah the Prophet.

Muslim residents, neighbors of this holy place, also respect it, and when they have troubles, they come to this house to pray before their Creator of the World. They all receive answers to their prayers and requests.

And this is how this synagogue came to be built so far from the center of the town, this Synagogue of Elijah the Prophet.

7

Elijah's Three Gifts

here once were three friends who after a day's work would meet on the porch of the coffeehouse to talk. They often talked about what they wished to have in their lives, for in truth they all had very little. One evening, the first man said, "If only I had money, I would perform *mitzvot* and help the poor."

The second friend said, "If only I had wisdom, I would build schools, especially so the poor children could learn."

Then the third friend spoke. "If only I could find a good woman, an *eshet chayil,* I would marry her."

That evening, Elijah the Prophet, in the disguise of a jester, happened to be walking by. He stopped and ordered a cup of coffee and listened. Then he turned to the three young men and asked, "Are you speaking the truth? Would you give to the poor if they came to your door? Would you really practice what you say?"

"Of course," answered the first friend.

Elijah took one *grush* from his purse and gave it to the young man. "Take this coin on condition that you will use it wisely to help and sustain those in need."

Then he turned to the second young man and asked, "Would

you really do what you say, build schools, especially to educate the poor children?"

"Yes, I would," replied the second friend.

Elijah took a page from a book that lined his cap and gave it to the second young man. "Take this page and with it learn all you can while you build schools for the poor children, as you promised."

Now turning to the third friend, Elijah asked, "And would you marry a good woman if you found her?"

"Gladly I would do that," answered the third friend.

"In that case," said Elijah, "ask the young woman who lives next door to marry you."

The following morning, the first friend woke up and found that he was rich, very rich! Remembering his promise, he began to distribute money for charity everywhere. He helped people who came to him for money. He gave *tzedakah* wherever he traveled. But after a few years, he became tired of performing these *mitzvot* and stopped. Instead, he kept all his money for himself.

The second friend woke up and found that he could easily learn whatever he wanted to know. He built a few schools, but he began to accept only rich families' children. Finally, when there was no room in the schools for any additional children, he stopped.

The third young man had met his neighbor's daughter. She always appeared bad-tempered, but, he thought, why not? At least it was convenient to court her. And so they were married.

After several years had passed, Elijah decided to test these three young men to see how they were faring. In the disguise of a traveler, Elijah came to the mansion of the first friend. When the servant came to the door, he asked to see the master. After waiting a long time, the master himself came to the door and the traveler asked to spend the holiday with him.

"Servant, give this poor traveler a *grush* from the pile," was the master's reply, spoken in a brusque voice.

"In that case," said Elijah, "give me the original *grush* I gave to you years ago."

"What's the difference? One *grush* looks like any other—there's no difference. Who are you, anyway? A jester?" asked the master in a mocking tone.

"Exactly," answered Elijah. "Open your drawer and there you will find the original *grush*. Return it to me."

The master obeyed and returned the original coin to Elijah. As Elijah disappeared around the bend of the road, the mansion suddenly became a small cottage and the servants began beating the formerly rich man, demanding their wages.

Elijah, in the disguise of an old man, then went to the second friend. He had with him a poor child to register in the school. When the friend came to the door and saw the poor child, he called out, "We have no room here. I am fed up with accepting poor children who cannot pay."

"Well then, give me back my original page. You will find it under your pillow," ordered Elijah.

"Are you crazy, old man? How will I find a page after so many years, especially under a pillow? You surely are jesting," the second friend said with a laugh.

"I never jest," answered Elijah. "Give back that original page. It *is* under your pillow," he repeated.

The second friend lifted his pillow and found the page and returned it to Elijah. Elijah disappeared. Suddenly the children all ran from the school as black smoke poured from the building.

Meanwhile, Elijah, in the disguise of a poor man, came to the small cottage of the third friend. The wife was home, and when she saw a poor, hungry person, she invited him to wash before anything else. "I'm dirty and my clothes are ragged," said Elijah.

"No matter," answered the wife. "Here are some of my husband's clothing. They will fit you. My husband is at work but soon he will return home." And while Elijah washed and changed his clothes, the wife prepared some food. After eating, she led the poor man to the bedroom to rest. She closed the door and waited outside for her husband because she did not want to disturb the guest's sleep—and also out of modesty.

When finally her husband returned, she went toward him to greet him. She told him about their guest. "And husband, do not be angry with me for I gave him the food I had prepared for our supper."

"Dear wife, thank goodness I married you. I now see that although you first appeared to be ill-tempered, you are a good woman who performs *mitzvot* that save us from hard times," answered the husband.

Elijah heard all of this and gave them the coin and the page. And then, before he left, he blessed them, saying, "May you see many blessed days until the end."

And so may we all!

8

A Tale Retold at a Feast

here was a certain wealthy man and his wife whose home was open to travelers and scholars. Whenever strangers came to their town, they were directed to this house, where they were always received with hospitality and generosity.

Once three scholars from Eretz Yisrael, traveling through this city, stayed in this house. They were so grateful to be received with such hospitality that they wanted to reward the couple. For their gift to be something the couple needed, they asked the servants what the couple lacked. The servants told them that the couple had everything that money could buy. Then the servants told the scholars, "But there is one thing these good people do not have: a child."

When it was time for the scholars to leave, they approached the couple and thanked them for their good welcome and added, "And may it be God's will that you may be rewarded for all the good deeds you perform in welcoming the traveler. May God bless you with a child at this time next year."

In one year's time, the woman gave birth to a son, and the parents' hearts were filled with joy and great happiness. At the *brit,* they prepared a feast, inviting everyone in the city, the rich and the poor, and, of course, all the strangers and travelers. When the child reached the age of 3, the father hired the finest instructor to teach him Torah. And the child learned well and quickly, for learning was sweet to him.

After eight years had passed, those same three scholars were passing through the same town on their return to Jerusalem. They decided to stop at the same house of this wealthy couple. Now they saw how the family rejoiced because of their son.

One day the father said to the scholars, "My friends, it was because of your blessing that God granted us a child after so many years of marriage. Our son is a wise young man who studies Torah with a fine teacher. His mind is quick like the wind and he remembers what he learns. Now it is time for him to be with the great teachers of Torah in Eretz Yisrael. Therefore, I would ask that you take our son to Jerusalem and that he remain with you so that he may become a *talmud chakham*. I will pay for all the expenses that you will need for him and for all his studies. All I ask is that you watch over him carefully and teach him Torah and all the laws. When he has learned all you can teach him, I will then send for him so that he may return to us."

The scholars listened, and after careful consideration they came to an agreement. When it came time to leave, the father gave the scholars a great sum of money for the expenses of clothing, lodging, food, books, and travel, and a generous gift besides. The son kissed his parents and wept. Then the parents blessed him with the hope that he would grow to be filled with the wisdom and love of Torah and to do good deeds. "And our son, our child, may God grant us the merit of seeing your face in joy."

Together, the son and the scholars traveled to the port, where they sailed on a boat on its way to Eretz Yisrael. However, after two days, the wind died down and the boat was carried along by the sea current. They were close to some islands, and finally the boat drifted toward land. All the passengers decided to leave the boat and walk on land until there was enough wind to continue the journey. The island was a beautiful place filled with grasses and fruit trees of all kinds. There were waterfalls and streams, mountains and valleys. The passengers all walked in different directions, eating of the sweet fruits and drinking the clear waters, feeling happy to be on land for a little while.

Toward evening the wind began to blow. The captain sounded the horn, which was the signal that everyone was to return to the boat. From everywhere the passengers ran back to the boat so that they could continue their voyage. Within an hour, all except one were on board.

The boy had gone far from the shore and was exploring the caves and rocks, so he did not hear the horn. The scholars began to search for him, asking the other passengers if anyone had seen the boy. They could not find him, and no one seemed to know where he was. The boat was about to sail. The sails were raised. What could they do, the scholars? They were afraid to be left in this deserted place. "Perhaps the boy is on the boat, but just hiding," they assured each other with that hope. The boat began to move and was soon out to sea again.

When it was evening, the boy returned to the shore, but he could not find anyone there. He realized that the boat must have sailed without him, and he was filled with fear and sorrow. He began to recite his evening prayers, and tears filled his eyes and his heart. That night, he stayed in a tall tree to protect himself in case there were animals that could harm him. He could not sleep, as he was trembling with fright.

In the morning, the boy climbed down from the tree, washed, and recited his morning prayers. He then ate some of the fruit and began to walk, repeating over and over, "The Lord *is* my shepherd, I shall not want. He makes me to lie down in green pastures: He leads me beside the still waters."

Suddenly, as he was walking in a field, an old man appeared, walking straight toward him. The old man was Elijah the Prophet, may he be remembered for good. "Where do you come from, and where are you going, my child?"

The boy told the old man everything that had happened to him and how he came to be alone on this deserted island. "I do not know what to do. Please, can you help me?"

"Do not be afraid, my child. I will help you and lead you to a place where there are people," answered the old man in a gentle voice. "Come with me."

The old man led the boy back to the shore. There he took the boy's coat and spread it on the water. Then the old man said, "Come and step on the coat and we shall go together."

The boy was afraid to step on the water, fearing he would

drown. But the old man swept the boy into his arms and placed him on the coat. In an instant, they arrived at an inn in the famous city of Saloniki.

Then the old man said to the boy, "Listen well and take care to do exactly as I command you. Go into the town and ask directions to the home of Teo Moshon. He is a seller of old clothes. Ask to stay only with him. Tell him that in return for room and food, he will be richly rewarded. Take this money for all your expenses. I will come back from time to time and give you further instructions about what you must do."

The boy was amazed at what had happened and agreed. "I will do whatever you order me to do and I shall turn neither to the right nor to the left." And the old man departed.

The boy went into the town, found Teo Moshon, and went into his shop. "*Sholom aleikhem,* sir. I have a favor to ask of you and I pray that you will fulfill my request."

"Speak that I may know what you wish of me, my child," said old Reb Moshe.

"I am a stranger here in this country. I hope that if I have found favor with you, I may be able to live here with you."

"My son, I am sorry that I cannot take you in as a guest. My house is small and my house is empty. I cannot offer you hospitality," answered Reb Moshe.

"But I have money to pay for my room and food. Take these coins as an advance, and go and buy food, a bed, and a table for me," replied the boy.

Teo Moshon went and told his wife and daughter about this young boy who had come to the shop and about his request. They agreed to let him stay. So Reb Moshe took the money, bought what he needed, and brought it all home.

Then he went and brought the young boy home with him. The family welcomed him warmly, and he stayed there studying Torah with a grateful heart.

Now, when the boat reached Eretz Yisrael, the three scholars journeyed to Jerusalem and wrote a letter to the boy's family. When the parents received the letter, reading all that had happened to their son, they wept and mourned. Their hearts were broken and their lives turned bitter. They wore only black clothing, and no one could console them.

After a time, the parents could no longer continue living in their home, and they decided to move to the city of Constantinople. There they performed *mitzvot,* as they had always done. The mother began to fill her days with visits to the sick and collect funds for orphans and poor brides. She helped arrange marriages whenever she could, providing whatever the couple needed to start a life together. And the mother and father, still grieving over their son, always found money and time to perform many good deeds.

Years passed and all continued the way it was, until one day the old man reappeared and said to the boy, now grown into a young man, "I have returned to give you some good advice. Listen well and do as I say. Here is another gift of money. Go to the marketplace. There you will hear about a fine palace for sale. No matter how high the price, buy it for that price and take Reb Moshe and his wife and their daughter to live there with you. After you have become comfortable, then tell the parents that you wish to marry their daughter. They will agree, for they have become fond of you and see that you are a serious student of Torah. Prepare then for the wedding ceremony according to the law. I will soon visit you again."

"I will obey all that you ask of me. And thank you for all your good help through these years. But I have to tell you also what is in my heart. My parents do not know what has happened to me, and I am certain that this must cause them great suffering. I wish to see them, to comfort them, to assure them that I am alive and well. How can I do that?" asked the young man.

"I know how you must feel, my son. But this will happen at the right time. They will see you and rejoice in finding their son in good health, all with God's help. But for now, remember what my words are," replied the old man. And giving him the gift, Elijah disappeared.

The young man immediately went to the marketplace and bought the palace. With keys in hand, he took Reb Moshe and his wife and their daughter to the palace, their new home. They hired several servants, and the young man paid for everything with Elijah's gift.

A short while later, the young man asked the young woman's father for her hand in marriage. "My son, I have come to love you

like a son. We are blessed to have you ask to marry our daughter.
We give our permission as long as she also agrees."

The daughter agreed, and the wedding ceremony took place.
All the people in the town were invited to the great feast, the
wealthy and the scholars, the poor and the strangers. Money was
distributed to poor scholars and others in need.

A year later, the young couple had a child. Their tears of joy
were mixed with tears of sorrow because the young man felt the
sadness that his parents must feel not even knowing that he was
alive and well. For the celebration of the *brit,* they prepared a festive
meal and gave *tzedakah.* A year later, another child was born, and a
year after that, a third child. And with each child, there was a festive
meal and gifts to those who were in need.

When the young man, now a father of three children, was alone
in deep thought, Elijah suddenly appeared and said, "Soon you will
see your parents again. But you and your family must sell the palace,
leave this city, and move to Constantinople. When you arrive in
that great city, I will visit you and tell you what you must do."
Hearing this news, the young man rejoiced.

The young man immediately began to fulfill the old man's
orders. He sold the palace, took his wife and children and his wife's
parents, and they all traveled to Constantinople. When they
arrived, the old man again appeared and instructed the young man,
"Buy the large plot of land surrounded by a high wall. No matter
what price is asked, pay it, and then I will meet you there to tell you
how to proceed."

So once more the young man followed Elijah's instructions and
found the land with the high wall and bought it at the price
demanded. Elijah appeared again and told him, "Here are the plans
for the building. First, build a strong, large house of hewn stone on
one side. Choose trustworthy workers who can keep a secret, and
let them dig on the side where you will lay the foundation. When
you dig there, you will find a great treasure. Put the treasure in the
stone house and build the rest of the house according to the
instructions written on these plans."

And all came to pass just as Elijah had foretold. Before the stone
house was built, the foundation was begun. The treasure was found
and stored in the stone house. The rest of the building was
completed as the old man had commanded. There was a separate
house for an academy of learning; a big building that served as a

place for travelers to rest, eat, and sleep; a large house for the family; and a beautiful park with fruit trees and flowers of all kinds. When all was completed, the old man visited the young man once again and said, "Listen carefully. Should you meet your mother and father, do *not* let them know who you are until I give you permission. Only then will I tell you how to approach them. All will be well."

The news of this great house with the gardens, the academy, and the place for travelers spread throughout the city.

* * *

One day, the young man's mother and two other women were collecting money for a poor orphan who was about to be married. When the three women arrived at the door of the wealthy young man, he welcomed them and invited them to come in. When the young man saw that one of the women was his mother, and that she was wearing black, he quickly ran into another room and wept bitterly to see his mother's suffering. But he remembered that Elijah had warned him not to reveal himself before he instructed him how to act. Gaining control of himself, he returned and gave the three women a generous donation, treating them with every honor. The mother, seeing the respect he gave her and the pleasant way he spoke, remembered that her son would be about the same age and with the same sweet manner had he lived. She got such pleasure just from looking at this young man that she found it difficult to leave. Finally the women got up and left, thanking the young man for his donation.

Whenever she needed a donation for a good cause—and it happened quite often during the next few weeks—the mother, along with some friends, approached the young man for a donation. She grew to love him like a son. And the young man regretted so much that he could not yet tell her who he really was.

One day, Elijah returned, and the young man told him about his mother's visits. Elijah listened and advised him this way. "I will now tell you how you may reveal to your parents who you are. But it must be done gradually, or else the shock may be too much for them. Prepare a great feast and invite all the important people of the town. Tell them that it is a special occasion celebrating a miracle that happened to you. Invite your mother and father also. When everyone is seated at their places around the table, you with your father at the table with the other men, your mother at the women's table opposite your table, announce the following: 'My friends, before we begin the feast of celebration, I wish everyone to tell us about his life. After the first story, we will serve the first dish. After each person's story, we will serve another dish.' When your turn comes, you must begin your story and tell it slowly. But then tell the guests that since so much has happened to you, you will have some food served between the parts of your story. In that way, your mother and father will gradually realize and understand for themselves that you are their son. Only then make yourself known. All will be well until the end of your days." And Elijah went on his way.

The young man began preparations for the feast with great haste and with great joy in his heart. But at the same time, he was also filled with another feeling, perhaps terror. In three days' time, everything was ready. The food, the wine, the silverware and china, the tablecloths, everything was fit for a king's feast. All the respected citizens were invited to come, and among them were his mother and father. Two tables were set in the dining room opposite each other, one for the men, one for the women. The host began to wash and then to recite the *hamotzi*.

But then, just before the servants began to serve the first course, the host stood up and announced, "My friends, thank you for coming to help us celebrate a miracle that has happened. But before we begin to eat, I would like to request that each one in turn tell us his life story. After the first guest has completed his tale, we shall eat one dish, then the second guest will tell us his story and we shall eat a second dish, and so we shall continue through the meal."

Now, whatever a host asks, the guests must do. And so the first guest began to tell about an event that happened to him during his life, and the first course was served. And this continued until it was the turn of the host himself. And so he began his story.

* * *

"I was an only son, born of parents in their old age. My parents were wealthy people who devoted themselves to good deeds and acts of charity and loving kindness. They were especially hospitable to the travelers and scholars journeying from the Land of Israel.''

(His parents listened, wondering at how similar their stories were.)

"One day three scholars came from Eretz Yisrael and stayed at our home. My parents treated them with great respect and honor and when they were about to leave, seeing that my parents had everything but a child, the scholars blessed them so that with God's help they would bear a child.''

"Tell us more! Continue your story, please!'' cried out the parents. But the young man answered, "My story is long and there is much to tell. Let us eat a little first. Then I will continue.'' And when they had eaten, the host continued.

"A year after their visit, my mother gave birth to me. And my parents were as joyful as Abraham and Sarah, for they had been deemed worthy to have a child in their older years. They taught me Torah and the commandments until I was 8 years old.''

The parents both began to weep when they heard this story. They tried not to cry, and yet how could they not when they heard that what had happened to this young man was so much like their own story. The host, seeing this, stopped his narration and called for another part of the meal to be served. Then he continued.

"Eight years later, the scholars returned, and when they were about to leave, my father begged them to take me to Jerusalem to become a scholar, to learn Torah and the commandments with the great teachers of Israel. The three scholars, who had been treated with such honor, were willing to do whatever my father asked of them. My father gave them money for all expenses and asked them to take good care of me. I bade my parents farewell and got on the boat.''

While the host spoke, the father and mother did not take their eyes from him. They listened to the story of how the wind died down and how the passengers went ashore on that beautiful island. The young man described all he saw there, the fruits he ate, and the fresh water that fell from the mountain. But then the host once more called for a pause so as to eat a little more food. The parents were anxious for him to continue. They were filled with a strange hope. But the host cautioned them to have patience and he would continue the long story.

Finally he began again, this time telling of how the captain sounded the horn but he did not hear it. The boat sailed away, leaving him on the island. He told of how he had cried and recited his evening prayers and climbed a tree for safety during the night.

Then, as he continued to the end of the story, the parents realized that he was indeed their son. And they began to give thanks to God for all the good He had performed for them. The mother and father rose from their places and approached their son. They embraced him and rejoiced with all those present when they heard of the great miracles that had happened to them all.

And Elijah, too, listened and witnessed all this happiness.

The son and the parents and the entire family continued studying Torah, performing good deeds, and giving *tzedakah*, in loving kindness and hospitality, as they had always done. And they spent their days in good and their years in pleasantness.

9

Things Could Be Far Worse

here was once an honest merchant who prospered in all that he did. But he was never satisfied and always complained that things were not good enough. As time went on, his business success began to change. Slowly, slowly he began to earn far less profit. In fact, he made barely enough to pay his bills.

One day, as he was walking through the street, Elijah the Prophet approached him and greeted him. "*Sholom aleikhem,* my friend. Tell me, how are you? I see from the way you are walking that you are filled with worry."

"*Aleikhem sholom,*" answered the merchant. "You are correct. I cannot hide my worry, for my business is not going as well as it should."

Elijah answered, "My friend, you should not worry so much. Things could be far worse. After all, you still earn a living."

And Elijah disappeared.

Some time passed and the merchant lost all his livelihood, all his business. He had to borrow money from others. What else could he do?

One day Elijah met the merchant and asked, "My friend, how are things going with you?"

The merchant answered, "Terrible! Worse than ever, for I am so ashamed that I have to live on money from others."

Elijah replied, "Don't worry, for things could be far worse."

And again Elijah disappeared.

More time passed. The merchant had borrowed money from everyone he knew and still his debt grew. Soon no one wanted to lend him money or even to meet him on the street.

Once more Elijah met the merchant and asked how he was faring. The merchant answered, "I will tell you the truth: I would now be willing to eat at other people's homes and to live on borrowed money, but now there is not a single person who wants to lend me anything more."

Elijah replied, "Don't complain, because things could be far worse."

And the merchant said, "*How* could things be *worse?*"

But when he looked up, he realized that he was talking to himself, as Elijah had vanished.

Now the merchant began to go out begging for charity, since none of his former friends or business merchants wanted anything to do with him. He felt ashamed to go knocking on doors and begging.

And when he met Elijah, he told him the state of his affairs.

And Elijah again assured him, "My friend, things could be *far* worse."

As he was begging for alms one day, along came a man who decided to be the merchant's "partner," and insisted that whatever money the merchant got would become his.

And so when Elijah encountered the merchant one day and heard about what was happening, Elijah repeated "Things could be far worse," and left him.

Well, one day, the man who had become his partner died. What could the merchant do but carry him to a cemetery? But the body was heavy and, oh, it began to smell. The merchant could not beg for charity while carrying the body. He thought that this would be the end of him, too.

When he got to the cemetery, he buried the body and then walked along the country road. He sat on a rock and cried. Elijah happened by and asked him what was wrong.

The merchant replied, "I see now what you meant by the expression 'Things could be far worse.' There seems to be no end to this bad luck. And so what's the use of complaining?"

When Elijah and the merchant returned to the city, Elijah blessed him and wished him well.

From that time, things began to improve for the merchant, and soon he had his business and his livelihood again. And he never again complained.

10

The Healing Fruit

t happened in Morocco that there was once a God-fearing, wealthy couple who had two sons. When the parents died, the two sons inherited all the wealth and land. One son was generous and openhanded, always practicing charity to help the hungry, the orphans, and the poor brides. But the other brother was a miser and kept all his wealth for himself. When the kind and generous brother used up his entire treasure of gold, he began to sell the land he had inherited and to distribute that money to help others. Meanwhile, the wealthy, greedy brother bought up all that land, the other half of the inheritance, so that he now owned everything.

Now David and Hannah, the generous couple, were left without anything at all. But although they were poor, they still kept their faith in God. They tried as best as they could to celebrate the holidays by going to the synagogue, by rejoicing and singing the prayers, by reciting the blessings over the wine and the *challah*. And this is also the way they taught their children to do.

It was the festival of Hoshana Rabba. After the husband and his children had returned from the synagogue, where they had prayed for dew while beating the willow branches on the ground, the wife said, "My husband, take this *dirham* and buy something for the children, something special to eat for the festival."

The husband took the coin and left for the marketplace. As he was about to enter the marketplace, an old person approached him and said, "Can you give me some money? It is the festival and I have had nothing to eat in honor of it."

What could David do? How could he not give—not perform a *mitzvah?* So, of course, he gave the *dirham* to this old person. But then David was afraid to return home without something for the children. He began to wander through the streets until he came to a synagogue. There he found the children playing with dozens of *etrogim,* citrons, that were no longer needed after the Hoshana Rabba morning service. What use were they to anyone now?

David began to pick up some of these citrons and to fill his pockets with them. Then he walked down to the waterfront. There he saw a ship about to sail to the king's city. He boarded the ship and soon he was sailing on the sea.

When he came to the city a few hours later, he was approached by the king's servant, who said, "The king has become ill with a stomach ailment and the doctor has sent me to find the merchant who is to arrive on this ship because he may have something to sell that will cure the king. I see that you are a visitor here. Do you by any chance have any such medicine to sell?"

David looked at him with great surprise. "No, I have nothing to sell, for I am a poor man. But you are right—I am a stranger here and live in another city."

"But I have been told to come to the ship to greet you and that I would know you when you came ashore. The doctor instructed me to bring you with me to the king's palace, so perhaps you have the remedy after all," replied the servant.

David followed the servant to the king's palace. When they arrived there, they went directly to the king's chamber. The doctor greeted David and said, "So you have the remedy we need to cure the king. Sell us one of the citrons that you carry with you."

David was surprised to hear the doctor's words. How did he know what David had brought with him? Slowly David took one of the citrons from his pocket and handed it to the doctor. The doctor gave the citron to the king to eat. And as soon as he had finished, the king sat up in bed fully recovered from his illness. Everyone was overjoyed, the king more than anyone.

Then the king said to David, "Do you have more of those citrons? And what are they used for, anyway?"

David emptied his pockets while explaining how the Jews pronounce a blessing over the *etrog* and the *lulav* during the festivals of Sukkot and Hoshana Rabba. And while the king listened, the doctor stood nearby, smiling and nodding his head.

When David finished, he looked toward the doctor, but suddenly the doctor was no longer standing there.

"Elijah!" exclaimed David under his breath. "So that's how the 'doctor' knew I had *etrogim* in my pockets."

Meanwhile, the king had ordered the servants to fill David's pockets with gold coins in payment for the citrons. "Ask whatever favor you will, and I will be happy to grant it," commanded the king.

"I would like to return home now, Your Majesty. I would also request that everyone in my town come to greet me. I do not want this honor for myself. Instead, I want everyone to know how *HaKodosh Barukhu,* the Holy One, healed you and helped me regain my wealth and my lands, which I can now buy back," David answered.

The king ordered a boat to take David back to his city, and a proclamation was sent out for the people of the town to come to welcome him. His family, along with everyone in the town, waited at the dock for David's arrival. He was to be greeted with great honor.

As David's ship approached the shore, he saw his brother coming toward him in a small boat. Suddenly a great wave swept over the boat and his brother was drowned.

From that time on, David and Hannah and their family lived in wealth and plenty. And as their wealth increased, so did their good deeds multiply. They continued to prosper for as long as they lived.

For He shall pay a man according to his works.

Job 34:11

11

*Her Wisdom
Is Her Beauty*

nce upon a time there was a girl who was born with the face of a beast. So hideous and frightening did she look that her parents hid her from the world. They could not bear to see how people would grimace or laugh at their child, nor could they bear the thought of the cruel things people would say about her.

"We must protect our daughter from such evils," they decided. And so, out of love for her, they kept the child at home, cut off from the outside world. When visitors came to the house, the daughter would stay in her room alone.

As she grew older, the girl began to ask questions and to listen to her father studying out loud. She eagerly absorbed everything she heard and asked more questions. Soon she was reading and learning Talmud, studying the *Mishnah* and the *Gemara*. Once, when her father began to ask her questions, he found to his surprise that he could learn something from his daughter.

One day, a particularly difficult passage of Talmud was being discussed in the synagogue and no one, not even the rabbi, was able to interpret it to everyone's satisfaction. When the father returned home, his daughter saw that he was deep in thought and she asked him, "Father, what did you discuss in the synagogue today?"

The father told her of the talmudic passage and the difficulty everyone had in understanding it. The daughter then began a discourse that made that passage crystal clear. When she finished, her father blessed her and thanked God for a daughter gifted with such wisdom.

The next day, the father went to the synagogue and presented his daughter's wise words. The men in the synagogue were amazed. "Elijah must have visited you in a dream," they said. "No woman could be as wise as that when not even our rabbi could understand how to solve this problem." But the father swore that the wisdom he had uttered came directly from his daughter. This experience was repeated many times, and everyone soon knew of the young woman's great wisdom.

One day, a young scholar came to this town in search of wisdom and knowledge. He had heard of a certain woman whose words were "pearls of wisdom," and when he came to the synagogue, he asked about her: Could he meet her? Where could he find her? He was told that he could only meet her father, and through him, he could ask any question, no matter how complex, and the daughter would give him the answer, but again only through her father as mediator.

So the young scholar asked her father to ask his daughter about a certain difficult problem. And the next day, the father brought his daughter's answer to him. The young man was amazed.

The young scholar asked two more questions, and each time the young woman unraveled the mystery and gave a clear explanation.

After the third answer, the young scholar said, with tears in his eyes, "I have been looking for such a woman to marry—one who is learned and wise. I would like to have such a companion to study with. I see I have much to learn from such a woman, for her wisdom is like that of Deborah the judge. I would be greatly honored if you consented to this marriage."

At first the father refused to consider this proposal, not that there were any others. Then the father hesitated. Perhaps he would consider it. The man persisted, even after being told that the young woman was different, that she had a blemish that marred her womanly appearance.

"No, I will have none other for my bride," the young scholar insisted. "Her wisdom is her beauty." Upon hearing this, the father decided to give his consent. And so the wedding took place.

That night, the bridegroom saw his wife for the first time, and her face startled him. The bride wept upon seeing how she had shocked him, and she said softly, "You mock at the work of the Creator, which no creature can change. But whatever could be learned, I have learned. Was it not Joseph's wisdom that brought him out of his prison, while his beauty caused him harm?"

Moved by his wife's words, the young scholar remained that night with her. But at dawn, leaving his ring and his *tallit* on the table, he left the house.

Months passed, and in time the young woman gave birth to a son. Her joy was mixed with bitter tears. As the child grew, it became more and more difficult to keep him hidden in the house. So one day the grandparents took the child to school, claiming that he was their own son. And that is what the child believed, too.

Once, the child overheard someone say, "Those old people could not be his parents. They are surely his grandparents. His father must have come and gone in the night." And they laughed.

The child returned home and said to his grandfather, "Tell me the truth. Are you really my father?" At first his grandfather lied, but the youngster kept doubting his replies.

Finally the boy's mother decided to answer her son's questions. "I will tell you the truth," she said. "You are old enough now and we cannot, we must not, keep it from you." And she told her son, in a gentle voice, everything that had happened. "And here is your father's ring and the *tallit* that belongs to him."

"Where is my father?" asked the boy. And the mother told him the name of the town her husband had come from. It was far away, in another land.

The boy took the ring and the *tallit*. He kissed them and held them close and said, "I will go and search for my father."

The boy took the ring and the *tallit* and set out to find his father. Months passed, and he finally came to the town where his father lived. He went directly to the synagogue and asked for his father by name. One old man heard the boy asking about the young scholar and he said, "I am his father. Who are you, and why do you ask for my son?"

The young man stared at this old man, and finally he said,

"Your son married my mother and then left her after the wedding night. I am your grandchild." The old man looked at the boy, not believing what he had heard, and yet the child, strangely enough, resembled him. It was like looking into the mirror of years ago, so much did the child resemble the old man in his youth. "Tell me, my child," said the old man slowly, "do you have any proof of this?"

The boy took out the ring and the *tallit* to show the old man. "These my father left with my mother."

The old man recognized the ring and the *tallit,* gifts he had given his son many years before. He embraced his grandson and in a trembling voice said, "Come, my child, I will introduce you to your father."

When the old man and the boy came to the house, the old man said, "Wait near the door, and let me go inside alone." He entered and saw his son sitting at the table. "My son," he began, "do you remember the ring I gave you many years ago? Well, could this be the ring?" And when the old man showed him the ring, his son gasped. The old man knew then that the boy had been telling the truth. And he continued, "So this must be your *tallit?*" And the old man turned to call in the boy, saying, "And perhaps you will also recognize that this is your son."

The boy, now reunited with his father, said after a time, "Father, we must return home. My mother is the most beautiful mother who ever lived and also the wisest. I love her so. And I love you, too. Let us become a true family." After much pleading, the father agreed to return home with his son.

When they entered the house, the boy's mother was sitting at the table absorbed in a volume of the Talmud. Only when she heard a voice whisper, "*Mother?*" did she look up. A smile came over her face when she saw her son, and she was very beautiful.

"You see, Father. Look well and see how beautiful my mother, your wife, really is," cried the boy. "Look, Mother, see whom I've brought home with me. My father! Your husband! Now we can be happy together!"

The boy's father stood at the door, not daring to enter in case his wife would not welcome him. When she looked up and he saw her face, he held his breath, for she was very beautiful. He waited, hoping she would invite him in.

As soon as the woman looked to see who was standing at the door, she recognized her husband. They looked at each other for a very long time, she sitting at the table, he standing at the door. Then she nodded, giving him permission to enter. So the husband and wife and their child joined hands in a blessing of thankfulness.

From that time on, the wife kept the ring next to a mysterious bottle that had a few drops of water in it. Whenever the son asked his mother about the bottle, she would laugh and say, "It came from Elijah the Prophet." "And what kind of water is inside it?" the boy would ask. And his mother's answer was always the same, "Miraculous water that washed away the veil from my face." And she would laugh a bit sadly and add, "I keep the ring next to it as a reminder of the miracle that brought us together again—your love for us both."

The reunited family lived in great happiness and wisdom.

So may we all.

12

Elijah's Partnership

hen someone has wealth, he is also considered a
chakham, a wise man. But if a person has nothing, even
if it is the same person who was once wealthy, and God
tests him with misfortune, then that person is considered a *nar,* a know-nothing. That's how Jews often looked upon
people, either as *chakhomim* or *naronim.*

Once there was a poor couple who could not earn a living. After
a time, the husband said to his wife, "Let me go where my eyes will
lead me. I cannot stand to see how you suffer on my account." And
the husband left his home and walked into the forest. But soon he
got lost. He was tired, and seeing a bed of pine needles, he lay down
and fell asleep.

Suddenly an old Jew awakened him. "Traveler," he called out,
"wake up and tell me what path will lead me out of the forest."

The husband sat up, surprised to hear a human voice, and said
to the old man, "Where I was going there seemed to be no path
out."

"Well then," replied the old man, "let us become partners and
we'll walk together to find this mysterious path that will lead us to

the village. Then let's walk from village to village and earn a few rubles before returning home."

"Why not?" answered the husband.

So the two men found their way out of the forest and came to a town. Since it was *erev* Shabbos, they went to the home of a rich man. The rich man came to the door, but seeing the two bedraggled partners, he gave them some coins but did not invite them for Shabbos.

It was getting to be late—the sun was almost setting—so they ran to a small cottage they saw from a distance. They did not want to be late for the start of the Shabbos. A poor Jewish family lived in this cottage. When they opened the door to the travelers, they said, "You are welcome to stay for Shabbos. However, we are ashamed that we have no meal fit for Shabbos. But whatever we eat, you will eat."

The old man nodded, and with a smile, answered, "At least we will have the pleasure of spending Shabbos with a Jew!"

As the woman was about to welcome the Shabbos queen, she turned to the guests and with embarrassment, her voice drifting off, explained that they could only afford to light sticks in place of candles.

"Oh?" replied the old man in a surprised tone. "I just glanced in the other room and there I saw candlesticks with candles." The woman went to the other room, and to her astonishment she saw candlesticks and a table covered with a fine white tablecloth, and in the center were two *challehs* covered with a beautiful cloth. And there on a chair was a hat and coat for her husband.

"Come, put on your Shabbos hat and coat and let us go to the *shul* for the evening prayers," said the old man.

"There is no *shul* near us, and there certainly is no *minyan*," replied the poor man.

"But I did pass a small House of Prayer not far from here. We will be just in time for the service," insisted the old man. And he was right. As the three men entered, they heard such sweet davening that it filled them with the Shabbos joy.

As soon as they returned home, everyone greeted the woman with Gut Shabbos! Then the old man said, "It's time for the fish."

The woman, knowing she had not prepared fish, went to the kitchen to bring in whatever she had, and there she saw platters of stuffed carp, roast goose, potato kugel, and so many other delicious foods for Shabbos. Well, as you can imagine, they enjoyed the meal, and the other two meals on the Shabbos as well.

Finally, after Shabbos was over, the old man turned to his hosts and announced, "We must leave, the two of us, but we thank you for your hospitality."

And as they were about to enter the woods to return home, the old man turned to the husband and said, "They will now prosper because the rich man's wealth will become theirs. And as for you, here. Take these rubles and you, too, will grow rich. Remember, anything is possible if God wills it."

"And you, my partner, who are you? After all, you have not even told me your name," said the husband.

"Your partner is Elijah the Prophet," replied the old man.

And Elijah vanished into the forest.

13

*Elijah the Prophet
and the Son of a Wise Man*

here once lived a wise man and his wife. Many women who were barren would come to the wise man and he would give them amulets and medicine, and they would have children. One day, a woman came to his house, and when she didn't find the wise man at home, she asked his wife, "Where is the wise man? I have been barren a long time. I have heard that anyone who comes to him succeeds in having children."

Just then the wise man arrived. He wrote out an amulet for this woman and gave her some medicine. And the woman left, feeling happy in her heart.

The wife of the wise man saw all this and became very angry. The wise man asked her, "What's wrong, my wife?"

And she answered, "Is it possible that we live without children while you give medicine and charms to other people so they can have children? I want us to have children, too—for our own good."

And the rabbi answered, "I agree, my wife. I will ask God to help us."

The wise man asked God for a child. And that night Elijah the Prophet spoke to him in a dream and said, "If you want a son, I will fulfill your wish. But I will come on the day of his *brit* and take him so that he will learn Torah with me for five years."

And the wise man answered, "I will ask my wife."

The next morning the wise man went to his wife and said, "If you will agree that on the day of the *brit* of our son we will give him to Elijah the Prophet so that he can teach our child, we will have a son."

"I agree!" the wife cried. "The main thing is that we will have a child. God should have pity on us."

A year passed, and a son was born to them.

On the day of the *brit,* the couple prepared a feast for the *mitzvah*. Elijah the Prophet arrived dressed as a poor man. At the end of the meal, Elijah said to the wise man, "Father of the son, do you recognize me?"

"No," answered the wise man. "But you are welcome at our feast."

"I am Elijah the Prophet. I came to take your son," replied Elijah.

And the wise man went to his wife and asked her, "If somebody gives you something and says, 'Take this and keep it for me and guard it for me until I come back after a certain time,' and he returns after that time and asks for this thing back, how would you answer? Would you return this thing to the person?"

"God forbid, whoever gives something on deposit has to have it returned to him," the wife answered.

"Well spoken. My wife, Elijah the Prophet has come to take our son to teach him Torah," the wise man said.

And with happiness, the wife agreed and gave her son to Elijah the Prophet. And Elijah told them, "Count five years from this day. At that time bring with you some good things and I will meet you and tell you where to find your son."

Five years passed. And the wife said to her husband, "Five years have ended. Go and bring back our son."

The wise man took some good things, and on the road he met Elijah the Prophet. Elijah said to him, "Go to the Beit Midrash and divide among all the students the good things you have brought. When you get to the place where your son is sitting, he will know you and embrace you."

The wise man went into the House of Learning and gave all the children the good things. Then a great miracle happened. After all, his son was only 8 days old when Elijah had taken him, and now he was a child of 5 years. And yet his son got up and kissed and embraced his father as though he had known him all his life. Then his father took him on his shoulders to return home.

On the way, the son and the father passed by a sea. The son suddenly saw something written in the heavens and it said, "There will come a time when your father will bring you water to wash your hands and your mother will do the same for your wife." And the son sighed.

The father asked him, "What is wrong, my son?" But the son did not want to say anything to his father. Knowing he was hiding something, the father became angry and threatened him. "If you don't tell me, I'll throw you into the sea." But his son still did not want to tell his father what he had seen.

In a burst of rage, his father threw him into the sea. At that moment a large fish swam up to the son and swallowed him.

In a certain town, there was a wise man who liked to eat fish for the third meal on the Shabbat. All during the week no one was able to catch anything out of the sea except for one large fish. A fisherman approached the wise man on Friday and said, "All week long we fishermen could not catch any small fish from the sea, as we do all the other weeks. I caught only this large fish, early this morning. What should I do?"

And the wise man answered, "We have no choice. Bring it."

Then the wise man's young daughter took the fish and hurried to prepare it for cooking. But suddenly she heard some sort of a strange voice coming from the fish.

"Be careful," it said. This was, of course, the voice of the child within the fish.

The daughter ran to her father and said, "Listen, the fish told me to be careful."

"Then be careful, my daughter. Open the fish slowly and see what is inside it," the father advised.

The daughter cut the fish slowly. From the inside of the fish came a very beautiful young boy.

Now, before Elijah the Prophet had left the boy after the five years of learning, he made him promise that he would fulfill this order: "A month of days you will not pray and you will offer no blessings. You have no permission to read anything until the thirty days are over."

When the wise man brought the child to the Shabbat table, he said to the boy, "Recite the blessing over the food. Say *Barukh*. . . .

Remembering Elijah's last instructions, the young boy answered, "I don't know it," and he ate without the blessing. He did not wash his hands. He did not read anything. It continued that way for a whole month.

The month ended. On that day the wise man's daughter was reading a passage in the Talmud aloud, and she made a mistake. The young boy said to her, "Listen, that is not correct. You made a mistake and didn't understand the passage. Go back over what you read."

The other members of the family had called the child ignorant because he didn't know how to read anything. So when the daughter heard what he had said, she said, "How do you, an ignorant boy like you, dare to tell me that I have made a mistake!"

And he answered her and said, "Open up the book and take a look and you shall see."

And the young woman saw that she had really made a mistake, and she admitted it. Afterward she went to her father and said, "This young boy understands Talmud better than I do."

The wise man was astounded. "How is it possible, my daughter? He doesn't even know *aleph bet*. How can he know Talmud? I want him to come to me. I will speak to him."

The young boy came to the wise man and the wise man asked him, "My son, do you know how to read?"

"Yes," answered the boy. "Now I have permission to read."

And the wise man thought, "There seems to be some mystery about this boy." Aloud he asked, "And what would you like?"

And the boy answered, "I want to give an explanation of the Torah on Shabbat in the synagogue."

On Shabbat, the wise man asked the congregation to invite the young boy who lived in his house to give an explanation of the Torah in the Beit Knesset. Everyone in the town knew that this young boy was ignorant.

The boy went up on the *bimah* and began to explain all the different verses of the Torah. The explanation continued for a long time, but the boy never seemed to tire. Everyone was amazed and listened to each word, each breath.

Afterward the wise man invited all the congregation to his house. He set a festive table and had a great Shabbat feast. He was happy, indeed, that there was such a brilliant student, a *talmud chakham,* in his house.

Years went by, and in time this young scholar married the wise man's daughter and became a great judge in the town. In fact, he became famous everywhere.

Now let us return to the scholar's father and mother.

When the father returned home on the appointed day without their son, five years after the child's *brit,* the mother was stricken with grief. But from that day on, the father stopped speaking, refusing to tell his wife what had happened.

The wife argued with her husband, constantly asking him, "Where is my son? I want you to tell me where my son has died." But still the husband remained silent.

After many years had passed, the wife finally said, "I want to go to the new judge in the town where our child was studying. We'll go to him and he will judge between us. He will force you to tell me where my son is and what you did to him."

The parents came to that town to see the judge, who in reality was their son. As he was looking out the window, he saw that his parents were coming to him. He turned to his wife and said, "Listen, on this day, my parents will come to us. We will invite them here for three days and they will stay at our house until I prepare the trial. Please do not tell them who I am."

When the parents came to the young judge, he greeted them with a hearty welcome. Then they said to him, "We have come to be judged by you. We have heard that you are an expert in law, and that is why we have come to you."

The judge said to them, "The law says this: Whoever comes will stay three days. After three days, I will prepare the trial."

The couple stayed at the judge's house for three days. And before each meal, the father would run and bring the judge a cup of water so that he could wash his hands. His mother would bring a cup of water to the judge's wife. And the prophecy came true, the prophecy that the young boy had seen in the heavens a long time ago. On the third day, the couple came to the trial.

The judge said to his father, "You must begin now and tell me the whole story." And the father told the judge the whole story and the whole truth. Afterward the judge said to his mother, "And you tell me your story."

The woman told the judge the whole truth, about how she had been barren and how she was asked to give her child to Elijah for five years and about how her husband, after five years, went to bring back the child and the child did not come back. And she continued, "And all this time, I have been pleading, 'Where is my son? Where is my son?' "

Then the judge asked his mother, "Do you know of some sort of a sign or mark on your son?"

She answered him, "My son has a long hair, like *tefillin*, on his hands."

The judge held out his hands and said, "Maybe like this? I have hair like that."

"Exactly like that!" she exclaimed. "Exactly like that!"

And the judge said to her, "Mother, don't be frightened. I am your son. Everything was written in the heavens. Whatever I saw came to be. And now, thank God, we will all live together in peace. Go, sell your home, sell all your goods, and bring everything you have here. We will live a good life, a peaceful life, with happiness."

And so his words came true.

So may it be for all of us.

14

Looking for His Luck

here was a poor man who lived at the edge of a village near the sea. He was a beggar, and somehow he never made enough for his living. Day after day he became impatient because he didn't see any hope where he was. As he looked around, all he saw were other people who also lived in poverty, like him. And he said to himself, "I will go look for my luck in another place. I won't come back here until I find it."

The others said to him, "*Mishaneh makom, mishaneh mazel*— Change your place and you change your luck." So what did he do? He took his walking stick and his bag, he took some food, and he left the village and became a wanderer. He went through mountains and fields, walking from place to place.

On the third day after he left the village of his birth, the man met a wolf at the entrance to the forest. This wolf was thin and scraggly: his hair was thinning, his eyes were half closed, and his stomach was empty. The wolf asked the wanderer, "Where are you going, my man?"

And the man answered, "I am going to look for my *mazel*, my luck."

"If you find your luck in the place of places, please do me a kindness. Tell them that I want to ask how I can change my bad luck to good because I am always sick and always hungry," said the wolf.

The wanderer promised the wolf to inquire about his luck, and he continued on his way.

After three days, he came to a city. When the people of that city saw the stranger, they brought him directly to the king. That was the custom of that city—to bring strangers to the king.

The king asked him, "Where do you come from and where are you going?"

The wanderer told the king the story of his poverty and said, "I am searching for my *mazel*, my luck."

And the king asked, "If you are going to find out about your poverty, then perhaps you can also find out why my government is so weak and what I have to do to make it strong."

"I'll be glad to ask this question when I find my *mazel*," answered the wanderer.

The next day he continued on his way. He came to an orchard where there was a spring. Next to the spring grew a fruit tree. The wanderer thought, "I will stay here to rest and then I'll continue on my journey."

As he sat down, the owner of the orchard approached him, holding out his hand in peace, and asked, "Where are you going, friend?"

The wanderer told him the story of his search for his *mazel*. Then the owner of the orchard said to him, "Good friend, when you find your *mazel*, maybe you can ask about this fruit tree I have. Half of its fruit is very sweet, but the other half is very bitter. And yet all the fruit comes from the *same* tree. Can you help me discover why this is so?"

And the wanderer answered, "Yes, I will inquire for you."

The next day he went on his way.

After three days, the wanderer met an old man, who was Elijah the Prophet. The old man blessed him with peace and asked him, "What is the matter? Where are you going?"

The wanderer told him all that had happened to him and that he was looking for his *mazel*.

The old man said to him, "I am a messenger from God and I

have come to tell you to return to your home. Your days of poverty
and want are over. Your *mazel* is waiting for you.''

The wanderer said to Elijah, ''Are you certain of this? Can you
promise that this is true?''

''Yes, it is true,'' replied Elijah.

The wanderer started on the path home, but he remembered
his promises to those he had met along the way. He turned around
and said to the old man, ''I have passed by many places, and people
have asked me some questions. Could you answer their requests?''

Elijah stood there smiling and agreed to hear the requests.

''In one place there was a tree. Half of its fruit was bitter and
half was sweet. What is the reason for this?''

And Elijah told him, ''The reason is because under the roots of
this tree there is a great treasure. Half of the growing roots are on
the treasure and the other half are not. Those roots that are in the
ground produce sweet fruit. But those that are resting on the
treasure have bitter fruit. If the owner of the tree will remove the
treasure from the ground, all the roots will grow in the earth and
the entire tree will produce sweet fruit.''

''Good,'' said the wanderer. ''And now, here is the second
case. I passed through a city and the king said to me that his
government was weak. He asked me to find out the reason for
this.''

And Elijah answered him, ''The king is a woman, but nobody
knows this. The government of a single monarch is always weak. If
she marries someone, and that person becomes her partner, then
the government will become strong.''

''Good,'' said the wanderer. ''And now for the third request.
I met a wolf who has been sick and weak for a long time and never
seems to get well. What is the reason for this?''

And Elijah said, ''Tell the wolf that if he can eat a foolish man
who doesn't have any *seikhl,* that will be the medicine to cure him.''

''Fine. I will remember all that you have said,'' replied the
wanderer. And he bade farewell to Elijah the Prophet and started
for home. On the way, he came to the owner of the orchard, who
asked him, ''Have you come back? And have you found the answer
to your question?''

''Yes,'' answered the wanderer. ''My poverty is over and my
mazel is waiting for me.''

"And did you ask about my problem with the fruit tree?" asked the owner of the orchard.

"Yes," replied the wanderer. "Under the roots there is a treasure of gold and diamonds. This treasure is the cause of the bitter fruit. When you remove the treasure, all the fruit of the tree will be sweet."

"Really! Let us go see if this is true," said the owner of the orchard.

"I have no time to stay and help you dig up this treasure. My *mazel* is waiting for me and I must hurry to get it," replied the wanderer.

With great happiness the owner of the orchard said to the man, "I've become old and I have no one to share this wealth with me. Come and live with me and we will be like brothers. Half of my land will be yours to plant and harvest. Half of this treasure will be yours."

The wanderer laughed to hear what the owner of the orchard said. "This treasure doesn't interest me. I must go back home to find my *mazel*, and when I do, I'll be richer by a hundred times without working," replied the man. And he hurried on his way.

Then he came to the city of the king. The king said to him, "You have come back, I see. Well, have you found the answer?"

"Yes, my *mazel* is waiting for me and I must return home," replied the man.

"And did you ask about my problem?" asked the king.

"I was told that you are a woman-king, and because you rule alone, your government is weak. But if you marry someone, the king and queen, as *partners,* will be able to take control and strengthen the government."

And the woman-king said, "No one knew this before. Come, let us get married. Then you will be the king of this whole city and I will be the queen."

The wanderer laughed when he heard what the woman-king proposed. "No, no, my *mazel* is waiting for me. The owner of the orchard promised me treasure and I didn't accept that. So why should I agree to your offer?" And he continued on his way.

Once again he passed near the entrance of the forest and met the sick wolf. "Well, I see you are returning home. Did you find out what you needed to know?" asked the wolf.

"Yes, I asked and I found out that my *mazel* is waiting for me. I also asked about the owner of the orchard whose fruit tree produced bitter fruit and found that it was all because of a treasure lying under its roots. He offered to share the treasure with me, but I refused. I also asked about a queen who wanted to marry me and share her kingdom with me. But I didn't want to do that, either."

"And what about me?" asked the wolf. "Did you find out why I am always sick and how I could get healthy?"

"It's very simple. If you will attack and eat a foolish man who does not possess any *seikhl*, then that will be your remedy and you will get healthy," said the wanderer.

"AAAAAH! Where will I find a man more foolish and stupid than *you?*"

Slowly the wolf got up and attacked and ate the poor wanderer who had gone looking for his luck.

15

*The Emissary of
Elijah the Prophet*

n the town of Lublin, there was a custom that had existed for many years. Whenever the rabbi of the town was about to die, he would appoint the new leader of the Beit Din to take his place.

Now that the rabbi of Lublin knew that he would soon die, he called all the benefactors of the synagogue and the advisers together at his house. They waited for him to tell them who should take his place, who would be their rabbi and their guide. With great respect, all the heads of the town came to hear from his mouth who would replace him and who would sit in the chair of the *rabbinut* after him. And they asked him, "Who will be our rabbi in your place, our teacher?"

And the rabbi said, "Don't ask me. Go to the first person who becomes sick after my death. He will tell you who your new rabbi will be. Do what he tells you and all will be well." Just as the rabbi said this, he turned his face to the wall and died.

Everyone in the city was very disturbed at the news because they did not know how to find the first person to become sick after the rabbi died. The city was big, and many people lived in it. Who could know who was sick in such a large city? They began to

discuss this situation and to offer advice. They looked around to try
to find out who would be the first person to get sick after the death
of their holy rabbi.

Finally they decided to tell the leaders of the *Chevrah Kadisha* in
Lublin what had happened. As a result, the *Chevrah Kadisha* issued
an order to all the people who collect money for the sick and who
belong to *Chevrat Bikur Cholim,* the people who visit the sick. ''If
someone gets sick in this town from this day forward, you must
immediately report this sickness to the *gabaiim* of the *Chevrah
Kadisha.''* And the *gabaiim* of the *Bikur Cholim* took it upon
themselves to fulfill this order. They promised to look around
carefully to find out who would be the first person to get sick.

But no one in the town became sick for thirty days after the
death of the rabbi.

After thirty days, a tailor got sick. He lived just outside the city in
a small, run-down house. This man was poor and alone. He didn't
have much to eat and only old clothes to wear. Most of the people
in the town didn't seem to know him. And if they had known
about this man and his work, they would know only that he was a
tailor and a very simple man. This same tailor was the first person to
get sick after the death of the rabbi.

After the *gabaiim* of *Chevrat Bikur Cholim* found out about him,
they immediately told the *gabaiim* of the *Chevrah Kadisha* about the
tailor. Then they told the rest of the town. All the honorable
gabaiim, together with all the leaders in the town, met to discuss
what to do. This sick man was a very simple man, not a *talmud
chakham.*

But they had promised to do what their rabbi had willed them
to do before his death. And even though they didn't want to do
this, they had to do what he said.

The leaders of Lublin went to the tailor's house, and they found
the tailor, very ill, in bed. And the tailor asked them, ''Honorable
people, where are you coming from and why have you come under
my roof?''

And the men answered him, ''We are the leaders of Lublin and
we have come out of respect for our holy rabbi to ask your advice.
Who is the right person to take the place of our dead rabbi, *zikhrono
livrakhah,* in our city of Lublin?''

The tailor said to them, "Have you come here to laugh at me? I don't know what you want from me. What are the duties of this rabbi? And why is it not possible for the people of Lublin to be without a rabbi?"

The people told him, "We need a rabbi who will guide us and show us the right way and the laws, what is permitted and what is not. We need someone who is wise and who will judge among us when there are disputes. For all these things we need a rabbi. And he will also show us how we should lead our lives."

The tailor looked at them and answered, "If that is the way it is, I understand why you need a rabbi. But why have you come to me to ask this question? Take one of the good people among you."

They said to him, "This order was given to us by our rabbi, *zikhrono livrakhah*, and we are fulfilling this promise because he ordered us to come to you before he died. And he said, 'Go to the first person who becomes sick after my death. He will tell you who will be your new rabbi.' We cannot change this order. It has been the custom in our town for many many years, and we must fulfill this order of our rabbi. And since you are the first person to get sick after the death of our rabbi, *zikhrono livrakhah*, we have come to ask your advice."

After hearing this answer, the tailor said to them, "Honored people that you are, you know the needs of the town. I am a simple man, a tailor, who has busied himself with his work all the days of his life. I still don't understand what you want from me."

Bewildered and confused, the men came together and talked about what they should do next. Then they decided to approach the tailor again. They said to him, "We are asking you just to listen as we read the names of different towns and the names of the rabbis, and all you will have to say is 'here he is' when you hear the right name. Then we will try to bring this rabbi to our town to replace our rabbi, *zikhrono livrakhah*."

And the tailor said, "You can do what you have suggested. I will listen."

The elders of the city sat and read the names of different Jewish communities all over the world. The tailor lay on his broken bed and didn't say a word.

But when they read the name of the town of Ostraha, the sick man lifted up his head and said, "Take the rabbi from the town of

Ostraha." The people became happy, very happy, and responded, "*Yehee Hashem imkha*, May God be with you. As you say we shall do."

As they were about to leave, the tailor called them back and said to them, "I have told you to put the rabbi from Ostraha on the chair of the *rabbinut*. But if the rabbi of Ostraha tells you that he doesn't want to leave the house of his father, then tell him in my name, 'The tailor of Lublin orders you to go with us to be our rabbi.' "

As soon as he had said this, he recited aloud, *Shma Yisrael Adonoi Eloheinu Adonoi Echad.* At the moment he said the word *echad,* he drew his last breath and his soul left him.

The people of the town buried the tailor with great honor next to the grave of the dead rabbi.

After the burial, the townspeople sent two *talmidei chakhomim,* chosen from the most respected people of the town, with a letter from the *rabbinut* in their hands, to the rabbi in Ostraha. They left Lublin, and when they arrived in Ostraha, they went directly to the home of the rabbi and said, "Honored rabbi, we have come here to bring you and place you on the chair of the *rabbinut* in our city. You will be our rabbi and teacher."

And the rabbi of Ostraha said, "Thank you for this great honor. However, I do not want to leave the city of my birth. This is the place where my father and my father's father were rabbis, generation after generation. How could I leave here and go to Lublin? No, I cannot do this thing. I will remain in the town of my birth, the town where I live, and the town of my fathers before me. And after my brief time on earth shall pass, I hope to be buried among them here."

So the people of Lublin returned to their town without the rabbi of Ostraha. Then the leaders of the community decided to send another group of emissaries to the rabbi of Ostraha. But the rabbi gave them the same answer, that he would never leave the town of his birth.

Hearing this, the emissaries told the rabbi that they would give him a greater salary. But still the rabbi refused to go with them to Lublin. When the emissaries of the town saw that nothing they said seemed to convince the rabbi, they said, "We want you to know that we are coming to you in the name of the poor tailor from Lublin, he should rest in Gan Eden. And this tailor ordered us, before his death, to go and to bring you to Lublin and to tell you, in his name, that you have been ordered to leave your community in Ostraha and become our rabbi and guide in Lublin."

And when the rabbi heard these words, he fell on the ground, ripped his clothes, and mourned a bitter mourning for the tailor. After a while he rose and said to them, "If these were not the words of a true *tzaddik*, I would never leave my city, my home, the place of my father and my father's father. But now I do not see how I can disregard the tailor's words. I will leave with you immediately, as was his order."

The rabbi announced this decision to the people of Ostraha—that he would be leaving them to go to Lublin as the new rabbi there. The people gathered together, then came to his house, weeping and crying bitterly. The officials of Ostraha also wanted to increase his salary, but this was the only thing they could offer to try to persuade him to stay. All their cries and arguments were of no use. This was a very important decision, and there was no choice in the matter.

Before the rabbi left the city, he asked the people not to be angry with him. "It is not of my own volition that I am leaving the city of my birth, good people; I am fulfilling a holy *mitzvah* and going to Lublin," he told them. And the rabbi left Ostraha and went to Lublin.

All the people in Lublin came to meet him and bring him into the city. They welcomed him with great honor and happiness. The people of Lublin made a reception, and everyone came to take part in the happiness of this *mitzvah*. All day long the rabbi sat at this party and gave *drashim*. At the third meal, *seudah shlishit*, after the *drashim* in the synagogue, all the honorable people came to his house. The leaders and the *talmidei chakhomim*, all sat in front of him. They ate and drank and were happy as they spoke words of *Torah*.

With such happiness in their hearts, they turned to the rabbi and asked him, "Dear rabbi, we have one small request to make. Would you please tell us who this poor tailor was, he should rest in heaven. All those days he lived among us and we didn't know who he was. If it wasn't for this command from our rabbi, *zikhrono livrakhah*, we still wouldn't know that this tailor had lived among us."

And the rabbi said, "I didn't know who he was either, except for something that happened. It was my custom, from the time I became a rabbi in Ostraha, to stay after the Shabbat services, or any services, in the Beit Knesset every day. After the prayer of Shacharit, all the people would leave the synagogue and I would close and lock the gates from inside. The windows were higher than a man's height so no one could climb in or out. As a result, there was no possible way for anyone to enter the synagogue. I would sit there alone, wrapped in a *tallit,* crowned with my *tefillin,* and study until the middle of the day. At noon I would open the gates and leave the synagogue and go home to eat. Afterward I would listen to the people who would come to me with their troubles and problems. That was my custom every day.

"One day I was sitting in the synagogue, studying the Torah. All of a sudden I heard a voice. I looked up and I saw a man approaching me. When I saw him, I became frightened because I knew that the synagogue was closed and locked from the inside. 'How did you get inside?' I asked with great surprise and shock. The man laughed and said, 'Why don't you ask me how I shall leave, as you yourself locked the gates and hold the keys in your hand.'

"The man stood in front of me and looked at my face. And when he saw that I was frightened, he turned to me with these gentle words: 'My teacher, my rabbi, do not be frightened and do not be afraid of me. I am a tailor from the town of Lublin. I am flesh and blood just like you.' Then I asked him, 'But why have you come to me?' And he answered, 'It was Elijah the Prophet, *zakhur latov,* who sent me to you to warn you of the evil things that will happen in this town. Because you are the rabbi of the place, order the Jews to seal the broken parts of the city wall wherever the stones have become weak or crumbled.'

"Then I said to him, 'If what you say is really true and you are the emissary of Elijah the Prophet, why can't I see him? I won't pay attention to anything you have said in his name until I see him with my own eyes.' And he said to me, 'I know that to see Elijah the Prophet face to face would bring fear to the person who saw him, and he would not be able to bear it.' Then I answered him, 'Whatever will come to pass, and the Holy God will be here with me to help me, it is my wish. The Holy Torah that I study day and night gives me this honor.' And the man came closer to me, and took a handkerchief out of his pocket, and put it on my face. I closed my eyes and I saw Elijah the Prophet. He stood before me, and I saw him face to face. And I *was* frightened. I stepped backward, and from all my fear and fright, I fell to the ground and fainted. When the tailor woke me up, he said, 'Didn't I tell you, my rabbi, my teacher, that there would be fear within you if you saw the face of the angel of God? And now you must fix the city wall as I have told you to and do it in the name of Elijah the Prophet, *zakhur latov.*' And he immediately vanished.

"I have not seen or heard of the tailor until this day. I wish I could see him in the next world, the world of truth. He should be honored among all righteous men, and they should protect us and all of Yisrael, *amen. Kein yehee ratzon.*"

Night fell. The stars appeared. The rabbi finished his story, and the people in the town of Lublin now knew who the poor tailor was, the man who had sat all the days of his life at the edge of the city and busied himself with fixing old clothes—he was one of the thirty-six hidden *tzaddikim* by whose merit the world continues to exist.

Then the people understood the command of their old rabbi, who knew all the great works of God. He had known that the tailor would be the next to die after him and that nobody else would die before then. He had also known that the rabbi from Ostraha would leave that place and come to Lublin to become their rabbi only through the direct order of the tailor, the emissary of Elijah.

16

The Man
Whose Words Came True

One day, a man called his three sons to him and said, "My children, I am old and I know that I will soon die. There is a place in the fir grove, near the yellow, sandy earth in the woods, where I wish to be buried. I ask that you bury me there, and I ask that each of you, in turn, stay three nights at the grave. Do not be afraid and it will turn out well." Each son promised his father to do as he requested.

Soon after, the father died and the sons buried him in the fir grove.

The eldest son spent the first three nights at the grave. At daybreak, on his way home, he met an old Jewish man. It was Elijah the Prophet, whom it is always good to mention. Elijah asked him, "Where are you coming from?" and the son answered, "As Father asked us, so we must do."

Elijah then said, "What do you prefer, a barrel of gold, a certain amount of good luck, or to be a *vortzoger* and possess the power to have your words come true?"

Without a moment's hesitation, the eldest son responded, "Gold!" The son turned his head and saw a barrel of gold under a tree. (He never even looked up to thank Elijah. And even if he had, he would have noticed that Elijah was no longer there.)

The same thing happened when the second son was leaving the father's grave at daybreak on the third morning of his watch. But this son wished to have good luck. As he was turning around, he found some gold coins at his feet. And even though good luck was with him all day long, he never even gave a thought to Elijah, who had granted him his wish.

When it was the turn of the youngest to be at the grave, and Elijah appeared asking him which wish he chose, the youngest said, "I'd rather have words come true."

When the two older brothers heard this, they began to make fun of their youngest brother. "Words coming true! Then say the word, brother!" How they laughed. But the youngest brother did not answer them. Instead he just turned and started walking into the forest.

In the forest, the young man spoke these words: "I say, may the tree fall and hook itself to my coat and drag after me as far as the emperor's palace."

And just as he uttered those words, it happened.

When he passed the emperor's palace, the emperor's daughter, who was sitting at the window, saw him and laughed. (After all, who could keep from laughing at this sight?)

However, the young man became offended and, as a retort, said, "May your belly be laughing!"

He had no sooner uttered those words when the princess became pregnant and gave birth to a child. A child! And you can imagine how astonished everyone was, no more than the princess herself. No one knew who the father could possibly be, so they convened an official meeting of all the counselors to decide this matter. After thinking and talking for many days, they concluded, "When the child reaches two years of age, he will be placed on a table and every man in the kingdom will be invited to come close to the child. We will then observe and see to which one the child reaches out with his arms. That is how we will discover who the father is."

And so it happened, but the child reached out to no one. So they started searching for any man they might not have included.

In the synagogue studying behind the stove was that young man, the youngest brother, the *vortzoger*. And when they found him they put this young man near the child, and the child stretched out his arms. "Are you the father?" they asked the young man. And he simply replied, "Yes."

"Then what should be done to you?" the counselors asked.

"Do what you like," answered the young man simply.

And again after much consultation, they decided to put the young man, along with the princess and the child, in a locked glass box, along with one loaf of bread, and float it down the river.

As they were floating in the box, the young man became hungry and ate the loaf of bread. "Leave half for tomorrow," pleaded the princess.

"Do not worry, my dear princess, tomorrow there will be more," answered the young man. And on the next day there was more bread.

"Since what you said about bread came true," reasoned the princess, "then say that we should float to the edge of the river."

And when the young man said those words, the box soon bumped against the edge of the riverbank.

"Say 'Glass box, open!' " requested the princess. And when the young man repeated those words, the box opened and the three of them stepped out onto the dry land.

Amazed and with great excitement, the princess then spoke. "In that case, since you are capable of making your words come true, say that you want a silver bridge with gold railings to appear, and may the bridge reach as far as my father's palace."

The man with the special power said the words, and soon a silver bridge with gold railings reached from that spot to the palace.

Again the princess said, "If you are capable of that, too, say the word and let a golden carriage appear, drawn by four horses, and let it take us to the imperial palace."

And everything happened just as he said those words.

When they arrived at the palace, the emperor came out and, dazzled by what he saw, he asked, "What is this? Who created all this?"

"Father," spoke the daughter, "this husband of mine brought all this through his words. All his words come true."

"In that case, young man," replied the emperor with joy, "you are not an ordinary person after all. I give you half of my empire, and may you be happy with my daughter!"

A great feast was held, and mead and wine were drunk.
Mead and wine flowed down the chins of everyone—
but none reached my mouth.

17

*Elijah the Prophet
on the Seder Night*

n the town of Salonika in Greece, there was a man who didn't have anything. One day, in the week before Pesach, the man went for a stroll on the beach. He was very bothered by all of his troubles. How would he celebrate the seder? After all, he still had nothing for the holiday.

He walked nervously along the beach. Directly toward him walked the Angel of Death, in the disguise of a person.

"Why are you so sad?" asked the disguised Angel.

"My house is so empty. Pesach is coming and I have nothing prepared for the holiday," answered the poor man.

"Come, we'll make an agreement," replied the Angel of Death. "I will give you a hundred gold *dinarii* and you'll prepare a beautiful and festive seder in your home. As soon as you bless the first cup of wine, I will arrive at your house and ask you three questions. If you answer them, you will stay alive and rich and happy with your lot. But if you can't answer them, then I'll take you with me and you will die. What do you say to this challenge?"

Because he had no choice, the poor man agreed to this suggestion, took the money, and returned home and told his wife

115

about the meeting. His wife was surprised. "Was it worth it to take the money on those conditions?" she questioned. "But Pesach is such a festive holiday and, after all, it is a big *mitzvah* to make a seder. So go buy what we will need and God will help us."

And so the man went out to buy everything they would need. His wife cooked and prepared and set the table with everything the way it was supposed to be. And the evening of the first seder came. Everyone sat at the table. No one dared to begin the blessing over the first cup of wine.

All of a sudden, a light tapping was heard at the door of the house. The door opened and in came Elijah the Prophet, disguised as an old peddler. He asked the family, "Is it possible for a guest to join you at the seder and to spend the night here?"

"Of course. You are welcome!" The man and his wife showed him great honor and gave him water for washing and made a place for him at the table. When he sat down, he saw that they were not starting the seder, always finding some excuse to delay the *Kiddush*.

"Why aren't you reciting the blessing over the wine?" Elijah finally asked.

The poor man then told him all that happened on the beach. Elijah calmed them down. "Don't worry. I am with you. Begin the first blessing."

Just then there was a knock on the door.

Elijah said, "Do not answer it. I will answer in your place."

And Elijah turned to the door and called out, "Who is it that is knocking on the door?"

And the Angel of Death answered from the outside, "Is that you, Elijah? Listen and tell me how I knew it was you, even though I was on the other side of the door?"

"Very easily, for you saw me from the keyhole," replied Elijah.

And the Angel of Death said, "Your wife gave birth."

"Oh what good luck!" answered Elijah.

"Yes, she gave birth to twins," continued the Angel of Death. Elijah replied, "It's God's will."

"And one of them died."

"He paid a debt. God gives and God takes away," replied Elijah.

And then the Angel of Death added, "And the second one is sick. And do you know why?"

"From the pain and the loss of his brother," answered Elijah.

And the Angel of Death saw that he couldn't enter, nor could he best Elijah with his words and questions.

Suddenly the Angel of Death disappeared in a gust of wind.

This is the way the poor man was saved by performing the *mitzvah* of opening his door to invite all those who are hungry to come and eat.

18

The Neighbors

n Lebanon there lived two women who were neighbors. One was very poor because her husband could never earn even a penny, no matter how hard he worked. The other was very rich, but she was never happy with what she had. She was always complaining to her husband about her ill fate.

Now Pesach was approaching, and in the house of the poor woman there was nothing for the festival. Her heart was sad about it, but in her heart there was also hope.

That day the woman decided to take all her children's clothes to the river to wash them. At least this way they would be clean and bright in honor of the holiday. The woman sat along the bank of the river, scrubbing and washing the clothes. And her tears became mixed with the water of the river.

All of a sudden, standing next to her was an old man. "What happened to you, dear woman?" he asked with great pity. "Do you need something? Why are you weeping?"

"Oh, no," answered the woman hurriedly. "Only some of the soap bubbles have gotten into my eyes, and this is the cause of my tears." And she quickly wiped her eyes with her apron.

"Have you prepared everything for the holiday?" asked the man.

"Yes, of course," answered the woman.

"And do you have *matzot* and wine?" he asked.

"Of course," she answered.

"And the candles and the tablecloth? Are they ready?" he continued questioning.

"Oh, a long time ago," she said.

"And the meals? And *everything* you need?" he asked.

"Yes, of course. Everything has been prepared," she answered.

"If that is so," said the man, "then I'll say good-bye and wish you a happy holiday!"

The next day, the rich neighbor also went to the bank of the river to wash the children's clothes. But she was grumbling about the hard work that accompanies the preparation of such a holiday.

All of a sudden, next to her stood this same old man. He started asking her the very same questions. But the woman answered these questions with anger and bitterness because she didn't have anything yet prepared for the holiday. And about her husband she spoke with the same anger, for he was a good-for-nothing.

The old man wished her a happy holiday and disappeared.

The evening of the holiday of Pesach, there wasn't anything in the poor woman's house. Darkness seemed to be everywhere, for there were not even candles. But the hungry children were dressed in bright, clean clothes, and the tablecloth on the table was white and clean.

But not so in the rich woman's house. There was much on the table but no happiness in their hearts. Instead, their mouths and faces were full of complaints and arguments.

All of a sudden, the old man with the white beard appeared. With his long walking stick, he knocked on the door of the rich household and said to the rich woman, "Whatever you wished on the bank of the river, this is what you'll have."

And then the old man turned to knock on the door of the poor household and said to the poor woman, "Whatever you wished for yourself on the bank of the river, that is what you'll have."

Suddenly the poor woman's table was filled with everything

good, with silver chandeliers hanging from the ceiling, and the house was filled with light and happiness and love, and songs for the holiday.

The poor woman wanted to thank this man who had brought these miracles, but he had disappeared and was never seen again. She then understood that he was none other than Elijah the Prophet, Eliyahu HaNavi, whose good name we should always remember.

19

The Modest Scholar

any years ago, there lived in Jerusalem a wise man, a scholar. But this scholar was a very modest and poor man who had a habit of always remaining in the back, behind everyone. Whether in the synagogue, at a *simchah,* and especially when it came time to accept money from the charity fund, this man would give everyone else the honor to sit in the front or allow someone else the place ahead of him. At Passover each year the rabbi distributed gifts to all the townspeople and money from a special charity fund to all the needy. This was the custom at that time. It happened, one year, in the month of Nisan, when the rabbi had finished distributing these funds, that he had overlooked this poor scholar and had not given him any money for Passover.

The holiday was approaching, and the scholar still had no money to buy all that was necessary for such a celebration. His children began to complain and said, "Father, it is almost *yom tov*. We need *matzos* and wine and so much else so that we may properly honor the holiday. It is almost time to clean the house of all leaven. What should we eat during the holiday? Should we then die before your eyes?"

When the father heard these words, he began to weep bitterly and to pray with a great outcry because of his poverty and need. And these cries reached up to Heaven, to God Who Sits in the Heavens. And when God heard these cries, God grew angry at the city where no one could have pity on and help this poor man and his family. God's wrath was so great that He was ready to destroy the city of Jerusalem.

At that moment, Elijah came before God and said, "O God, Merciful God, do not destroy Your city and Your people. This scholar was not overlooked on purpose or from some evil intent, but rather because of his great humility. Let me go down and I will see that things are set right." And God agreed to this offer.

The scholar finished praying and weeping and went out into the town to see what he could borrow. As he was walking, Elijah, whom it is always good to mention, appeared in the disguise of an ordinary man, a traveler, and greeted him with "*Sholom aleikhem.*"

The scholar returned the greeting and asked, "I see you are a stranger here. Can I be of any help to you? Perhaps you are looking for someone who lives here?"

"I am a stranger here in this place and so I do not have an invitation for the seder tonight. Do me the honor of inviting me and I shall reward you with all that you need," replied Elijah.

And the scholar answered, "You do not need even to ask. Please stay as long as you wish, and you will be our welcome guest. What is your name, so that we may show you proper respect?"

"My name is Rabbi Nissim of Egypt," replied Elijah. "Please take this money so that you can buy what you need for the holiday." And he handed the scholar money to pay for his lodging and food.

The scholar returned home, his grateful heart filled with happiness. He called out to his wife and children to hear his story of meeting the stranger. "Go quickly now to buy all that we will need for the *yom tov.* Our guest will soon be here to join us for the seder. Treat him with great honor, for he is our guest. You will see that he has a face like an angel of God."

Passover eve came, and the scholar looked around the synagogue for his guest. He began to ask people, "Have you seen a man by the name of Rabbi Nissim of Egypt?" He walked through the marketplace and the streets asking after him. But it seemed that no one had seen him or heard of him. The scholar returned home but, before beginning the seder, he and his family waited at the seder table for their guest to arrive.

After a time, the scholar said, "I am certain now that our guest was not an ordinary man but Elijah the Prophet himself. Of course, that is why he called himself Nissim of Egypt, just like the miracles God performed in Egypt to set the Jewish people free, and the miracle that happened to us so that we can observe the Passover festival. Let all who are hungry come and join us. Let us begin, with song and praise, and with the symbols of the feast, the memories of our past." And the scholar stood up and recited the *Kiddush*.

But on that same Passover eve, the rabbi of Jerusalem had a strange and frightening dream. In his dream, he saw someone who seemed to be an angel of God about to attack him with an upraised fist. At the same time, the angel cried out, "How could you have forgotten that poor scholar? The Blessed One was so filled with wrath that He would have destroyed the city. Only Elijah, of blessed memory, saved you and the entire city from this fury by offering to help this poor man."

In the morning, the rabbi awoke, shaking from fright. He sent for the scholar and told him of this dream. The rabbi pleaded with him for his forgiveness. And from that time on, the rabbi always searched for all the poor and all the modest persons in the community, in order to support and sustain them.

And from that time on, the scholar's family had enough money to celebrate all the holidays with whatever was needed and to live a comfortable life for all their days.

20

A Blessing in Disguise

any years ago it happened that there was a good couple who lived in Baghdad. The husband studied Torah and performed *mitzvot,* giving charity to the poor and helping whoever needed work. The wife, too, was a good woman, distributing charity and offering hospitality to anyone who knocked on their door. They had one son, and the parents taught him the ways of God and to follow the Commandments, as they did.

When the son grew old enough to marry, his parents arranged a marriage with a good family who had a beautiful and learned daughter. At the wedding, everyone, the rich and the poor, were invited to celebrate in the *simchah*.

However, as time went on, the couple still had no child. It was hard for them to see other young couples with their babies. At night they wept bitter tears because they had no child to hold in their arms. During the day they saw the looks of pity in the faces of the people, and they would go out into the marketplace or synagogue only when it was necessary.

It was soon to be Pesach. They prepared everything according to the tradition. On the night of the first seder, they read the

Haggadah. As she heard the words of the Exodus from Egypt, the wife began to cry. Her husband looked up and saw her tears, and he understood why she was weeping. He spoke gentle words to her and, as he had said to her often before, he once again repeated, "My wife, do not worry. *HaKodosh Barukhu,* the Holy One Blessed Be He, will not forget us. We will have a child."

Suddenly they heard a tapping at the door. When the husband opened the door, they saw a weary traveler. Without hesitation, the couple invited this old man to enter and to join them for the seder. They sat and recited the *Haggadah* together and ate together, enjoying a lively discussion about the story of the Exodus.

When the old man got up to leave, the couple invited him to stay the night. But he insisted that he had to leave. And as he rose from his place, he did not thank the couple but spoke these words instead: "I asked *HaKodosh Barukhu* that I may merit to visit you next Pesach at the seder and that your table will be filled with disorder at that time."

The couple was astonished at this and even somewhat angry that this traveler would say such an ungracious "thank you." However, they did not want to offend him, since he was their guest and they had offered him hospitality with their whole hearts, without a thought for a reward of a "thank you."

Soon after Pesach, the wife knew that she was expecting a child. A beautiful child was born three months before the next Pesach, and they knew great joy.

When Pesach arrived, the couple once again sat down to begin the seder and the reading of the *Haggadah*. This time they held a baby on their laps, and the child behaved like all children do. He wiggled and laughed, he reached for the glass of wine, and he pulled at the tablecloth, he tore a page from the *Haggadah,* and he squealed when he threw a plate down. And what did the parents do? They behaved like all new parents. They laughed with joy, and watched with laughter, and spoke with delight at their child's "work." And the seder was in disorder and certainly not *b'seder*.

Suddenly there was again a tapping on the door. And when they opened the door, the couple saw the same traveler who had come the year before. They recognized him and again invited him in. But suddenly, as they stared at the man and also at the table, they recalled his words, his "thank you," and understood for the first time that those words had really been a blessing.

The couple began to talk at the same time, thanking the old man for his blessing, which had come true, and asking for forgiveness because they had regarded his words in a different light.

And the old man smiled with a beautiful smile and said, "There is no need to ask my forgiveness. How could you have understood my words at that time? May you be worthy to bring your child to study Torah and do good deeds and to bring your child to the *chuppah*."

And the old man disappeared.

Then the couple understood that the traveler had been the Prophet Elijah, may his name be remembered for good.

21

The Ignorant Beadle

here was once a beadle in the Beit Midrash. He was a simple man, and he always had faith in God. He was so innocent and naive when he was young that, after all the students, the *talmidei chakhomim*, left, he would stay in the Beit Midrash and the Beit Knesset, which was above the House of Study, and clean and work, without any wages. He tried to learn, but he could never learn anything. Nothing ever stayed in his head.

After he grew up, he needed some sort of an income, and he would mutter aloud about this from time to time. Somebody in the Beit Midrash heard him. From that time on, on every Thursday, this anonymous benefactor would leave him a little packet of money, and that would be his "pay." When he had finished cleaning and washing the floor on Thursdays, he would kiss the *mezuzah* and see this packet and think, "It's as if God has given me this money so I'll have something to live on." And he would work faithfully, knowing that he could expect this money each week.

One day the beadle got married, and even after his baby was

born, he continued to work in the Beit Midrash. This was his only business and his only work.

The amount of money he continued to receive was always enough. The beadle's family never lacked for anything. Every week he would bring the packet home to his wife and she managed the money. If it was *erev* Pesach, the anonymous benefactor would give him enough for Pesach. If it was *erev* Shavuot, he would give him enough for that *yom tov*. And that's the way it was—until the anonymous benefactor died.

One day, not long before Pesach, the beadle had finished fixing, washing, painting, cleaning. He then went out, expecting to find the packet so he could prepare for the holiday. But he didn't find anything. "Maybe I forgot something? Maybe I didn't prepare the lamps?" he thought. So he went back inside and cleaned them, filled them with oil, and again he dusted. But still there was nothing—no money, no packet, nothing.

That's the way it was for that one day, and then a second day. Two weeks passed and three weeks—and soon it was *erev* Pesach.

But the beadle still had faith in God and said to himself, "Good! Maybe *HaKodosh Barukhu* stopped giving me my income here in this world and will give it to me in the next. But I will never hold out my hand to ask for help. I have never, in my whole life, ever asked for charity or depended on the generosity of others. Go ask someone else? Never!"

But then he thought, "But how can I celebrate the Passover holiday with a fast? To be tortured in such a way during the holiday? It can never be."

So what did he do? He went to his wife and told her what had happened, how he had been without an income for many weeks. He told her how he had tried different things, how he cleaned and washed more than he normally did during the whole year. And still he never found any money.

"Maybe *HaKodosh Barukhu* wants us to live in another city and that was why He stopped giving us money," he reasoned. "It's better to die in the streets from hunger in a strange city. After all, the neighbors know us in this town and that we have an income. They know we have to buy *matzah* and *charoset* and all the things to prepare for Pesach. And now the holiday is in two more days and we still have nothing. Come, my wife, we must leave this town."

His wife didn't argue with him and accepted everything her husband told her. They closed their house, and taking their child, they left the town during the night so no one would ever know.

Because the beadle had always stayed so close to the Beit Midrash, he didn't know the way to the next town. So instead of traveling on the king's road, they went into the forest. It was dark, and they walked in the fields and forests all night. After some hours, they were very tired and weak. They found no one in the forest. Of course, they had no food, no drink. They were hungry and thirsty, especially the poor child. Although the child couldn't ask for water, the mother felt in her heart that he was thirsty. So she said to her husband, "My husband, I am thirsty."

The husband answered, "I have been thirsty for half the night, but I didn't want to say anything for fear I would remind the child of his thirst. What can I do? I don't have any water for him."

At that moment, the child began to cry and the father was filled with pity. His wife then said, "My husband, I have no more strength to walk. We will stay here and you must go to look for water." So leaving them in the forest, the beadle started searching for water.

He took one step, then lifted his eyes to heaven and cried and repeated the names of Avraham, Yitzchak, and Yaakov, of Sarah, Rivkah, Rachel, and Leah. When he looked up, he saw ahead of him a downhill path that led to fresh grass. As he walked along, he saw a waterfall with a small spring of fresh water at the bottom. He immediately took some water and drank it and found that the water was sweet. He had never tasted such sweet water. When he tasted it, he felt as though he had eaten the most delicious food in the world.

He immediately turned and called out to his wife, "Look how great God's miracles are. God has given us a place to spend the holiday. We don't have to prepare anything. It is all here. This water has such taste that a person can live from this water alone. As soon as I tasted it, my hunger and thirst left me and I was satisfied."

The wife also drank the water. She said to her husband, "I'm sure that this water comes from the Garden of Eden. This will be our place, and here we will live. And if God has brought us to this place, then we will never feel the heat or the cold, we will never be afraid of the animals of the forest or the devils and spirits. And if He does all these wonderful miracles for us, then we have found favor in His eyes. We will celebrate the holiday of Pesach here.''

They slept there and remained there.

A few miles away, there was a sea. A ship was passing by and, by the power of God, its supply of water suddenly gave out. The owner of the ship observed the couple on the beach. When he saw them again on the second day, he thought, ''These people must have water in order to live there.'' Bringing the ship as close to the shore as possible, he came ashore and found the beadle and his wife and their son playing in the grass.

''Good people, could you please sell me some water?'' he asked.

''Who are you?'' they asked, thinking all the time that perhaps he, too, was sent to them by God.

He answered, ''I have a ship with many people, but we have no water, and we must have water to survive. I will give you a large amount of gold for some of your water.''

''This water is not ours,'' they answered. ''This water belongs to God. Take as much as you want.''

''No, I can't,'' answered the man. ''I will pay you.''

''From the time I tasted this water,'' explained the beadle, ''I felt there was some sort of a miracle in it.''

''But I can't take the water without your permission,'' insisted the man. ''I know that it is because of you that I am here.''

Then the beadle and his wife told the shipowner everything, about what had happened, and how poor they were.

''Then what can I do for you?'' asked the man.

''If you really want to do us a favor, then take us to a land where there are Jews.'' asked the beadle.

''Is that all you ask?'' said the man.

The man gave an order, and the sailors brought many large barrels and filled them with water and took them to the ship. Afterward, when they returned to fill the barrels again, they took the beadle and his family to the ship. After a few days, they sailed to a country where there were many Jews.

The ship docked at the port, and as the beadle and his family left the ship, the shipowner bade them farewell, saying, ''A few miles from here you will find a city where there is a very honorable community of Jews.'' And then the ship departed.

But the poor man, instead of going in the direction of the city, again wandered into a forest. The family walked and walked. When the beadle saw that they were lost, he began to cry, "*Ribono shel Olam*, Master of the Universe. . . ."

But then he became angry with himself. The Master of the Universe had brought them to a place where they could live an easy life, without work, without worry, and they had left that Paradise. Now he was sure that the Master of the Universe would punish him. Now the animals of the forest would eat them. And he had all these terrible thoughts. And meanwhile the child was hungry and crying.

Suddenly two rough-looking men from the city appeared. They were just walking around in the woods, as people from the city sometimes did when they had nothing else to do. They saw the beadle and his wife and child. "What are they doing here? We came here to be alone, but why are they here?" they wondered.

They approached the family and asked, "Who are you?"

Because he was afraid, the beadle did not know what to say. Who were these people? If they were Arabs and he told them he was a Christian, maybe they would kill him, because at that time the Arabs hated the Christians. But if he told them he was an Arab, maybe they were Christians. And if he said to them he was a Jew, maybe then they would still kill him. So he decided to tell them "I am the son of the Name. God created all of us."

"You are really the son of the Name?" the men scoffed. "If that is so, then ask the Holy One, Blessed be He, to cure me. My leg always hurts and causes me to limp. I am in pain all the time."

"Therefore," said the beadle, "God will send you a complete recovery in His Name." He had only to say these words, with such force and with such feeling, that suddenly the man stopped feeling pain and even danced a few steps to test his leg. "This is the son of the Name!" he shouted.

But then the other man said to his friend, "But maybe this is God Himself." "Oh, no," said the first man. "He said things in the way that we understand." So they both ran immediately to the city and told everyone about the righteous man in the woods who had arrived. "You know me and how my leg is always causing me pain and making me limp. From the second he asked God to cure me, I was cured by the Almighty in Heaven."

Representatives from the whole city were sent to the woods to

find this righteous man and his family. They went with wagons.
They brought clothes, different kinds of cakes, fruit, wine, and
other good food. The beadle was astounded and didn't know what
to do. What should he say? So he said what he had said before,
without thinking. "I am the son of the Name. God created all of
us." It was just something to say. When the people heard his
words, they immediately took him, with great honor and fanfare,
and put him in a wagon and welcomed him with great honor. They
already knew him as the man who brought complete healings.

After they took him to the city, they began to argue and fight
among themselves. Who would receive him? At whose house
would he be a guest? Then the rabbis came. "Thank God, we have
a person, who is the richest man of our community, our mayor. He
is a good man and a good Jew, fearful of God. Why should we
argue? This family will be a guest at our mayor's house." And that's
the way it was decided.

So the family was given several rooms in the mayor's home until
the community could build a house for the beadle's family and
support them. The poor beadle saw that God had brought him to
this place, after all, and he said, "It is because of the Torah and
because of the place I kept clean that people have brought me here
and now give me more and more and more."

From that very day, all the people of the town, the innocent
ones, the wise ones, even the fearful ones, learned that this man had
some sort of magic power, that anyone who had any kind of pain
had only to go to him and ask, "Sir, please pray to God for me."

So what could he do, this poor man, this poor beadle? When
people asked him to pray for them, he prayed. He lifted his eyes
toward the heavens, he prayed—and he saw that his prayers were
accepted. So from that day on, anyone who mentioned this beadle's
name spoke it with a blessing. And from that time on, anyone who
had any reason would come to this holy man. And also, along with
the charity boxes for contributions in every house, there would be
a money box marked "For the son of the Name." And when
people saw that the money boxes were full, they would bring them
to the beadle. Especially when a woman was pregnant and about to
give birth, they would bring him a special gift and he would pray to
God for the woman to have a safe delivery. And that's the way life
continued for years . . . and years . . . and years.

Then the beadle became old. And of course the community helped him and worried about him. They built him an important house and of course he had a Beit Midrash and of course a yeshivah. But remember, he was an absolute *am ha'aretz,* a foolish man, an ignorant man.

As his son grew, he also could never learn anything—nothing, nothing, nothing. Just like his father. He was fearful of God, but he couldn't even learn one letter of the *aleph bet.*

A few more years passed and the beadle died. The whole community gathered, and with great honor, mourned him for seventy days—just as in the Bible the Jews had mourned for Yaakov our Father. And why? Because it was known from this day forward that whoever was sick would remain sick. And there was nothing they could do. Furthermore, if anyone had something stolen, it would remain stolen. When the beadle was alive, he could help everybody. He would cry to God, and God would answer him immediately. "But now we're finished." And the community bemoaned their fate with a heavy heart.

Months passed.

There was a widow who had one daughter whom she raised by the sweat of her brow. This daughter got married and became pregnant. When it was time for her to give birth, she had terrible labor pains, for one day, two, three, and still she did not give birth. The mother didn't know what to do. Everyone tried different ways to help the young woman, but nothing seemed to help. Finally they implored the mother by saying, "At least go to the beadle's house, and ask for pity for your daughter. Take *tzedakah* and give it to his widow."

But the mother replied, "Oh, to my great misfortune, there is only the beadle's son, who is worthless."

"But go anyway," they pleaded with her. "Only kiss the wall of the house, give charity, and leave. Maybe this will help. Otherwise your daughter is lost. She will soon die because she is suffering so."

And when the mother heard this same advice from everyone who came to her, she took some money and started for the beadle's house.

On the way she saw the beadle's son. She thought, "What did that great righteous man leave after him? Such a son! Such a simpleton! He doesn't know anything."

When the son saw that the woman was in such a panic, he pitied her, much like his father would, and he asked her, "Why are you running, dear woman?"

"Oh, leave me alone. I'm in terrible trouble, for I have a great misfortune. How can I explain this to you?" she answered.

Then he said to her, "Tell me anyway what is troubling you. Maybe I can help you."

"How can *you* help?" And the poor woman began to scream at him.

But he calmed her and again offered his help. Finally she said to him, "My daughter is already in labor with terrible pains for five days. I'm going to your father's house, *zikhrono livrakhah alav shalom,* to kiss the wall and give *tzedakah,* and maybe that will help my daughter."

And the son said to her, "You don't need to do anything. Go back to your home. Because of my father, this will happen before you arrive back at your home. Some woman will approach you and say to you, 'Your daughter has already given birth. She is well. She is only worried about you and keeps asking about you.' "

"What? Are you crazy? What are you telling me?" she started to scream. He didn't let her finish, but continued, "My dear woman, return home. It is only by the right of God and my father that I am telling you this. And this is the exact way it will be. Your daughter has already given birth and is asking for you. Everything has turned out well."

Since he was not letting her pass, and was only repeating with such force what he had already said, she turned around and went back home.

On the way back, she began to curse him. "That ignoramus stood in my way. What does *he* know?"

But suddenly some women approached her and cried out, "*Mazel tov!* Your daughter has given birth, and she is fine. She is asking about you. Where were you? She is worried about you and wants you to be near her."

The woman could hardly believe what she was hearing and said, "Do you know that the son has even stronger powers than his father? He didn't even pray. He just said that this is the way it would be, and that is the way it turned out."

The people began to run to his house. They realized that whatever he said was as though it was already decided in Heaven.

Many years passed. One day a rabbi came from the holy city of Jerusalem. He was collecting contributions for the good of all of Israel. And as he was traveling to this same town, he also took a wrong turn and went into the forest. He didn't know what to do. Some people were walking in the forest, and when they saw this rabbi, they asked who he was.

The rabbi was frightened of them and answered, "I am the son of the Name."

"Oh, then you should know that your brother died many years ago. But his son lives here in this city." And then they said, "Come in the wagon and we will bring you to his home." And they told him of the young man's greatness.

Some of the men ran ahead to tell the son that his uncle had arrived from Jerusalem and was coming to see him. When the wagon of people arrived and the rabbi approached the beadle's son, the son accepted him as his uncle and greeted him.

But the rabbi thought, "These people are crazy. This young man is simple." But he told the young man how everyone had spoken so highly of his father, that he had been a *tzaddik,* a truly righteous man. And so the rabbi stayed on as the guest in this house, accepting the role of the uncle. And the son served him and waited on him, just like a child.

But suddenly the son began to cry, "My father died but I don't want to say *Kaddish.*" And his mother also cried, "My husband has died, and he is not saying *Kaddish.* It is like a nation without Torah. It is like the time of Moses our teacher. When he died and went up to Heaven, the people became idol worshipers, and they made the golden calf. And the whole nation just sat, ate, and drank. No, I want my son to know that he should say *Kaddish* for his father."

And the rabbi said to her, "I only came to collect contributions for the people of Israel. I can only stay for a few more days."

"Just tell us; we will give you what you need to collect for *tzedakah.* But the most important thing is for you to teach my son Torah." Then she asked him, "How long do you plan to be away?"

"An entire year," he answered.

Then she said, "If you will teach my son Torah, I am prepared to give you as much money as you want, for I have continued to receive great amounts from the people of the town, more than I can ever use. The most important thing is for my son to learn Torah."

The rabbi finally agreed. He reasoned that in this way, he would get what he came for, the money to bring back with him, and without the hardship of collecting from the people in the whole town. It was even performing a *mitzvah* at the same time. He saw with his own eyes that the son could perform miracles, but also that he didn't know how he did it.

The son said to the rabbi, "Honorable Rabbi, you will stay here, and when there are only three days left, this is what will happen. On the first day, I will give you your money. On the second day, I will be your witness. On the third day, you will get to Eretz Yisrael."

The rabbi was astounded by what he heard. "How is this possible? Even if he were a rabbi and a righteous man, he wouldn't be able to accomplish such miracles. How can a simple, ignorant man perform these miracles?"

In spite of his doubts, the rabbi started teaching the young man. Six months passed, and the young man had learned nothing. He would sit with the rabbi for whole days, and still he learned nothing.

After six months, the rabbi went to the mother and said, "You should know, my dear woman, that your son's brain cannot learn anything. He has studied for six months. And now I have no more strength for this task."

"For the sake of God, just teach him the main points," pleaded the mother.

And so the rabbi started teaching him the *Shma Yisrael*. He would repeat it over and over, "*Shma Yisrael Adonoi Eloheinu, Adonoi Echad.*"

He taught it again and again, until the son finally learned this prayer.

One day the rabbi said, "You should know that the way between here and Eretz Yisrael is a long way, a very long way, and it will take me a whole month of days to arrive there."

And the young man said, "Because of my father and because of

Torah, with God's help, you will get to Eretz Yisrael as I promised."

When there were three days left before the rabbi's departure, the son gave him a considerable contribution, even more than the rabbi had expected. The son himself had gone to the rich people, to the tax collectors, and to the villagers, and he collected a great sum. The money filled the entire wagon.

On the second day, the rabbi started on his way, but the young man said to the him, "Don't go anywhere. Just sit in the wagon and let the horses pull you. You will get there *b'shalom,* in peace, and God will guard you from Satan and the evil eye."

And the rabbi believed him and blessed him. Then the rabbi said to him, "I want to hear the *Shma* from you."

And the young man recited, "*Shma Yisrael Adonoi Eloheinu Adonoi Echad.*"

With great happiness, the son returned to his house, the place where he had sat, with God's help, for a whole year and had studied.

His mother approached him and said, "My son, thank God, the rabbi has gone in peace?"

"Yes, Mother," he answered.

"And what have you learned? Can I hear you recite something?" asked his mother.

"*Shma Yisrael Adonoi Eloheinu Adonoi . . .*"

He had forgotten the last word. He didn't know how to finish. He asked his mother to help him.

"Why are you asking me? I didn't study," answered the mother.

"Well, then, I'll go back and ask the rabbi," he answered without concern.

And the mother cried out, "Master of the Universe, it is already four hours since the rabbi left. My son, how will you reach him?"

"I will reach him," answered the son. He immediately got on a horse and caught up to the rabbi. But when he found him, the rabbi was suffering from a great thirst. He didn't have any water and the sun was very strong. He could barely speak to the young man. "If you hadn't come now, I would have died," said the rabbi. "And now please get me some water."

The young man ran until he came to a cave. He hurried into the cave and there he found a door. He opened the door, and, yes, there was water, which he quickly brought to the rabbi. The rabbi drank the water and again taught him the *Shma.* The young man had forgotten only the last word, *echad,* but they went over the entire prayer a few times. The young man blessed the rabbi and returned to his house.

When his mother asked him what had happened, he told his mother with great happiness, "I found the rabbi and he taught it to me again. Now I know the *Shma.*

"So recite it for me, my son," she asked.

He immediately began, "*Shma Yisrael Adonoi Eloheinu Adonoi* . . . What now, Mother?"

"Again you forgot?" said the mother.

"So what, Mother. I still have strength. I will go and find the rabbi and he will teach it to me again," assured the young man.

So the young man again got on a horse and again was able to reach the rabbi. But a long time had passed, and he again found the rabbi parched and without water. The rabbi again asked the young man to bring him some water.

The young man went to the same place, but when he went to the door in the cave and started to push it open, all of a sudden, a man came in and said to him, "What do you think you are doing that you push a door open like that? Do you think this is a vacant place? That there isn't some kind of a guard? You should know that this is a holy place. The only people who can enter are *tzaddikim,* righteous people, for this place is like Gan Eden, the Garden of Eden. No one has the right to come in just like that. The first time I allowed you to come in. But know that I am the guard here. I am Elijah the Prophet. The first time I let you come in was because of your father. But this time, the second time, you pushed your way in without permission."

The young man replied, "You are right, sir. But I did all this not for me, not for my father, but because of Torah, so I could learn Torah. If you don't believe this, I am ready and willing to accept any kind of punishment you will give me. And if you really are Elijah the Prophet, you probably already know all of this."

And it *was* all known already.

And the young man continued, "You probably know how much suffering I have endured just to learn one word of Torah."

And Elijah said to him, "If this is the case, then come in. I will give you a pitcher of *mayim ohayim,* the water of life, and when you drink from it, you will drink Torah. Everything has already been decided in Heaven. Everything so that you should come here to learn Torah. Why? That you should know what your aim in life is. But remember, don't forget to drink."

And Elijah gave him a pitcher filled with the water of life.

The young man drank from the pitcher and he knew all of Torah and all the wisdom of life because he drank.

And Elijah said to him, "Listen, I will also give you other water to give to the rabbi to drink. Tell him that he will get to his house at eight o'clock at night and that you will get to his house before him, at four in the afternoon. You will live in Jerusalem, the holy city, and his daughter will become your wife. Now listen carefully. This daughter always studies and always learns. She has a special room where she reads and studies all the time. And I will cause it to happen that she will make a mistake and you will correct her. In this way she will know you, and you will be married. But it is forbidden for you to say one word from Torah until I come and say to you, 'Yes, student.' Remember all that I have spoken."

The young man drank the water and all of a sudden he was transformed into someone else, absolutely someone else. He then went to the rabbi and said, "You should know that I cannot live without Torah and so I must live with you and learn from you. You will arrive in Eretz Yisrael, with the help of God, at eight this evening and my mother and I will arrive at four this afternoon. There will be four hours between our arrival and yours. I'll bring all my possessions and we will live together."

When the rabbi heard all that the young man said, he was very happy. He then drank the water the young man had brought him and they bid each other *sholom.*

The young man returned home and said to his mother, "Mother, there is no reason for us to be here any longer, not even for one more minute." They gathered whatever they needed and filled a wagon with all their things. And then a miracle happened.

Before then, the young man had been performing miracles for others, but now it was a miracle performed for him.

Before the rabbi left, he had told his family that if he did not arrive in his town by *erev* Pesach, it would be a sign that he had been killed

or had met with some misfortune. He had bid farewell to his wife
and daughter, whom he loved like the apple of his eye.

The rabbi's one daughter was perfect in everything she did. She
was also very, very wise. She swore that she would not marry
anyone except a man who was wiser and greater in learning than
she. Young men came from all over the world, but there was no one
who proved wiser than she. And so she remained without a
husband.

Erev Pesach came. All the great rabbis came out to wait at the
various places of entry to the city. But the rabbi did not arrive.

When the rabbi's family and the people in the town saw, after
waiting a long while, that he had not arrived, they began to mourn.
Everyone thought something evil must have befallen him.

When the young man arrived at four o'clock, he found the
people crying, in mourning. He approached several people and said
to them, "I have arrived here at four o'clock. Don't worry. The
rabbi will be here at eight." When the people heard this, they
thought he was crazy, that he was making fun of them. There were
even people who cursed him. Some wanted to beat him. "You are
just talking stupid nonsense! The rabbi has been away a whole year.
How would you know the exact time of his arrival?"

When they heard that the rabbi had actually arrived at eight that
evening, his wife and daughter came out to greet him. All the great
rabbis came to greet him. But the rabbi said nothing to any of them,
because he was worried only about the young man, the beadle's
son.

When the rabbi didn't see the young man there, he thought,
"Maybe something has happened to him." And he remembered all
the favors and *mitzvot* that the young man had done for him. And
for a whole year he saw miracles done everywhere but did not realize
that it was the young man who was performing them.

During this time, the rabbi did not meet with anyone, not even
with his beloved daughter. He was only concerned about the young
man. He worried so for him that he had no interest in anything else.
He spent his time in prayer. It began to upset a lot of people, and
they began to address the rabbi in a different way. "Honorable
Rabbi, what has happened to you, dear Rabbi, that you do not
speak to any of us?"

"Maybe you have seen a strange young man? A young man with his mother?" And the rabbi told them what the young man looked like. And when they heard this description, they answered, "Oh, yes, Rabbi, we have seen this young man. He is a crazy man."

"Crazy? Yes, I must meet with that young man." And he did not rest until he saw the young man. Only after that did the rabbi meet with the great rabbis of the city and tell them what the young man had done for him, that it was only because of him that he did not speak with the rabbis.

Then he called his daughter and said to her, "My daughter, during a whole year I sat at this young man's house, and all the money I brought here was because of him. He is a righteous man and modest. Because of this I was afraid that something happened to him. Now there is great happiness."

That year they celebrated Pesach the way it was supposed to be celebrated. In his life, the rabbi never thought he could be as happy. "I only wish my daughter could marry the young man. But the young man is such an *am ha'aretz,* a stupid young man, and he would never know what to say to my daughter. She, who has rejected great scholars, would certainly never consider him for a husband. After all, she has sworn to God that she will marry only a *talmud chakham,* a very wise scholar, so this could never be a match."

Meanwhile, the young man followed Elijah the Prophet's instructions, and did not speak words of Torah to anyone.

One day, as he heard the rabbi and his daughter discussing a point of Torah, he listened. He noticed that she had made a mistake, but he said nothing. Later he pushed a note under her door, correcting her mistake. It happened a second time. Then a third time. Then she made a mistake on purpose and waited near the door. When the note appeared, she immediately opened the door and found, to her amazement, that it was this young man.

"Why didn't my father tell me the truth about you?" she asked. "You are a scholar after all, not at all the way my father has described you."

Then the young man spoke to her. "I was warned from Heaven not to tell this to anyone but my wife, but I will tell you. But you should also know that if you tell this to anyone else, you and I will no longer be allowed to live." Then he told her exactly what happened to him, about meeting Elijah the Prophet, and how he was blessed with being in upper Paradise, how he brought water to her father. All this he told her. But he also told her that he was forbidden from saying even one word of Torah until it was announced from Heaven that he could speak.

The young woman told her father that she was pleased with the young man and that she wanted to marry him. "Father, you and I will both teach him," she said happily.

The father listened with great surprise, but also with happiness. Then after a long while he said, "But do not get your hopes too high. I know how hard it is to teach this young man, and he cannot learn. How can you marry him when he is without Torah? It is true that those who are learned cannot perform the miracles he does, but he. . . ."

The daughter interrupted her father and said, "On the day of the wedding, he just has to begin. . . ."

And her father said to her, "Do not say even one word about this for the time being. After all, people will talk and wonder how you could wait so long and then choose this ignorant young man after rejecting scholars and other learned young men. How will it appear to everyone?"

The daughter said to her father, "Don't worry, Father. I will teach him."

"*You* cannot teach him anything. *I* will teach him," he replied.

"Father, only women can outshine the men. Even you are embarrassed in front of me. When he sees a beautiful young learned woman, he will surely be embarrassed not to know as much as I do. Then he will begin to learn," she said.

But to the rabbi's great sadness, on the day of the wedding the young man did not say anything. The groom was waiting for Elijah the Prophet, who had not yet arrived. But the rabbi, not knowing this, was sorry that he had approved this marriage.

Then the young man stood on the pulpit and began, "Ladies and gentlemen. . . ." Although the rabbi knew that the young man knew nothing, it was only proper for him to say something, to speak a few words of Torah at his own wedding.

But then the young man did not continue, and why? Because he didn't yet have the right, the permission. Because everything comes from Heaven.

At that moment, the rabbi spoke aloud, but not to anyone in particular. "He isn't worth anything since he cannot even begin to speak." As soon as the rabbi said this, insulting the young man, Elijah the Prophet appeared and said, "Yes, student."

And then when the young man began to speak, it was as if all the heavens had opened. Even the Holy One Blessed Be His Name and His Court came down to earth. And the angels were listening to the true Torah. All the people listened, and they were astonished.

The young man spoke for one hour, two hours, three hours. People normally would have gone to eat, for it was the time for the second meal. But the young man continued speaking until the bride came. She approached him with the blessing that only she could speak to him. Then she said, "Enough. It is Shabbat and it is forbidden to fast on Shabbat."

The rabbi was astounded. "How is it that yesterday he was only an ignorant man and today he can speak such words of Torah?" The rabbi did not sleep all night. Suddenly Elijah the Prophet came to the rabbi in a dream and said to him, "You should know that what you said insulted him. Heaven passed a difficult sentence over him. You must ask his forgiveness and save him. You should know he did not do this from pride. He could not do this before he was given permission from Heaven. Do not think he is a great misfortune."

The next day the rabbi bowed down before his daughter's bridegroom and began to ask his forgiveness for saying the insulting words. Of course the young man forgave him. The rabbi asked his mercy. And then he asked the same from his daughter.

All this came from Heaven in order for the daughter to find a man who was wise in Torah, who was righteous and right and true.

The young couple saw only good days from that time on.

22

Laughter and Tears

here once was a king who loved questions and riddles. He also liked to hear clever answers. One day he said to his advisers, "Is it possible for a person to laugh and cry at the same time?"

His advisers were not certain if this was possible. They began to ask all the wise men of the kingdom. No one seemed to know. Perhaps no one had ever asked that particular question before. The king began to ask this question of everyone who came to the palace and finally, since he could not find the answer, he decided to have a contest.

"Whoever can make me laugh and cry *at the same time* will win one hundred gold coins," the king announced.

The advisers tried to make the king laugh and cry at the same time, but they did not succeed. Many other people tried, but usually the king sat on his throne either laughing at their attempts, or else becoming sad because he could not find anyone clever enough to succeed in this feat.

News of this contest reached the village where a beautiful young peasant girl lived. She was known for her wisdom even more than for her beauty. This young woman kept thinking, day and night,

159

how she could make the king laugh and cry at the same time. She talked with the old people in the village to find out if they knew any remedies to make a person laugh and cry at the same time. But no one seemed to have heard how to do this.

One day, the young woman was in the marketplace when an old merchant approached her and said, "Buy this basket of onions. They will come in handy."

"But I have come to the market to buy fruits and flowers today. Thank you, dear sir, but I do not have need of any onions," answered the young woman.

The merchant, however, kept insisting that she buy the onions. And after a while he said, "Dear gentle young woman, come sit next to me while I tell you a story." And he began to hum a tune while they walked to a place under the shade of a nearby tree. And then the old merchant began to tell the young woman a witty story while he began cutting an onion. As the young woman listened, fascinated, she began laughing. But then a stranger thing happened—tears began rolling down her cheeks at the same time. By the time the old merchant had finished the story, the young woman was drying her eyes on the corner of her apron. When she looked up to thank the merchant and to buy some onions, after all, from this kind man, the old merchant had disappeared. But there, next to her on the ground, was the basket of onions. She ran quickly around the marketplace to find the old man, to pay him for the onions, but he was nowhere to be found.

"Strange indeed," she said out loud. But when she looked at the cut onion, she realized, "I cried and laughed at the same time. Only Elijah the Prophet could have taught me this wisdom."

What did she do? She went directly to the palace of the king. When she arrived at the palace, she was brought before the king.

She sat down next to the throne and began humming a tune. The king was startled by what this young woman was doing, just sitting there singing. He began to listen. After a while, the young woman began telling the king a humorous story as if she were just talking to him like a friend. Then, while she was telling the story, she began cutting the onions into pieces. Holding the slices in her hands, she continued telling the story, gesturing wildly, often bringing the onions close to the king's nose. Smelling the strong onions, the king's eyes began to tear, while at the same time he was laughing at the comical story. The laughter and tears happened at the same time.

From all around the palace, the advisers and servants came running when they heard the king laughing. And when they saw the young woman cutting onions, they all began to laugh so loud and so hard that tears rolled down their cheeks.

When the story ended, the king dried his eyes—and suddenly realized that he had been laughing and crying at the same time.

Looking around the room and seeing his audience of advisers and servants, the king stood up from the throne and proudly announced, "Here is a wise and clever woman! She wins the gold coins—and my gratitude!"

From that day on, the young woman was a welcome guest in the palace, and she also became the royal storyteller. And the king always enjoyed her stories.

And that's how the king laughed and cried at the same time!

23

The Jewels of Mitzvah

any years ago, there was a wealthy man, Reb Yitzchak, learned in Torah and generous in distributing charity. Once, several rabbis came to his city and asked him for money. "We are collecting money to redeem captives," they explained.

Reb Yitzchak welcomed them and showed them great honor. After talking and hearing why they had come, Reb Yitzchak invited them to a meal. "Come and have dinner with me and I will give you the entire amount that you need."

At the dinner, they engaged in discussion about the Torah commandment of redeeming captives and of the great pleasure to perform *mitzvot*. "For the reward of performing *mitzvot* is both in this world and in the next," they agreed.

Listening to all of this, Reb Yitzchak replied, "May I have your permission to tell you a story that illustrates what we have been discussing? This happened when I was a young man, and it all happened because of a *mitzvah* that I had the opportunity to perform. Of that I am certain."

The rabbis were eager to hear his story and answered, "Let us hear, for it is always good to hear about the miracles performed by *HaKodosh Barukhu,* the Holy One Blessed Be He.''

And the wealthy Reb Yitzchak told his story.

* * *

When I was a young man, I married and my in-laws provided all that I needed for my wife and for me. But then I decided to leave their home and try earning my living. I had only 400 silver shekels with me, and I went out into the world to see how I could provide for my family. It was the time of the great fair at Leipzig, and I thought, "Let me try my luck there." After all, my father and his father were merchants in precious stones. Perhaps that is what God had in store for me, too, to become a jewel trader.

When I arrived at the fair, there was a crowd of thousands of people. The sounds of music and entertainment intermingled with the shouts of merchants and filled the air. As I walked through the crowds, I was pushed, almost against my will, toward a corner where I heard, above the voices, the cry of a woman. I saw her there, wrapped in a shawl, weeping as though her heart would break. I approached her and asked, "Why are you weeping so? Perhaps I can help you. Are you lost? Are you hungry?"

"No one can help me. My daughter is betrothed, but I need 400 silver shekels for her dowry. I could not save enough and now, if the money is not paid before three days, the wedding will not take place. Then what should we do? We will suffer such shame, and my daughter will not be able to marry. There is no one who is willing to help us." And the woman again wept.

When I heard her words and saw her tears, I, too, wept and felt such compassion. I realized I had just 400 silver shekels in my purse, but what did they mean to me when I heard the suffering of this woman? I took the money and gave them to her, wishing her *mazel tov.*

As soon as I turned, I felt a lightness and happiness in my heart. Here I had just given away all the money I had and still I felt happy. Strange, yes. But listen.

As I turned to leave the fair, not knowing, or even thinking, what I should do next, I met a merchant jeweler who suddenly appeared. He greeted me and, of course, I greeted him in return. In his hands he held pearls, the most exquisite pearls I had ever seen. My eyes must have opened very wide, because then he asked, "My friend, do you wish to buy these pearls?"

"Indeed, I would buy them at once, except for one thing. I do not have any money. Thank you for your offer, but you will do well to find a merchant with a full purse," I answered.

"My friend, I approached you because I see you are an honest man. Today you have no money, so I will wait until you sell these pearls and then, I am sure, you will pay me what you owe. I give you these in trust," the jeweler replied. I had never met such a man before and did not know what to say.

Then the man put the pearls in my hand. And just as I was walking away, two men approached and said to me, "We have heard that you are the merchant who has fine pearls to sell. We come from the king, who is in need of certain perfect pearls for his new crown. May we see your merchandise?"

So I took one of the pearls from my pocket and showed it to the royal representatives. They grew very excited. "And do you have more? This one is perfect. We will buy it." And I showed them all the pearls I had. They bought all of them at a very good price. Well, you can imagine how happy I was. I could now repay the jeweler who had trusted me with his pearls, and with the profit I could buy more merchandise.

The next day, I went back to the fair and met the jeweler again. I paid him what I owed him and asked to buy still more merchandise. This time the jeweler had even more wonderful jewels, rubies and diamonds and emeralds. But the jeweler insisted that I take them on credit and that I should pay for them on the following day—*after* I had sold them. I saw that that was the way he conducted his business. So what could I do? I thanked him for his trust and went on my way. I never noticed, at the time, that I did not see where the jeweler went or where his stall was placed.

Again, the next day, the royal representatives found me and asked me if I had more jewels for the royal crown and also for the queen, who had need of exceptional jewels for a new necklace. I showed them my new merchandise, and again they were enchanted when they saw what I had. They bought everything for a large sum. Because of this I saw that I had become extremely wealthy.

The next day, I went searching for the jeweler to pay him for his generous loan of the jewels. I searched everywhere but could not find him. I became worried. After all, I owed him a great deal of money. Perhaps he would think that I ran away without paying my debt. I searched in every market stall and street. I asked everyone-about this merchant. I described how he looked. But this man, this trusting merchant, had vanished without leaving a trace. Then I was certain that the merchant had to have been Elijah the Prophet, may his name be remembered for good.

Every year when I go to the fair, even now years later, I still look for that wondrous merchant, but I have never seen him again. But you see, my friends, I am certain that I became a wealthy man because of the *mitzvah* I performed of helping to marry off a poor bride by supplying the needed dowry.

Because of supplying the jewels for the king and queen, I have always been welcomed in the royal court. As a result, the king and queen think kindly of the Jews and are ready to hear our petitions with an open heart.

And now, my friends, that you have listened to my story, I am ready to give you the sum of money that you will need to continue your good work of ransoming the captives and other *mitzvot.*''

Saying that, Reb Yitzchak went to his money box and took out the money that he had promised, saying, "May God help us, and may we always be worthy of performing good deeds.''

24

The Inheritance

yrkanus was a happy man. Every morning he awoke with joy in his heart and recited his prayers, filled with gratitude and thanksgiving for what he had—his strong, handsome sons, fields that were rich with good soil, full granaries, and flocks and herds that were multiplying. God had been good to him, and he felt proud of his work and what he would be able to leave as an inheritance for his sons.

"Working with the land is the best occupation a man can have!" Hyrkanus would say whenever he passed one of his sons in the field. It soon became an expected remark, repeated like a song's refrain. But every time he said it, it was like a fresh thought to him, and he felt good about being his own master. And when he saw the rewards of his labor, the fruits, the harvest, the calves, the lambs, the baby goats, he thanked God for these riches and the life of a farmer.

"Yes, my sons, to be a farmer is the best life of all. Working with the land is the best occupation a man can have! Cities! Let others go to the city and work in other jobs. Not the sons of Hyrkanus! For us it is the life of a farmer, connected to the land, to the planting and harvesting of our own food, of feeling the joy of

working with the earth and our own animals. I am satisfied that I
will be leaving my land in good hands and that you will continue
working the land with your sons and your grandsons." So Hyrkanus spoke to his sons.

One day, as Hyrkanus visited one of his fields, he saw his
youngest son, Eliezer, sitting on a rock and weeping.

"My son, what is the matter? If the work is too hard, come and
you'll work on another field that has already been plowed," said the
father. And it happened again that Hyrkanus came to that field the
next day and the next, each time seeing how his son Eliezer was
working without heart, or just sitting and sighing.

This sadness puzzled Hyrkanus, and so finally, one day, he
approached his son, asking, "Tell me, Eliezer, what causes you to
weep? What disturbs you that you cannot work with your full force?
Open your heart to me."

And Eliezer replied, "Father, I do not love working on the land
the way you and my brothers do. I find it to be like a prison.
I. . . ."

"Well then, my son, I understand. Although I wanted you to
follow my path, to succeed on the land as I have done, I will help
you change your occupation if that is what you desire. Tell me what
you would like better: to be a weaver, a carpenter, a blacksmith?
Perhaps a silversmith? Or to work with leather and make saddles? Or
even a. . . ."

"No, Father, those are not even in my dreams. I have only one
idea in mind, to study Torah and become a scholar. I want to devote
my whole life to learning, Father," answered Eliezer.

"That is pure nonsense! To become a scholar! You need to get
married and have children. Then let one of your sons become a
scholar. This is *your* place, Eliezer, where your father and your
brothers are. The land is for Hyrkanus and for the sons of
Hyrkanus! This is a place for workers, not for idle scholars." Saying
this, Hyrkanus left and returned to his fields.

Every day seemed so hard for Eliezer. He could not sleep. He
refused to eat. He thought only of wanting to know more about
God and God's laws. And he felt so ignorant and so trapped.

After several weeks, Eliezer had a dream. In the dream he saw
Elijah the Prophet, and Elijah said to him, "I know that you have
a great sorrow upon you. What is your desire that will give you
peace?"

"I want to study and learn. I am so ignorant that even the birds have more knowledge than I do. Can you help me? You help all those who call upon you. What can I do to attain my heart's wish?" pleaded Eliezer.

"If you love knowledge and would devote your whole life to learning, a life more dedicated even than plowing the fields and harvesting the wheat, then go to Jerusalem. Find the school of Rabbi Yochanan ben Zakkai, and he will teach you," answered Elijah.

Eliezer did not hesitate. Without bidding farewell to his parents, not even to his brothers, he left home and arrived in Jerusalem. He immediately asked where Rabbi Yochanan ben Zakkai's home was, made his way there, and waited outside the door.

The rabbi noticed the young man standing by the door, weeping. "Who are you? Who is your father? Why are you weeping?" asked the rabbi. But Eliezer answered only with his own name and then added, "I weep because of my desire to study."

"And how much learning have you already?" asked the rabbi.

"Nothing. That is also why I weep, because of my ignorance. Teach me, Rabbi, for without knowledge I cannot live," replied Eliezer.

Ben Zakkai took the young man into his home like a son, spoke gently to him, reassuring him, and began teaching him the *Shma,* the grace at meals, and to pray.

"I recognize an honest heart. I shall teach you as long as you study well and become a light to your people." And every day, ben Zakkai and Eliezer studied two sections of the *Mishnah* and at every meal they spoke words of Torah, and when they walked, ben Zakkai talked to him with stories. And the rabbi's judgment proved true. Eliezer was a good student with a quick mind, reasoning, questioning, learning, remembering, connecting, and applying what he had learned to his life. It was only a short time later, admired by all the other students and teachers in the academy, assured of his place as a great scholar, that Eliezer finally told Rabbi Yochanan ben Zakkai that he was Eliezer ben Hyrkanus, the son of the rich landowner and farmer, Hyrkanus.

What was happening all this time in his father's house? Did Hyrkanus grieve for his son? Search for him? Did he think to find him and bring him home forcibly or perhaps ask forgiveness and send him to study with his blessing? Who knows? Because no sooner had Eliezer left than the brothers began to condemn him, talk against him, reminding their parents that their youngest brother had brought disgrace to the family by rejecting the family land.

"Since he despises the land and its inhabitants, he should have no share in the inheritance," they all agreed. Urging the father to take this action, repeating this over and over, the father finally decided to disinherit Eliezer. To do it legally, Hyrkanus had to travel to Jerusalem.

When Hyrkanus arrived in the Holy City, he was amazed at the crowds. People from everywhere seemed to be there. The streets were filled with people, their arms filled with baskets, the air filled with excitement. How different from his quiet, distant fields! How insignificant his houses and land seemed compared with the magnificent white stone buildings and roads in Jerusalem!

Turning a corner, Hyrkanus met an old friend. "Come, Hyrkanus, and let us go to visit Rabbi Yochanan ben Zakkai today. There is a great dinner with many prominent people who are in Jerusalem. Surely we will hear great words of Torah."

And so Hyrkanus joined his friend, and when they arrived at the home of ben Zakkai, they found many people seated at tables. When ben Zakkai learned that Hyrkanus, the father of Eliezer, was his guest, he instructed that Eliezer be seated at the same table with Hyrkanus. The father did not recognize his son, for he never even imagined that his son Eliezer could be associating with such prominent and learned people. And in the time he had been away from home, Eliezer had changed.

After the feasting, ben Zakkai turned to Eliezer and said, "It is time to hear words of Torah. Honor us with your wise words."

"Oh, that I cannot do at this time, my teacher. For is it not written that a student can be likened to a well and cannot give forth more water than it possesses. All I know I have learned from you, and as it is written, 'Talmid al yoreh halakhah bimkom rabo' [Sanhedrin 5b]—'A student should not teach halakhah in place of his teacher unless he is at a distance of 3 parsa'ot.' Besides, I still have much more to learn," answered Eliezer.

But ben Zakkai spoke again, and again urged him to speak, saying, "A good student like you may be compared to a fountain, an inexhaustible spring, that gushes forth fresh water from its own source.''

Reluctantly Eliezer agreed, but only after ben Zakkai left the room, for he understood that his presence overwhelmed his student and that Eliezer would then feel freer to speak.

Eliezer began to speak. And when he spoke of holy things, about the beauty of creation, of life and its wonders, of death and its mysteries, of the world in its grandeur, and the human soul, his face shone with a radiance and his voice grew wondrously eloquent. The people listened, awe-inspired.

Ben Zakkai had meanwhile returned to listen from the back, and when Eliezer had finished, he could not restrain himself and rushed to the front and kissed him on the forehead, saying, "Oh, blessed son of Hyrkanus! O blessed Israel, to have such a teacher as you!"

Everyone began to applaud, and when the echo of the admiring comments had barely faded, Hyrkanus turned to ben Zakkai and asked, "Of whom are you speaking? Which Hyrkanus do you refer to?"

"Why, to you, of course. This great teacher is your son, Eliezer, here standing at your side," replied ben Zakkai.

"My son!" And turning to Eliezer, he searched his face for a sign of recognition. "Yes, you are my son Eliezer." And they embraced. "Blessed am I to have such a son! I must confess that I came to Jerusalem—yes, I will be frank—to disinherit you. But now I shall disinherit your greedy brothers, who persuaded me to take this action. Instead you shall be my sole heir!"

"No, Father! Let each brother have his portion. Each one works the land and deserves to inherit what is rightfully his. I bear them no ill will. If I desired fields, I could pray to God for them, for He is God over the earth. If I desired gold, I could pray to God for it, for God is the God of all the wealth that exists in our world. But my prayer was for the opportunity to devote myself to the study of the Torah. And this blessing I have already been granted."

Then after asking about his mother and his brothers, the father and son continued to speak more words of Torah.

25

All Because of a
Loaf of Bread

In the city of Vormeise there lived a wealthy land-owner. His name was Reb Shmuel ben Yaakov, and he had a daughter Peninnah. When his daughter reached the age of marriage, the father went to the academy to choose a young scholar for her. And he chose a young man, 15 years of age, who was a *talmud chakham,* already known for his good mind. When the betrothal agreement was drawn up, it was agreed that Reb Shmuel would pay for all expenses so this young man could go to the academy of the Maharshal and live there and study for three years, without any worries about money. Everything was to be paid in advance. The young man agreed and left to begin his studies with one of the greatest sages of the generation.

But, as we know, nothing is assured forever. The wheel turns, and Reb Shmuel's fortune was lost. He entered into a business venture that destroyed his entire wealth, money, and land, and the only things that grew were his debts. (May none of us know about such creditors who made his life bitter like gall.) The only person left who gave him some pleasure was his beloved daughter—and what could she do but wait for God to have mercy and pity them.

All this time, the bridegroom-scholar was in the academy of the Maharshal, devoting himself to the study of Torah. He did not need much money, for he spent his entire days and nights learning, studying, praying. Of course, he did not know—how could he— what had happened to Reb Shmuel.

After three years, the scholar received a letter from Reb Shmuel, who wrote: "Our sages say that when a young man reaches the age of 18, it is the right time to marry. But know that I am now unable to pay the dowry and fulfill the other conditions written in the betrothal agreement. I do not want to bind you to this, and so I am informing you that you are free to arrange a marriage with anyone you choose. Please forgive us."

When the scholar read this letter, he replied in writing: "I am of course very unhappy to hear what you have written. I know that God will help you out of your plight. Have courage and patience, for God helps in mysterious ways. I would still desire to marry your daughter under any condition. But if you, sir, do not wish to bind your beloved daughter to me, then you are also free to do as you wish, and you may betroth her to someone else. Then I will decide what to do."

Both bride and groom waited for God's mercies. She sat alone in her parents' house. He remained in the academy, devoting himself to the study of Torah.

When the matchmakers heard about the broken engagement, many approached the young scholar with proposals of all kinds. But his only reply was, "I only desire to study Torah." And although many students left the academy after a certain number of years, many to return home to marry, the young scholar stayed on. Soon he gained a reputation as being strange, and people referred to him as "Reb Leib the-one-who-prefers-to-remain-alone."

When Reb Shmuel's fortunes did not improve, his daughter Peninnah decided to do something to help them. She opened a small shop and sold bread and cakes to make a living for her parents. More and more people outside of the neighborhood heard about the delicious baked goods and came to buy. From this Peninnah earned a modest income. At least they did not have to accept charity from anyone. And this continued for ten years.

At this time war broke out in the state. Armies marched through Vormeise, and the streets and markets were filled with soldiers.

One day a troop of cavalry marched by in front of Peninnah's shop. At the very end of the troop, which had just passed through, came a rider on a very handsome horse. He stopped in front of the bakery. He got off his horse, looked around to see if anyone was watching, and with his sword pierced a loaf of bread that was on the counter and then rode off. Peninnah came into the shop just as this happened. She ran into the street shouting after the horseman, "Come back! Do not steal from a poor girl who is trying to support her elderly parents! We have nothing but the money I earn from this bread!"

The horseman, hearing her cries and words, slowed down, returned to the shop, and said to her, "But I have been riding for three days without food. I am very hungry, so what could I do? I wish I had money to pay you for this bread." And he thought a moment and then said, "Good woman, I'll tell you what I'll do. I have two saddles that I'm sitting on. I'll give you one in payment for the loaf of bread." And as he spoke, he pulled out one saddle and flung it into the shop with great force. Then he spurred his horse and rode off.

The young woman cried bitterly. That soldier had taken a loaf of bread, and what he gave her in return was an old, torn, worthless saddle. She went over to the saddle to pull it out of the way—but when she did, to her amazement gold pieces spilled out. She could not even lift it because it was so heavy with gold coins.

Quickly Peninnah ran off to her parents to tell them all that had happened. "We will keep it for three days," the father answered, "and if the soldier does not return, then it is a sign that this is a gift from God."

But no one ever came to claim the saddle and its contents. The parents thanked God for not abandoning them in their old age. "That soldier must have been Elijah the Prophet," they agreed.

Reb Shmuel sat down and wrote a letter to the scholar, telling him that a miracle had happened and that he was now prepared to arrange the wedding as planned and to fulfill all the agreed-upon conditions, that is, if the scholar was willing.

When the scholar received this letter, he was overjoyed with the news—and not surprised. He wrote back agreeing to all the conditions.

On the day of the wedding, the young scholar arrived in Vormeise, and the wedding was held with joy and happiness.

Everyone in town had been invited to share in the *simchah*. And some even said that there was a mysterious handsome soldier who had come in to witness the couple being led to the wedding canopy and that he had wept tears of joy.

26

The Proper Response

here was once a young man who inherited a great deal of money. With the money he bought great tracts of land. To plow this land, he needed oxen. So one day, taking a full purse of gold coins and mounting his finest horse, this landowner started for the marketplace in a nearby town to buy the oxen.

Elijah the Prophet, who was also on his way to the fair disguised as a merchant, met the young man and asked him, "Where are you going?"

And the young man replied, "To the great fair."

Elijah began to ride along with him (for he, too, was riding on a horse) and continued his questions. "And what will you buy at the fair?"

"I will buy the best oxen to plow my land," answered the young man with great pride in his voice.

"Say, 'If it please God,' " cautioned Elijah.

"There is no need for that!" replied the young man. "Since I have the money in *my* purse, I will buy the oxen *I* choose, whether it pleases God or not." And he spurred the horse to go faster.

Elijah, catching up with him, called out, "But not with good fortune"—and he rode off.

When the young man arrived at the fair, he chose a fine pair of oxen. But when it came time to pay their price, he discovered that his purse was missing. He searched everywhere but could not find it. With great annoyance, he had to return home to get more gold.

He filled a purse with money and once more set out for the marketplace. Again Elijah met him, but this time Elijah was disguised as an old man. As the young man stopped to let his horse drink from a stream in the woods, the old man, Elijah, approached and asked the young man where he was going.

"To buy some oxen at the fair," he replied without courtesy.

"Say, 'If it please God,' " said the old man.

But the young man gave the same reply as before and rode off in haste. And again Elijah called out, "But not with good fortune."

And when the young merchant arrived at the marketplace to pay for the oxen, he again discovered that his purse was missing.

For the third time, he had to return home for more money to purchase the oxen. But this time, when he started riding to the fair, he began to think what had happened to him along the way—*twice*.

"Perhaps this was because of my arrogance, thinking I could do whatever I wanted just because I have money. Maybe there is a power greater than that. Maybe the power to do what I wish depends on God." And so he decided to add, "If it please God, then I will succeed in purchasing the oxen."

As he was deciding this, in his mind and his heart, there suddenly appeared a poor boy who asked the young merchant, "Can you use a strong helper? I need work and will be glad to help you."

"I am going to the fair to buy some oxen, if it please God. Perhaps you can help me bring these oxen back to my lands. I can offer you some good pay for this service," answered the young man. And so the two of them arrived at the fair, completed the sale, and started on their return trip with the pair of oxen.

As they were returning through the forest, the oxen suddenly broke loose and started to go in a different direction, off the path. The man and the boy started running after them through the forest as fast as they could. Then they saw that the two oxen had stopped in front of a huge, flat rock. When they reached this place, the young merchant saw, on the top of the rock, his two lost purses and his money.

Amazed and grateful, but also filled with wonder, the merchant took his purses, saying softly to himself, "If it please God."

Afterward they brought the oxen safely home. The hired boy, who was Elijah, may his name be remembered for good, disappeared.

Later, when the king heard about this fine pair of oxen, he offered the young man a handsome price for them. And so the young man became even wealthier. But whatever he did from that time on, whether he sold or bought, he always remembered to add, "If it please God."

27

Rachel and Akiva:
A Love Story

here lived in Jerusalem a wealthy man by the name of Kalba Savua. His only daughter, Rachel, was filled with wisdom and beauty. And, of course, many young men sought her hand in marriage. But none of them found his way to Rachel's heart. And her father expressed his displeasure at her judgments.

"Father, I will not marry a man only because of riches or because of a good family name," Rachel told her father. "The only man I will marry is one who has a noble character and a good heart."

Rachel walked in the meadows, enjoying the beauty of the hills, the sky and the clouds, the trees and the flowers, often singing the psalms of David and the song of Miriam. She would watch the shepherds attending her father's flocks, listen to the tunes they played on reeds or flutes, and wonder how the sheep and cattle understood the shepherds' commands.

One of the shepherds, Akiva, won Rachel's heart. He was wise, modest, kind, and gentle. And they loved each other.

One day, as they spoke, Rachel said to Akiva, "You are worthy to be a teacher of Torah in Israel. Promise me that you will study Torah after we are married."

"Study Torah? Begin my studies now, at the age of 40?" asked Akiva. "How can I do that? What can I achieve?"

"Akiva, you have seen how the round stone around the mouth of a well is ridged and grooved. Well, how do you think those ridges were engraved in hard stone? It is the rope, a *soft* rope that runs down over the stone every day, many times a day, that cut those ridges," argued Rachel.

"Oh, I understand what you say, Rachel. For if a soft rope can cut into hard stone, then how much more can the words of *Torah*, which are hard as iron, engrave themselves on my heart, which is merely flesh!" answered Akiva.

So Akiva promised Rachel, and they were secretly betrothed.

One day, Rachel approached her father and said, "Father, I have decided whom I want to marry. It is Akiva."

"Daughter, that cannot be! You are a daughter of a wealthy family. Akiva is a poor, ignorant shepherd. He cannot even recite the blessing after meals. Forget him and choose another, or soon I will choose a husband for you. It seems that you are not as wise as I thought you to be, for you lack good judgment!" answered the father with impatience and anger.

"Very well, Father, you may think of me as you wish, but I will marry only Akiva! My heart tells me that he is not what you see, a simple shepherd. Trust me, Father, as you always have. Why should my judgment mislead me now?" pleaded Rachel.

"Marry him, if you insist, Rachel. But know that if you choose to marry Akiva, then you both must leave my house. Then you will have plenty of love to live on, but very little else. At that time you will regret your decision and see that I was right," replied the father.

Rachel and Akiva married. Kalba Savua took an oath that his daughter would not inherit any of his property. And the young couple fled to begin a life filled with poverty and discomfort.

They found a little hut to live in outside the city of Jerusalem and lived on dry bread and slept on a bed of straw. But even though they had so little of the comforts and luxuries that Rachel had been accustomed to, nevertheless it was she who was always happy and singing, who bolstered Akiva's spirits when he was unhappy.

"Rachel, my beloved, I can give you nothing but sorrow and a bed of straw to sleep on. Look how you must suffer because of me!" cried Akiva.

"My husband, my beloved, I would rather live with you in poverty than without you and have all the riches in the world," replied Rachel.

And Rachel kept reminding Akiva of his oath that he would begin the study of Torah. "But they will laugh at me. They will say, 'Forty years old and he knows less than a child beginning his *aleph bet.*' How will I be able to endure this and study?" Akiva replied.

"Akiva, listen to me. If I brought an injured donkey to the marketplace and put dirt on its wounds and healing herbs all around it, the people would laugh and have a good story to tell afterward. Then if I brought the same donkey to the marketplace for a second day, they would again laugh. But then on the third day, they would no longer laugh. They would accept what I do as my habit of doing things. The same will be with you, Akiva. You must begin your study soon," counseled Rachel.

"If only I had some money, I would buy for you a golden crown with the shape of Jerusalem engraved on it, and place it on your head to wear, and you would look so beautiful, my Rachel, my beloved," answered Akiva. And he wept.

As they were talking, there was a knock on the door. When Akiva opened the door, the cold wind scattered the straw from their bed. There stood a man, a poor man. They quickly invited him in so they could close the door against the cold night.

"What do you wish?" they asked him.

"My wife has just given birth and I am too poor even to supply her with enough straw for a bed. Could you please give me a small bundle of straw for her?" asked the man.

Without a moment's hesitation the couple gathered up the straw they had and gave it to the man, with their blessing. And the man, who was the Prophet Elijah, departed.

Akiva turned to his wife, feeling consoled, and said, "I understand something now, my beloved, that there are people in this world even more unfortunate than we are."

Then after a moment, he said, with a gentle laugh, "But one day, mark my words, that Golden Jerusalem will look very beautiful on your head."

Years later, Akiva became a great teacher and scholar, with the support and help and patience of Rachel. After twenty-four years Akiva and Rachel and her father, Kalba Savua, were all finally reunited in happiness and blessing.

Still more years passed, and in his old age, Akiva saved some gold and made for Rachel a crown of gold that had large precious stones and pearls. For the design, he engraved the sun and moon, the stars and constellations, and the city of Jerusalem. And with great love and honor he gave this crown to Rachel, his beloved wife, and she wore the Golden Jerusalem, remembering his promise and the straw.

28

A Beggar's Blessing

lijah, disguised as a beggar, was walking in the city. As always, he observed people to see how they acted toward one another, how they spent their money, and how they gave charity.

One day, Elijah came to the mansion of a wealthy merchant. He knocked on the door. When the merchant saw from the window that it was only a beggar, he ordered the servants to take a basin of water and fling it over the beggar's head. When the basin fell into the street, just missing him, Elijah walked away as though nothing had happened.

Walking farther down the street, Elijah came to a small, poor cottage. In this little house lived the merchant's brother. But while the wealthy merchant was stingy and mean, the brother was generous and kind.

When Elijah knocked on the door, the brother and his wife invited the stranger in. "Come in and wash and rest. Then we will be happy to share whatever food we have with you," they both said.

After reciting the blessings after the meal, Elijah turned to the couple and said, "May God reward you! May the first thing you wish to do be blessed, and may you go on doing it until you say 'Enough!' "

And Elijah disappeared.

The wife turned to her husband and said, "What shall we wish for? If we wish for money, then we can help others."

"You speak pearls of wisdom, my wife. Let us wish for money," agreed the husband.

The husband and wife sat around the table and began to wish out loud, "We wish for gold coins." And gold coins, piles and piles of gold coins, began to appear everywhere—on the table, under the table, on the beds and under the beds, on the chairs and under the chairs, in the cabinets (and there were plenty of empty spaces, you may be sure, but now they filled up with the coins). When they saw that there was enough for their needs and for giving charity, they looked at each other and shouted, "Enough!" And the gold coins stopped multiplying.

The couple took the coins, counted them, and put them into separate boxes: one for the family needs, one for the future when their children would marry, one for charity, one for orphaned children, one for poor brides, and one for the synagogue.

One day, the greedy brother heard about his brother's good fortune. When he saw for himself how his brother and family had become rich, he asked, "Well, well, brother, how did you gain this good fortune? Surely you can tell me your secret. You know I always have your best interests at heart."

"Brother, a beggar came to our house. In return for our hospitality, he granted us his blessing," answered the generous brother.

"Beggars are always coming to my house, so I built a wide vestibule and that way I don't have to hear their pleading for alms when they come to my door. Describe this beggar to me, brother. Perhaps I'll keep my eyes open to see if this same beggar comes to my house. Then I'll really show him some hospitality and he'll grant me an even greater blessing, of that I am certain," said the greedy brother.

And the good brother described the beggar, adding, "And brother, I will pray that he visits you, too."

The greedy merchant watched for this beggar day and night. And one day, Elijah came to his house once more. When the merchant saw him, he quickly ran to the door to invite him in. Then he ordered the servants to lock the door, not to allow any other beggars in, and to bring the best food and the rarest wine, which was to be served on the finest china and crystal.

The merchant could hardly eat or drink. He just kept his eyes on the beggar and waited expectantly for the blessing.

After Elijah had eaten and recited the blessings, he turned to the merchant and his wife and said, "May the next thing you do be so blessed that you will go on doing it forever."

And Elijah disappeared.

No sooner had he vanished than the wife and husband turned to each other and said, "Let us wish for gold! But before we wish, let us drink a toast to congratulate ourselves." They took out their best bottle of brandy, poured two glasses, lifted the glasses, and called out, "To our gold! To our riches!" And they drank the brandy.

But then the "blessing" of the beggar began to take effect— because the couple could not stop drinking the brandy. They poured another two glasses full, toasted each other with "To our gold! To our riches!" and drank the brandy. And over and over they kept drinking the brandy until they fell into a drunken sleep. The next day, when they awoke, they started over again drinking and toasting, drinking and toasting, drinking and toasting until, one day, they woke no more.

As for our good brother, he and his wife and family continued to live in their good ways, in wealth, wisdom, and charity.

And so may we all!

29

The Bride's Wisdom

 here once was a wealthy man whose wife was not only beautiful but also wise. Together they taught their only daughter, Deborah, Torah, the laws of *tzedakah*, and kindness. Since the daughter loved to study Torah, she also learned to question what was not right or not just. Deborah and her father and mother—oh, yes, her mother was also very learned—often talked late into the night and on Shabbos about the interpretations of the law, using examples and stories and quotations from the Torah.

As she grew older, Deborah's mind became quick as the wind, as deep as the waters, as solid as the earth, and as brilliant as fire. Her parents were proud of their daughter, of the way she acted, and the way she spoke.

When Deborah became a young woman, her parents arranged a marriage for her. She had many suitors, since she was beautiful and wealthy; but the young man her parents chose attracted her particularly because of his ability to refute a statement of law. (What she never heard from him was the positive side, but she never realized that.) So she consented to the marriage, and they were wed. As happy as she was on the day of the wedding, as great was her sorrow when, that night, the bridegroom died a sudden, unexplained death. The bridal gown had to be changed for a gown of mourning.

Time passed, and once more Deborah was betrothed to a young man who was drawn to her wealth. Once again, the young bridegroom died on the wedding night.

After a while, the young woman married a third time, and this time also the bridegroom died. The wedding night turned into a morning of bitter grief.

Then Deborah resolved that she would never marry again. "Three times have I wed," she cried, "and three times have my bridegrooms died. Where is your great pity, O God, to cause such young men to die? Enough! If this is how it is to be, then I will remain alone, *not* just as a widow but also as an *agunah*, so I cannot marry anymore. And I will remain an *agunah* until You in your Heaven will see my suffering and sorrow and will have mercy."

And so Deborah remained alone for a long time.

Deborah's father had a brother who lived in another country with his wife and ten sons. Every day, the young woman's uncle and his eldest son went into the forest to collect firewood. They would sell the wood and thus earn a living for the large family.

One day when they went to the marketplace to sell their wood, no one came to buy. That night, they returned home with no money and no food. This bad luck continued until, one night, the father's eyes filled with tears and he said, "My son, let us remain in the forest to sleep tonight. I cannot bear to see how my wife and children cry for food and how they suffer because of me."

And the eldest son, whose name was Sholom, also wept.

The next day Sholom said, "My father, you have often told me about your brother, who is a wealthy man and a kind one. Let me go to him and perhaps find some work. In that way, my father, I can help you and the family." His parents saw that Sholom was determined to go. What else could they say to him? What reason could they have to prevent him from going? So they gave him their blessing, and Sholom set out on his journey.

When Sholom arrived at his uncle's house, he was welcomed with great joy. After he had rested and eaten, Sholom's relatives asked about his father and mother and his brothers.

When Sholom related how poor his family had become and how hard life was for them, his uncle gladly agreed to give the young man work, and he also sent cartons of goods and money to his brother.

After seven months had passed, Sholom approached his uncle and said, "You have been very good to me and to my family, my Uncle. But with everything I have now, I would ask one more request of you, which would bring me the greatest happiness. If you do not grant it, then I fear I shall have to return to my home."

The uncle was puzzled and said, "I don't understand. Tell me what you mean."

"Promise me that you will grant my request, Uncle," Sholom said.

"My dear nephew, I have grown to love you like a son. You would never ask for anything that is not according to the Law. So Sholom, I promise with all my heart to grant your request."

After a long while, Sholom said, "My uncle, I would like nothing more than to marry your daughter, Deborah. I want to make her my wife."

The uncle began to weep. "Don't do that, my son. Don't, my child. I cannot grant it. Ask anything else of me, but not permission to marry my daughter. I love you as my own son, as I love my brother. Three times she has married, and each groom has died on the wedding night. What has happened must have been on account of my sins, so I cannot keep the promise I have just made. I would be leading you to your death."

"Uncle, Uncle, I know what has happened," said Sholom. "I also know you have given me your promise, your word, to grant whatever request I made. You have given your word, Uncle, and I ask that you keep it."

"Don't marry her, Sholom," commanded the uncle. "I'll give you plenty of silver and gold. You are a wise young man with a good head. Don't put yourself in danger."

"No, it's not for your money that I want to marry Deborah," said Sholom. "What is money compared to the love I have found? Uncle, you have sworn an oath to grant my request. I have faith in God's love, that He will help us and protect us. He watches over Israel, just as a person watches over the apple of his eye. Isn't that what the Bible says?"

The uncle then realized that he would have to give his consent. Immediately he went to his wife and to Deborah to tell them about his promise. When Deborah heard the proposal, she began to weep, and she cried out bitterly, "*Ribon HaOlamim,* Lord of all the world, better you should turn your hand against me, but do not cause others to die because of me. My love for Sholom is so great. Do *not* take him away from me."

Hearing this, her parents wept together with Deborah and they prayed, asking God to guard the young couple from evil.

Then they began the wedding preparations. A great feast was planned, and all the people in the town, from the most important elders to the poorest of beggars, were invited to join in the wedding celebration. No one was left out.

It was the day of the wedding. Deborah was dressed, once again, in her wedding gown. Her tears of joy mingled with tears of fright and pain, and she prayed silently to God as she waited to be led to the *chuppah*.

In another room sat Sholom with the men, praying and singing—and also waiting.

Suddenly there appeared a stranger who motioned Sholom over to him and said, "My son, I am here to give you some good counsel, and you must follow it exactly." This stranger was Elijah the Prophet, may he be remembered for good.

And Elijah continued, "At the feast, a poor man will approach you. You will know who he is, because he does not resemble any other person in the whole world. His look will be wild; his clothing, black and torn. He will be weary. When you see him, get up from the table and place him next to you. Feed this stranger with the best foods and give him the finest wine. Serve him with honor and with your heart. Do not forget to obey everything I have told you. I wish you well, as I must leave you now." And Elijah disappeared.

After the marriage ceremony, the guests sat down for the festive meal. The bride and bridegroom sat at the head of the table, both happy in their love for each other. As everyone was eating and drinking, a stranger, a poor man bedraggled beyond description, appeared at the door. When Sholom saw him, even from a distance, he knew that this was the man he had been told to expect. As the man approached the table, Sholom stood up and invited him to sit next to him. And the bridegroom served this guest with honor and with his heart, as he had been counseled.

At the conclusion of the feast, the poor man called to the bridegroom, "I must speak with you for a moment." The bridegroom followed him into a room, and the poor man began, "My son, I am the messenger of God, the Angel of Death, and I have come to kill you and to take your soul."

"My lord," replied Sholom, "if it is God's will, then I can only obey. But give me a year, or even half a year, to share just a short span of time with my bride. Then I will go with you."

"No, I regret that I cannot grant even a moment more," answered the Angel of Death.

"Give me thirty days then, or let me enjoy just the seven days of feasting, as is the custom for a bride and bridegroom," pleaded Sholom.

"Impossible," responded the Angel of Death. "*This* moment is *your* time to come with me. I cannot delay what I have come for."

"Very well, I will come with you, but allow me to bid farewell to my dear wife," said Sholom. "At least wait for me just a few more moments. Will it matter so much?"

"You have been hospitable and kind and have shown me great honor," said the Angel of Death. "Therefore, in return for this good deed, I will grant you a few moments more. But be quick, for I must return with your soul on schedule."

When Sholom returned to the feast, he saw that his bride was not at the table. He went to the bride's room, where Deborah was sitting, alone, weeping and praying to God. Knocking gently on the door, Sholom called out her name. When Deborah came to the door and saw her husband, she embraced him and asked in a frightened voice, "My beloved, why have you come?"

"I have come to say good-bye to you, because the Angel of Death has called me to go with him," replied Sholom.

"*You* will *not* go with him!" she said with such force that even she was surprised. "*No,* my love, *you* stay here and *I* will go to him. *I* want to talk to him *myself*."

And Deborah went and found the Angel of Death waiting impatiently outside the room, and she asked, "Are you that angel who has come to take the life of my husband?"

He answered, "Yes."

"Well, he cannot die now," declared Deborah, "because it says in the Torah: 'Is there anyone who has paid the bride-price for a wife, but who has not yet married her? Let him go back to his home, lest he die in battle and another marry her' (Deuteronomy 20:7). So it's clear that when a man marries, he must stay with his wife. You cannot take my husband at this time."

"I must. I have been sent by God as His messenger. But you do have a good argument," replied the angel, weakening.

"Furthermore," continued Deborah, "it is written in the Torah: 'When a man has taken a bride, he shall not go out with the army or be assigned to it for any purpose; he shall be exempt one year for the sake of his household, to give happiness to the woman he has married' (Deuteronomy 24:5). Well, this would become a feast of mourning if my husband died now. Is this what God calls happiness and rejoicing? But God is true and his Torah is true. If you take my husband's life, then you will make a sham out of the Torah. So if you accept my words, good. If not, then I will take you to a *Beit Din,* to a rabbinical court, and we'll let the rabbinical judges decide. God would not break His own Laws."

And Deborah stood there looking at the angel eye to eye.

The angel, feeling pity for the young couple, looked away as he said, "I will go and consult with God." The angel flew directly up to Heaven.

That evening, the bride and bridegroom consecrated the marriage and slept peacefully.

The parents of the bride, however, could not sleep that night because of the dread of what might happen to their daughter's husband. All night they wept and prayed and, in the middle of the night, they got up and prepared a grave. At dawn, as the sun was rising, they entered the house again and, to their great surprise, heard sounds of joyful laughter filling the house.

When the young couple opened the door of their chamber, the parents saw that the young husband was alive and well. The faces of the bride and bridegroom shone with such beauty and love.

Well, as you can imagine, those seven days of feasting were truly days of rejoicing for the whole family.

As for the Angel of Death, when he presented the bride's argument before God in Heaven, God had to agree that the bride was right. So instead God sent the angel on other missions. The angel did not visit the bride and bridegroom for many, many, many years. And when he did, it was their true time to go with him.

30

The Repentant Rabbi

he young rabbi had completed his studies and was ready to leave the academy. He was ready to return home, his heart filled with hope. And he had a new title, which he had earned with the highest honors. He felt the pride of accomplishment—and why not? For years, had he not worked hard, studying, learning, questioning, attaining the admiration and the highest rank among his companions? And now it was time to bid farewell to his friends and to the head of the academy.

The head of the academy addressed all the students before they left: "My students, or rather I should say, my masters, for all these years I have learned most from you, my devoted students, what advice can I give you as you leave the academy? You have great knowledge, strong ambition, and you have gained my sincere respect. Yours is a holy purpose that you must not abuse. Remember always that the responsibilities of a gifted teacher are the most sacred. I will give you this rule to guide you. Let this principle be as an angel guiding you on the way: *Be pliant as the reed—that is, be kindly to all; and never be unbending as the cedar—that is, unforgiving to him who insults you*. My dear friends, why was the reed chosen to be used as a pen for writing the *Torah* scroll, the *tefillin* and the *mezuzot?* It gained this merit because of its special quality. You, too, will gain merit if you remember this principle and apply it."

After the farewells, the young rabbi began his journey home. As he rode, he could hardly keep from thinking about the reception waiting for him. After all, he was returning with the title of "rabbi," and the town would shower him with honor for his learning as well as for his title. It was a beautiful bright morning and, as he rode, he listened to the birds and enjoyed the flowering meadow, all the time imagining the welcome he would receive.

"Master! Master!" a hoarse voice called out, interrupting his daydream.

He turned to see who had called out, but his mood was one of anger. Who was pulling him out of this wonderful dream, this young rabbi, whom all delighted to honor?

When he looked down, he saw that it was a poor dwarf, crouching in the road. When the dwarf happily saw that he was noticed, he called out again, "Master! Master!"

At that point the young rabbi exclaimed in a scornful tone: "Tell me, have all the townspeople faces as ugly as yours? I would like to know before I continue my journey."

The dwarf was used to contempt, but this time he felt the pain even deeper than ever and he replied, "I do not know. Why not go to the Artist who made me and reproach Him for His handiwork. It was not my doing."

Suddenly, quick like an arrow hitting the mark, the rule *"pliant as the reed,"* his rabbi's parting advice, sprang into his mind. And now how had he applied it? Had he been kindly to this poor broken *nefesh?* What good was all his learning compared with the dignity of a human soul that he had treated with such contempt? Overwhelmed by a sudden sense of worthlessness, the young rabbi went over to the dwarf and threw himself to the ground and exclaimed, "Forgive me for my rudeness! I was hasty in my reply. I have sinned against you, but I ask for your forgiveness!"

The dwarf did not so easily accept this apology. Words that have stung cannot be taken back so quickly. The dwarf made only one reply. "Go reproach the Artist for His work! Perhaps you consider yourself a better artist!"

They continued walking to the town, and what a strange pair they were, with the dwarf walking first, followed by the rabbi, half pleading and half reasoning with the dwarf. But the dwarf would not be comforted. And all this caused the rabbi to lose his golden dreams. The very landscape had changed. The sun no longer seemed to shine as brightly. The birds were no longer singing.

Everyone in the village knew that the young rabbi, who had left years before as a child, was returning. There was great excitement in the town because the people there had always regarded a religious teacher with great esteem. And to have their own rabbi, born in that very town, and such a rabbi of learning and reputation, gave them an even greater *koved* indeed. There was joy and anticipation.

Knowing that this was the day of his arrival, the people gathered and started walking down the road to meet the young rabbi even before he would reach the town. Seeing him in the distance, they ran toward him, shouting, "*Sholom aleikhem,* O master! Peace be unto you, O teacher!"

The young rabbi did not know how to respond, as he felt such deep humiliation and self-reproach over what had happened on the road. But the people understood his silence as a sign of his modesty, and their admiration for him increased even more.

All this time, the dwarf mingled with the crowd and heard all the praise lavished on the young rabbi. But after a while the dwarf called out, "*Who* are you honoring in this way?"

"What! You don't know that this is our new rabbi, a scholar and a learned teacher? One of our own?"

"Scholar! Rabbi! Learned teacher! Keep us from such teachers! Listen, people, and judge between me and your rabbi." And the dwarf told them of the insult he had received. Everyone listened in silence, and one look at the young rabbi's face confirmed that what the dwarf was saying was what had happened. The people saw his anguish and his sorrow.

And then the young rabbi spoke, and his words came from a wound in his heart. "I have wronged this man. It was a shameful, cruel action, and I am truly sorry for my foolish words. I confess it openly. What more can I do? I have asked him to forgive me, but he is as unbending as the cedar. I had hoped to come to you with joy, but my soul is filled with sorrow and grief."

"Pardon him! Pardon him!" cried out the people. "Pardon him for his wisdom's sake. Look in his face and you can see his true repentance."

"Yes, I shall pardon him," replied the dwarf after a silence. "I shall pardon him for your sakes and that he may never commit again so grievous a sin." And when the young rabbi lifted his face to thank the dwarf for his forgiveness, the dwarf was nowhere to be seen.

"Perhaps the dwarf was Elijah the Prophet," he wondered. And for the first time since the morning, he had a smile on his face and the sorrow in his heart had lifted.

The next day was Shabbat. The young rabbi was to preach his first sermon, so people came from everywhere to hear him. The young rabbi did not feel any fear, but rather a new kind of excitement. After all, he had learned more from one day's experience than from years of study and thought. He had felt humility and compassion in a way in which he had never understood these feelings before. He realized that it was a valuable lesson and that more could be learned from studying people than from studying only books. He felt a new sense of gratitude and joy.

Wrestling with these thoughts, the young rabbi got up from his chair and approached the pulpit to begin his sermon. People grew quiet, and everyone's attention was on the rabbi.

The rabbi began to speak: "*Be always pliant as the reed, and never be unbending as the cedar.*"

31

*The Agunah, the Rabbi,
and the "Sheep"*

here was once a great rabbi who was also a very rich merchant. He and his wife had everything they desired—a mansion, wealth, a good name—but they didn't have a child. This rabbi would sit and plead with God, "Who are all these riches for if I don't have any children? God, I am begging you and asking for your mercy. Please give us a child."

One night, at midnight, the rabbi dreamed a dream. And in this dream he was told, "Your prayers are answered, and you will have a son. But he will have to go through many troubles. And he will bring you sorrow. Are you ready to accept this?"

The rabbi answered, "Yes. I am ready to accept this. I will do everything for him not to have troubles. I will protect him and watch him carefully. I won't let him have problems."

And the voice in the dream replied, "Very well. But you are warned."

The next morning, the rabbi awoke with a happy heart and immediately said to his wife, "Are you going today to the *mikveh* to immerse yourself?"

"And tell me why you ask," said the wife.

"Let us go together to the bathhouse and then to the *mikveh,*" answered the rabbi. And so they went together. First the wife and then the rabbi entered the bathhouse. Afterward, they went to the synagogue. There in the synagogue was the well of water. The rabbi's wife immersed herself seven times in the cold water. When she had finished, the rabbi immersed himself seven times. Then they returned home. That day, the rabbi did not leave home but recited psalms and studied Torah and prayed to God. That same evening, the rabbi's wife became pregnant.

All during the nine months, the rabbi was concerned for his wife's health and worried about her. After so many years, since the couple was no longer young, they had to be very careful. Nine months, nine days, and nine hours passed, and the rabbi's wife gave birth to a beautiful son. How can you describe such beauty! And their hearts were filled with joy and thankfulness.

The rabbi said to his wife, "My dear wife, now you must sit in this room forty days. Do not move from this place, not you and not our son. We have many servants, and you will have whatever you need. Just ring the bell and they will bring whatever you need."

After those forty days, their child remained in the house. He never went outdoors. The mother nursed him, and they coddled him and spoiled him. Whatever he wanted he had.

When he was 3 years old, they hired a teacher, an old rabbi, to come to the house to teach their son Torah. But the father insisted that the child be taught only in the house. And this is how it was. The child did not go out of the house for seven years. And all the time, the old rabbi taught him Torah. And the child learned Torah well and became almost as learned as his father.

And seven years passed. Then another seven years. By then the child knew *Torah* even better than his father. Since he was always home, he was constantly studying Torah, without any other activities or interests to interrupt his study.

When the young man reached the age of 18, he said to his father, "Father, there is so much I have not learned or seen. I live in this mansion so closely guarded, while outside there are people I have never seen. I don't know what an animal looks like or what it feels like to touch one. I don't meet with anyone except for my teacher and you, my parents. I don't know any other person. Even though I know a lot of Torah, and I hear what is happening in the world, I have never seen anything. I feel that now I must see the world for myself. Allow me some freedom, Father."

And the rabbi told his son, "Listen, my dear son, I am worried for your safety. I'm afraid for you—that you might get into trouble."

And the son answered, "Are you afraid for me? What is there to be afraid of? Let me go out into the world."

The rabbi could not stand to hear his son's pleading. Finally he said, "I agree. I will let you go out for ten minutes every day." And that's the way it was—the son went out of the house, but only for ten minutes every day. And the son was very happy.

After a few weeks, the parents allowed the boy to stay outside for a longer time. And so it continued in that way—each week he remained outdoors for a longer period of time. After a year, the boy became a merchant like his father. He would go out and come back, traveling only to the marketplace and returning home; everything was good and fine.

One day the son fell in love with a young woman, the daughter of a rabbi. And the son told his father, "Father, I want to marry this girl. She is very beautiful."

The father answered, "My son, I do not object. After all, she is the daughter of a rabbi, and she is very beautiful." And so they arranged the engagement party, the *kiddushin*. According to the law, they were betrothed, and it was as though she was his wife and he was her husband, although they had not yet come together under the *chuppah*.

One day, after the *kiddushin,* some merchants approached the young man and said, "Why are you trading only in this town? Go to Bombay. There you will find some extraordinary merchandise, merchandise such as you will not find here. You are wasting your time just sitting around here." Well, the merchants convinced the young man in such a way, and with such words, that the young man felt that if he didn't go with them to Bombay, he would never have such an opportunity again.

So the young man turned to his father and said, "Father, I *must* go to Bombay."

And the father said to his son in a pleading voice, "My son, please tell me why you want to go so far away. What makes you think of leaving here? Is it money that you need? You have great sums of gold, all you will ever need. This money will never end. Is something else lacking? Why do you want to go to Bombay to trade?''

And the son answered, "I want to know what merchandise they have there. I want to see a big city for myself. And I want to see another country. *I must go to Bombay, Father*. If I don't go, my life will end."

So again the father could not stand his son's pleading and entreating, and when it seemed that there was no other choice, he agreed. But then the father went to the merchants and said to them, "Dear sirs, you have gone to Bombay at least twenty times. But this will be the first time for my son. You know that he has only been out in the world for one year. Before that we had protected him by keeping him at home with us. I would ask you, please, to guard him carefully. Keep him close to you, advise him, be with him. As for money, that is not a concern. I will give you all you ask for. The most important thing is that he should return to us safely."

The merchants said to the rabbi, "You don't have anything to worry about. We have gone to Bombay and returned at least twenty times, perhaps even thirty times. And nothing has ever happened to us. What is there to worry about?"

Hearing these words, the father was calmed, but added, "Good. I am glad to hear your words. But please watch over him."

But in truth, the father in his heart, did not approve of his son's journey to Bombay.

The ship set sail from the port with the merchants and the rabbi's son. But when the ship was in the middle of the sea, the captain lost his way and didn't know which was the route to Bombay. The ship stopped near an island in the middle of the sea and the captain announced, "We have come to an island to rest and enjoy being on this little piece of land. Everybody should leave the ship and stay on the island for three hours. After three hours, the ship will set sail." So everybody went to the island. There they did not find any inhabitants, but there were many fruit trees of all kinds. The people ate the fruit and after the three hours, they took much fruit back with them to the ship.

Just two minutes before the end of the three hours, the young man remembered that it was time for prayer. He thought, "I will pray here in this beautiful place. Then I will return to the ship. There is just enough time."

In the meantime, everyone was back on the ship, and no one noticed that the young man was missing. The ship began to sail.

As soon as he had finished his prayers, the young man ran quickly to the shore. When he saw that the ship had already sailed far from the shore, he started to cry out. But who could hear him? What could he do? He remained on the island.

After two days, the travelers on the boat realized that the rabbi's son was missing. They searched everywhere for him. Finally they decided that he must have fallen from the ship into the sea. What else could have happened to him? They did not even begin to imagine that the young man would still be on the island. Since there was nothing that could be done, the merchants continued on the journey to Bombay. There they bought their merchandise and returned home.

When the ship had docked, the father was already at the dock waiting to greet his son. Everyone began to leave the ship, but his son was not there. As everyone passed the father, they put their heads down and could not look at him. The father sensed that something was wrong. "What has happened? Why are people putting their heads down as they pass by me? Why are they angry at me?" The father did not understand what was happening. Finally he pleaded with some of the travelers, "Tell me what is happening? Why have you avoided looking at me?" And then the travelers told him. "Your son has disappeared," they said.

"What do you mean? How has he disappeared? Where? When?" cried the bewildered father.

"We think he fell off the ship into the sea," answered the travelers. "But we are not certain. We did not realize that he was missing—but he is not on the ship."

The father returned home, crying and tearing his clothes. When the mother heard the news, she, too, began to weep. And so, too, the young woman who was to be married to the rabbi's son. Now she would never be able to marry. And they all mourned for the young man who would never return.

During the entire summer, the fruits were in such quantity that the young man had plenty to eat, always hoping another ship would soon come to the island and take him home. But all this time his clothing became more and more worn. Each time he washed them in the sea, they would become more threadbare—until there was hardly any cloth left. In the winter he shivered because of the cold at night, and he almost died from it. "Dear God," he began to cry and plead, "give me something to warm my body, something. . . ."

And God gave him extra hair like a sheep, and the hair grew long and curly and full all over his body. And the young man was happy because the new hair warmed him. But soon he began to see himself as a sheep. And he began to act like an animal. Soon he became hungry because he didn't have any more fruit. So he began to eat grass, like a sheep. And all this time—from eating the grass—his tongue changed and he could no longer speak. And in this way, three years passed.

After waiting for three years, the young woman went to the Beit Din and claimed, "There are enough young men who want to marry me. My betrothed is dead at sea and will not return. Release me from my promise of marriage. It is enough to be an *agunah* for three years. I am too young to remain alone and unmarried."

So the eleven rabbis of the Beit Din came together to consider this case. Ten of the rabbis saw that it was right to release the young woman from her vow and to give her permission to marry someone else. Only one rabbi did not agree with this decision. And if the decision in such a case was not agreed on by the entire Beit Din, then there was nothing else to do. The young woman would not be allowed to marry anyone else.

The ten rabbis told the eleventh rabbi, "If you don't accept our opinion, and you don't want to let her marry someone else, then we no longer consider you a rabbi in our community. You must leave our Beit Din."

But the rabbi was stubborn and replied, "I don't agree. The law of the Torah does not allow me to accept your opinion. Where is the dead body? Where are the witnesses that saw how and when he died? Maybe he clung to the trunk of a tree floating in the sea and was saved. Maybe he is still alive. Who knows? The most important thing is that, according to the Law, we cannot let her marry any man other than the young man she promised to marry."

All the people of the community sided with the young woman

and felt sorry for her. And the ten rabbis were also on her side. And everyone who saw the dissenting rabbi would curse him and even tried to hit him. This poor rabbi was not able to go out of his house. He remained at home, not going to the synagogue even for prayers. And meanwhile, the young woman remained an *agunah*.

Another three years passed. At this time, the ship sailing for Bombay again lost its way and found that it was near the same island. The people left the ship to walk on the island. When the young man saw the people from the ship, he started to run to them, happy to see people finally. But the people became frightened and said to one another, "What sort of animal is this? Who knows what harm it can do?" Because of their fright, they started to run back to the ship.

When the young man saw them running, he stopped rushing toward them because he did not want to frighten them. He suddenly understood their reason for running away from him. But he couldn't speak the human language anymore and he could not tell them who he really was. When the people saw that he was not going to attack them after all, they began to grow less fearful and to approach him slowly. They started to pet and stroke him.

Then they started to say, "*Ribono shel Olam,* this is just like a person. But what is this wool, like sheep's wool, all over his body? Master of the Universe, what sort of animal did You create?" When they wanted to leave and return to the ship, the creature started to follow them. He did not want to be left again on the island. They called the captain to ask what to do with this strange creature. When he saw this strange animal, he thought, "All my life I have been on the sea leading a very lonely life. Enough of this kind of life. Now God has sent me some sort of unique animal that is gentle and kind and willing to go with me. This is a rare opportunity. Why shouldn't I take him to the city and there I'll show him off, just as the gypsies lead their monkeys. I'll dance with him in front of an audience and people will pay me a lot of money. I'll command him, 'Get Up!,' 'Lie Down!,' 'Stand Up!' And this sheep will obey all my orders just like a monkey. And I'll collect a lot of money. I'll have a much easier life than my life now on the sea." And the captain quickly began to like this idea very much. So he took the sheep on the boat and tied him up with a chain.

When the boat returned to its home port, the captain went immediately to the owner of the ship and said to him, "I am giving you back your ship. I will no longer remain as captain, for I am sick of life at sea. Give me the money you owe me and I will go my own way.'' So the captain received his full salary and began to walk around from neighborhood to neighborhood in the city with his new animal.

People gathered and watched them. So the captain thought of a plan. ''First I will dress him up nicely so that no one will see that he is an animal. And then slowly we'll take off his clothes, piece by piece, and show him the way his mother brought him into the world on the day he was born. And in the meantime, I will teach him to obey all the commands I give him in front of an audience—how to sit, how to get up, how to dance.''

This strange creature learned everything the captain taught him and in a very skillful way. Going from place to place, from neighborhood to neighborhood, from town to town, the people marveled at this strange creature when they saw how he obeyed all the captain's commands. The captain collected a great deal of money from the people. And that's how they continued—until they came to the town where the creature's parents lived.

In the meantime, more than six years had passed since the day the young man left this town. One day, the captain and the creature passed through that town, going from neighborhood to neighborhood and from house to house, until they came to the house of the rabbi–merchant and his wife. Some of the people looked out of the windows and saw the captain. And the captain announced, ''Ladies and gentlemen, come and see the creature that I have here! Do you want me to bring it into the house? Look and enjoy it!'' And the captain went into the house, and the people gathered around him. The captain started giving the creature orders, ''Dance! Sit! Stand! Spin around!'' and on and on.

All of a sudden, the wife of the rabbi-merchant came into the room and, when the creature saw her, his own mother, he couldn't contain himself. He began to hug her and tried to kiss her. He didn't have a tongue for speaking. He tried to explain things to her with his gestures. He cried. But the rabbi's wife didn't know what to do. She didn't understand what was happening. How could she know that this was her son? Seeing this, the captain started to hit and beat the creature, pulling him away from the rabbi's wife. All of a sudden, the creature realized that his father was standing there.

He immediately began to run up to him and to jump on him and to hug him and kiss him. And when the rabbi saw this strange behavior, he fainted from all the fear and shock. Of course, he, too, did not know that this was his son. And while the captain wanted to leave quickly, the creature did not want to leave the house and kept pulling him back.

But the captain kept on beating the creature unmercifully, and only when there was blood running from one of the wounds did the creature finally leave the house. Again they went from house to house, house to house, until they arrived at the house of his betrothed. And again, when he saw the parents of the young woman, he began to hug and kiss them. Suddenly he saw his betrothed. He sat next to her, and gently he touched her hand. No one understood the reason for this. No one knew how to explain what was going on or why this was happening. The captain did not understand the creature's strange actions. Again afraid the animal might harm someone, the captain wanted to get him out of the house, but the creature did not want to leave, until again he got such a beating from the captain that he left.

Again they went from house to house until they came to the rabbi's house, the rabbi who had not agreed with the other ten rabbis of the Beit Din, the only rabbi who had refused to release the young woman from her vows to the young man. The creature and captain went into the house to perform their act. But when the rabbi saw the creature, he called out, "*Ribono shel Olam,* what is happening here? Isn't this an animal? But no animal such as this was created in the world. There is no mention in the Torah of such an animal." And the rabbi turned to the captain and asked, "Tell me, where did you get such a strange creature?"

"And what is it your business to know?" replied the captain. "I found it on an island in the middle of the sea. And that's where I brought it from."

And the rabbi said, "And what would you say to my offer if I asked to buy it from you? Would you sell it to me? I would like to buy a creature such as this."

"Just a minute," replied the captain. "Let me think." And the owner of the creature, still shaken from all that had happened, began to think. "A creature like this could make some trouble for me. Today it caused me embarrassment in two homes. It's a good thing it didn't kill anyone. Tomorrow it could kill someone. Then the authorities would arrest me and hang both of us. I better get rid of it, the quicker the better. I've earned enough from it. Now that I'm rich, very rich, I don't need it anymore." Then he turned to the rabbi and asked, "Are you willing to pay one hundred *dinars*?"

"Yes," answered the rabbi. "I'll agree to your price." And the captain took the hundred *dinars* and gave the creature to the rabbi.

At first the rabbi tied up the creature because he was a little afraid of it. But soon, after watching it for a while, the rabbi began to pet it, to stroke it. The creature became content and sat quietly. But when the rabbi brought it food, it didn't eat. Only when the rabbi brought it grass, did it eat. After it had gotten used to grass, it couldn't eat any other food, except for fruit. The rabbi put the creature in a room and brought it grass every day.

A few weeks passed. The rabbi said to himself, "Whenever I bring him grass for a meal, I'll mix in a little bit of meat. And each day I'll add more meat and bread and a little less grass." And so he did this every day. And with the water, he would add some milk. In this way he hoped to give the creature more strength, perhaps even to speak. The rabbi wanted so much to hear what this creature had to say. For six months this is the way their life went on. In this way the rabbi was less lonely, too, since he stayed at home alone all of the time, never going out of the house. After this time the creature began to speak, at first like a little baby speaks. Slowly, day by day, his speech became clearer and clearer. At the end of a year the rabbi began to understand the creature's speech. Then one day, this is what he heard: "I am the son of the rabbi-merchant from this city. You have done the *mitzvah* of saving my life."

The rabbi was shocked when he heard this. "Is it you?"

"Yes," answered the creature.

"Thank God! The people of this community are preparing to force me to leave this town because they don't want me here. It's good that your betrothed didn't marry someone else. The most important thing is that I was right and the majority was wrong. As long as there was no body and as long as there were no eyewitnesses, I, alone, kept the possibility open that you were still alive—even now after seven years."

"But now that I have begun to speak, there is the problem of this skin of sheep's wool. I have had it for such a long time," said the young creature.

And the rabbi began to worry, too, and he prayed fervently,

"Dear God, if You have done me this great kindness and You have brought me this young man after leading him from country to country, and city to city, from neighborhood to neighborhood, and house to house, give to my heart some sort of an idea, dear God, how to get this woolen skin off him."

At midnight, Elijah the Prophet, *zakhur latov,* appeared in his dream. And he asked him, "Rabbi, what is causing you to be so distressed? What is wrong?"

And the rabbi answered him in his dream, "Many problems have come to me. How can I not be distressed? What shall I do now? Please advise me how I should act."

And Elijah explained to him, "Tomorrow, go to the bathhouse. Rent the bathhouse for three days. Order that wood be burned in all the ovens until all the water in all the tubs is boiling. On the third day, take the creature to the bathhouse. Immerse him three times in the water and take him out. All his skin will be burned. So take this lotion and rub it on him. Then his skin will be like a newborn baby's." And Elijah took out a special bottle and handed it to the rabbi. Then Elijah continued with his instructions. "After this, take the young man and wrap him in cotton. When you have done all this, take him home and put him into bed. Every day feed him three teaspoons of pure olive oil and also milk, as much as he can drink. Continue this for forty days. After forty days, unwind the cotton dressing and see how he has healed. He will be in a faint, like a coma, and he won't be able to speak at all. He will remain like this for another forty days. After that time he will get up, healthy and healed, as he was before." Suddenly Elijah disappeared and the rabbi woke up. Feeling happiness and hope in his heart, he could not sleep for the remainder of the night.

In the morning he went to the owner of the bathhouse and said to him, "I want to rent your bathhouse for three days. And I ask that nobody else enter for those three days. Not one person must be allowed in. And furthermore, I ask that you fill the oven with wood and heat the water until it is boiling." And the rabbi paid the owner what he asked for the use of the bathhouse for three days.

On the third day, the rabbi brought the creature to the bathhouse. He had wrapped him up well so that no one would see what he was bringing with him. And the rabbi put the creature into the boiling water. After a few moments, the creature began to scream. But the rabbi held him firmly with all his might and immersed him in the water three times. When he took him out, there was no more sheep skin. It was just as Elijah had described it to him during the dream. Then the rabbi opened the special bottle and rubbed the lotion on the creature's body. After that, he wrapped his entire body in cotton, from head to toe. He wrapped him very well and took him home. Afterward, every day for forty days he fed him pure olive oil, three teaspoons, and plenty of milk, as much as he would drink, just the way Elijah had instructed him to do. After forty days, the rabbi unwound his cotton dressing, and the young man was in a faint. And so he remained for forty days. After he woke from this faint, the rabbi took the young man once more to the bathhouse to wash him. The young man looked at himself in the mirror and said, "How good it is! How good it is! I am myself once more, thank God!"

But his speech was still not very clear. Every day the rabbi sat next to him and talked to him. The two of them began to read and argue between them about Torah. And that's the way, very slowly, that the man's sounds returned to normal speech.

And again he knew Torah very well and his *neshamah* returned to him. One day the young man said to the rabbi, "Rabbi, this Shabbat we must go to the synagogue." The community was not very big, and in that community there was only one synagogue.

The rabbi answered the young man, "My son, if I were to go to the Beit Knesset, the townspeople would beat me. I am very careful not to go out of my house."

But the young man said, "If I go with you, they will not hurt you, because I am here as your guest." The rabbi agreed and gave the young man money to buy some clothes for Shabbat. On Shabbat morning the two of them went out to the synagogue. Everyone who saw them spat on the rabbi. One of them even blocked their way and called out to the young man, "Why are you going with *him?* This is an evil man. Beware of him! Why do you want to befriend a villain like him?"

The young man answered, "Leave that to me. Leave him alone. We are on our way to the synagogue. If you want to ask about certain things and clear up certain matters, come to the synagogue and you will find out what has happened."

They honored the guest's request and left the rabbi alone and accompanied them to the synagogue. When the two of them entered the synagogue, all the men who were already there got up, and each one took off his *tallit* and began to leave the synagogue.

So what did the young man do? He got up on the pulpit, next to the ark, and said to the congregation, "Gentlemen, listen to what I have to say. If you have been hurt or insulted by my coming, a Jewish guest in your community, I will leave the synagogue. Why should you have to leave? I will leave alone."

The people who were there called out to him, "It is not because of you that we are leaving, but rather because of the man you have come with. We don't speak with him, and we don't want to see him."

And the young man said to them, "Gentlemen, only this I ask of you: if you have complaints, let us hear them *after* the prayers. First let us pray."

Everyone agreed. And even though the mother of the young man was sitting upstairs and his father was also sitting in the synagogue, neither of them recognized their son. More than seven years had passed since he had disappeared.

After the prayers, everyone stayed in their places. Then once again the young man rose to his feet and asked, "Gentlemen, why are you angry with my host? Why are you all so upset?"

The young man then went up on the *bimah* and said, "Please allow me to tell you a story. This is how it was." And he began to tell the whole story of the son of the rabbi-merchant, from the very beginning.

"There was a great rabbi who was a very rich merchant. But he and his wife didn't have a child. And for many days, and for all his days, the rabbi was very depressed and every day he would ask himself, 'For whom are all my riches if I don't have any children? Dear God, I am pleading with you and begging you for your mercy. Give us a child.' " And the young man continued to tell the story. And those present understood that this young man was telling the story of the birth of the son of the rabbi and the story of his disappearance on a lonely island. And then the young man told of the creature who had grown the skin of a sheep and how he had begun to hug his parents and how they didn't recognize him.

Suddenly his father, sitting in the synagogue, burst out and asked, "Was that my son? And I didn't know?"

And the young man said, "Please do not interrupt my story."

And the mother, who sat with the other women, burst out with a scream, "Was that my son and I didn't know? Where will I find him now? Where is he?"

And the young woman, who sat with the other women in the balcony, cried out, "Where is he? Where is this creature—the one who sat next to me? Was he my betrothed?"

And the parents and the young woman were happy that the young man was still alive, even though he had a strange shape with strange, woolen skin. They kept wanting to know where he was. They didn't realize, nor could they even imagine, that this young teller of tales was telling his own story.

The young man continued to tell all about his experiences as though these things had happened to someone else. Near the end of his tale, the young man called up the rabbi who was his host and announced to the congregation, "And this is the man who saved me, and, thank God, who is responsible for me living and being here with all of you. This story that I have just told you is my story. I have told this story about myself."

And when those present heard these things, they were shocked and happy at the same time. The parents came forward to welcome their son and embrace and bless him.

Then the rabbi who saved the young man turned in prayer to Heaven: "*Ribono shel Olam,* I have no more reason to live on this earth anymore. I have fulfilled the *mitzvah* that you have given me to fulfill. I have no more need for life. God, if You understand me, take me to You."

And that was exactly how it was. The rabbi died in the synagogue. And the community gave him a very honorable funeral. They showed him great *koved*. And everyone asked for forgiveness for what they had done to him.

The young man went back to his parents and to his betrothed. And everybody has lived, since then, in happiness, in good, and in *sholom.*

32

The Greeting

Rabbi Meir of Peremyshlyany, the renowned wonder-working rabbi, once told the following story.

When I was a young man, I wanted to see Elijah the Prophet, whom it is always good to mention. I read everything I could about where he appears, and to whom he appears. I recited prayers and read of his adventures out loud, hoping, always hoping, that he would appear. I even walked through open fields looking in every direction and talking to every traveler I met on the way. Maybe this one would be Elijah, perhaps that one. . . . Finally I talked to my father about my desire to see Elijah. And my father answered, "If you study Torah with complete devotion, you will become worthy of seeing Elijah the Prophet."

So I applied myself with my whole heart and soul to my studies. I studied the sacred books day and night for four weeks without stop. At that point I went to my father and said, "Father, I did what you said I should do, and still Elijah has not appeared. You assured me that he would. . . ."

"*Nar groiser*, you are so impatient! Youth is often impatient. But remember, if you deserve to see Elijah, then he will appear."

Well, one night, as I was reading a portion of Torah while sitting
in my father's Beit Midrash, a poor traveler came in. His clothes
were dirty and torn, with patches one on top of the other. He was
ugly besides, and he was carrying a heavy pack.

As he put the pack down, I was disturbed to see that it was only
an old beggar with his dusty, dirty things who was bothering me,
rather than Elijah. This made my anger and annoyance explode, and
I shouted, "Hey, take your things away from this place. It's a place
of holy study, can't you see that?"

"I'm very tired," replied the traveler. "Let me rest a while and
then I'll go to find a place to sleep."

But I would not let him stay, and instead told him how my
father does not like strangers to come with their dirty packs to stay
here. And the traveler left.

As soon as he was gone, my father came into the room. "*Nu,*
have you seen Elijah the Prophet?" he asked me.

"No, not yet. I'm trying to have patience," I replied.

"So tell me, my son, was anyone here tonight?" he asked.

"Yes, but no one who mattered. Just a poor traveler with a
heavy pack that was filthy," I answered.

"And you, my son, did you greet him with *Sholom aleikhem?*"

"Of course not. Such a tramp, disturbing my holy thoughts!"
I said.

"But why didn't you, my son? Didn't you know that it was
Elijah the Prophet who came to visit? Now I fear that it is too late,"
my father told me.

"So from then on," Rabbi Meir concluded his story, "I always
make sure to greet every person I meet with a warm *Sholom
aleikhem.* And I say it with my whole heart, no matter what that
person looks like, no matter who that person is, no matter what his
position may be. *Sholom aleikhem!*"

33

A Choice of Years

here once lived a wealthy man, Yitzchak ben Shimon, and his wife, Sarah Leah. They had children, and all went well with them for many years. But the circle turned, and soon they found that they had lost their fortune. What could the man do? Since he needed to earn some money for their daily needs, he became a laborer in the fields, earning a few coins daily. His work was hard, but Yitzchak did not complain. Instead, he gave thanks to the Almighty for helping him find a way to keep food on the table and to provide sometimes a little something special for Shabbat.

One day, as Yitzchak was working in the fields, a man riding a handsome horse suddenly appeared. The man was dressed like a nobleman, wearing rich clothes. His saddle was covered with a cloth made of the finest twined linen embroidered with blue, purple, and crimson threads. The reins were studded with jewels.

"*Sholom aleikhem*," the man greeted Yitzchak.

Yitzchak, amazed that he had not heard the man approaching, answered in a startled voice, "*Aleikhem sholom.*"

"I have come to bring you good news. You will enjoy seven years of wealth and honor, even greater than you once had. When

237

do you wish to have those good years—now, when you are young, or later, at the end of your life?" asked the man.

Yitzchak did not know how to answer this question. Thinking that this man wanted some money, or had perhaps something else in mind, Yitzchak replied, "I am sorry that I have nothing for you. I am a poor man and must work in the fields. Please do not mock me. Go in peace."

And the man left, riding so fast that the horse left a trail of dust. And when the earth had settled, the man was nowhere to be seen.

The next day this nobleman came in the same way, giving the same offer and asking the same question. And Yitzchak gave him the same reply. But when he came on the third day with this offer, he added, "The Holy One, Blessed be He, has so ordained that you shall enjoy seven good years. You must choose when you want the seven years to begin."

Yitzchak said, "I will go and ask my wife for her advice."

Yitzchak ran across the field, directly to his house. His wife was surprised to see him in the middle of the day and greeted him with concern. "Wife, I have come with a very unusual question that I need your help in answering, for I know that you are wise. For three days, a nobleman on a fine horse has approached me while I was at work in the fields. He seems to come suddenly, as though from the very earth where the horse stands, and leaves quickly in such a cloud of dust that I do not see in which direction he departs. Each time he offers to return us to days of wealth and comfort, but only for seven years. What he wishes to know is which span of seven years we wish to accept—seven years now or seven years later, at the end of our years? How should I answer this question, my wife? He said that he will wait for my return, since I told him I must consult with you first."

The wife listened carefully, and a smile spread across her face. "Husband, what is near is better than what is far. Tell him that we would like to begin the seven years now. That is my advice, my husband."

"Dear wife, I know that you speak always with wisdom, that what you say usually is good sense. But why should we take the good years now, when I am strong and can work? Would it not be better to take them later, when we are old and I will not be able to work in the fields?" asked Yitzchak.

"My husband, we must trust in God. Who knows how long we

will live? God does not allow us to know the length of our lives.
Only for King David did he make that exception. And when we
grow old, we must have faith that God will help us then, too. Take
the seven good years *now*. That is my advice, Yitzchak."

So Yitzchak returned to the fields, a little surprised that the
nobleman on the horse was still there, waiting for him.

"Well, my friend, and what were your wife's words of advice?"
asked the nobleman.

" 'What is near is better than what is far,' she said. We would
prefer to have the seven good years begin right away," answered
Yitzchak.

"Very well," said the nobleman. "Take this coin and return
home at once. In seven years I will visit you and ask for its return."

Yitzchak took the coin, put it in his purse, and looked up to
thank the nobleman but saw only the cloud of dust. He began
walking across the field. He even began to feel lighter and happier
in his heart, or so he thought.

Arriving home, his wife came running from the house shouting,
"Yitzchak, come quickly! Look what our sons found while digging
in the garden!" Just at that moment, the sons carried out a pot
filled with a treasure of gold coins. There was such joy and
happiness in the house.

To the youngest son, who already knew how to write numbers,
the mother said, "My son, get an account book and write down
everything I will tell you. We will keep an account of what we spend
for our daily needs, and also we will keep separate pages for what we
give for *tzedakah*. Begin today. While the Holy One has entrusted
us with this good fortune, we will practice charity."

And the child kept the accounts carefully, page after page after
page. There was not a day when the couple did not help someone
who needed some money for the birth of a child, for a bride, for an
orphan, for a teacher, for clothes, for a debt. There was so much to
do and so many people to help.

The seven years passed quickly. One day, a nobleman appeared on
his horse at the gates of the house. Yitzchak came out to greet him.
Asking one of his sons to take the horse to the stable to care for it,
he invited the guest into the house. After washing, they sat at the
table and ate a meal together.

Then the nobleman turned to Yitzchak and said, "Seven years have passed. I have come to ask you to return the coin to me. I hope that they have been good years."

Yitzchak replied, "Yes, they have been good years and we are thankful for them. But just as I asked my wife for her advice before accepting the coin, I will ask her for her advice now before returning the coin."

And turning to his wife, Yitzchak said, "My dear wife, how do you suggest that I answer this request?"

"Let me answer, my husband." And turning to the nobleman, Sarah Leah said, "Dear sir, I want to show you our accounts. Here are the books that my son has kept for us. On these pages are the monies we have spent for our needs." Then turning to the other section of the book, Sarah Leah continued, "And on these pages, and there are many, as you see, are the accounts of the monies we have spent on others to help them and to feed the hungry. We have devoted ourselves to good deeds, to perform *tzedakah* as our way of life. If you can find anyone else who would do more with what you have entrusted to us, then take the coin. However, if you agree that we have made good use of our wealth, then allow us to keep the coin and to continue our good work." And Sarah Leah waited.

The nobleman listened. Then he turned the pages, slowly, examining each one, and mused, "You have spent a great deal of money, I see. But I also see that it was always to do good."

Suddenly standing up, the nobleman said, "Yitzchak and Sarah Leah, keep the coin and continue in your good ways. You have also taught your children well. I bless you and your children, so that they may inherit the coin and your wisdom."

Then the nobleman, who was Elijah the Prophet, left the house, jumped onto his horse, and, in a cloud of dust, disappeared, even before the couple could bid farewell to their generous guest. When the couple ran out of the house to say farewell, what they found instead, on the gate of the house, was a beautiful embroidered linen cloth.

The couple and their children continued to live in great happiness and wealth, performing *mitzvot* as they had always done. And when the couple died, their children, and each generation thereafter, inherited the coin and the treasured, twined linen cloth.

34

*The King, the Adviser,
and the Jewish Boy*

here was once a great king who conquered many lands. He became the richest and most famous king in the whole world. One day the king woke from his sleep and said to himself, "Here I am, the greatest king in the world and there is no king like me in power and in riches. How is it that I live in such a palace that is so run down? I have to build a new palace, more beautiful than any other, a palace such as no one has ever built before. Its name will be famous throughout the whole world."

The king called an adviser and said to him, "Take money and precious stones, all that you need, and build a palace for me, one unlike any other in the whole world."

The adviser took a large amount of money from the king's treasury and gathered many workers from the whole world. Their wages were more than twice what they had earned in past years. After two years of hard work, the great army of workers finished building the king's palace. The king planned to hold a great reception in the beautiful new palace for all his workers, servants, and for the entire nation. The whole country gathered in the square in front of the palace for the dedication ceremony. To the sound of drums and trumpets and the accompaniment of dancing and singing, the king approached the door of the great palace.

Suddenly, there at the door of the palace, appeared an old man. An eerie quiet descended. And the old figure said to the king in a loud voice, "If you put one foot inside this palace, the whole palace will come crashing down."

"That is not possible," said the king in wonder and disbelief.

"If you don't believe me," said the old man, "take one of your workers, dress him in the king's clothes, and let him go into the palace, and see what happens."

The king did just that—for he did not want to risk his life in case the old man's words would come true. He dressed one of his servants in the king's robes and pushed him into the palace. Immediately the great palace crumbled and collapsed into a great rubble of stones. The king and his adviser looked for the mysterious old man, but he had disappeared.

The king said to the adviser, "How is this possible? A palace that took two years to build with so many workers should collapse in a few seconds?"

The adviser, who hated Jews, answered, "Many years ago I read in an ancient book that every new palace will crumble under the king at his entrance if he does not slaughter a blond Jewish child, 10 years old, so that his blood spills everywhere."

The king ordered the adviser to begin building the palace again. And at the same time, he announced, "Any Jewish woman who has a blond child, 10 years old, is commanded to sell him to the king."

But time passed and no Jewish woman came to the king. And the adviser, who was already busy building the new palace, with even more workers than before, said to the king, "You are a powerful ruler, and the life of your subjects is in your hand. Order your workers to bring you a Jewish child who is 10 years old. Why do you have to wait until some Jewish woman brings him to you?"

"It is known that I am a just and fair king," answered the king. "That is why I will not do what you say."

Not much time passed, and one day a Jewish woman arrived at the palace with a blond child, 10 years old, and asked the guards for permission to enter. Permission was given, and the woman was brought before the king.

The woman said to the king, "Here is the child you asked for." The king paid her a high price, and she returned home.

The child was taken by the king's servants, bound in iron chains, and brought into a little room to sleep. The child understood and felt what was waiting for him and he began to cry. He cried bitter tears, heartbreaking tears, until his cries reached Heaven and the throne of God.

The *Kodosh Barukhu* called Elijah the Prophet to him and said, "Go down and save the child from those evil people. If we don't save him, we'll bring the world back to chaos."

Elijah the Prophet went down to earth. He came to the child's room and calmed him down. Afterward he took out his cup and gave the child a drink from it. After he drank from the first cup, the child became as smart as King Solomon. Elijah gave him another cup to drink, and he became as strong as Samson the Hero.

And Elijah asked him, "Now will you succeed to free yourself from those who hate you?"

"I will succeed," answered the boy.

Then Elijah the Prophet left him and went on his way.

When the child heard that preparations were begun for the great celebration for the new palace, he broke the sealed chains and went to the square in front of the palace. There he saw the king. Standing to the right of him was his adviser, and to the left of him, the executioner. When the king saw the boy in front of him, he asked the adviser, "Who freed the boy from his iron chains?"

"I don't know," replied the adviser.

"Then how did you free yourself?" asked the king of the boy.

"With my own strength I freed myself of the chains," answered the boy and asked, "Your Honor, Your Highness, why did you all come here?"

"To slaughter you and to spill your blood all over, so that my palace will stand," answered the king.

"What did I do to you that was so terrible?" asked the boy.

"Your mother sold you," answered the king.

"If my mother went out of her mind, that still doesn't mean that you have to slaughter me," claimed the boy.

And the evil adviser interrupted the conversation and said to the king, "Why are you arguing with this Jewish boy? Kill him and get rid of him."

And the king answered him, "Why should I kill him? He is speaking very wise words."

And the boy continued, "And who declares that if you slaughter a blond Jewish child of 10 years the palace won't tumble down?"

And the king answered, "The adviser, who read it in a book."

"If that is so"—the child turned to the adviser and continued—"then bring me this book where these things are written. If you can produce such a book, then I will save the executioner his work."

And the king turned to the adviser and demanded, "Bring the book."

And the adviser replied in a trembling voice, "But I told you, O King, that I read these things a long time ago, in an ancient book that I cannot possibly find any longer."

And the boy said to the king, "Well, if that is the way it is, then I request the right to a contest. I will ask the adviser three questions. If he answers them correctly, I will surrender my life. If he doesn't answer correctly, then he will be slaughtered himself. He, too, will have the chance to ask me three questions. I am ready to answer his questions. Allow me this contest, Your Majesty, for my life is at stake."

The king agreed, wrote down these rules, signed and sealed the paper, and then asked the adviser, "Do you want to ask your questions first, or should the boy begin first?"

"Let the boy ask first," said the adviser boldly.

And the boy asked three questions. "My first question is: What is sweeter than honey? The second question is: What is harder than steel or stone? And my third question is: What begins light, becomes heavy, and then is light again?"

The adviser turned to the king and said, "Dear King, only you would argue with a Jewish child. Slaughter him and save the palace."

"I can't do that because we made an agreement and I signed it."

"I don't know the answers," admitted the adviser reluctantly.

The king turned to the child and asked, "Do you know the answers to these questions?"

"Of course," said the child. "The answer to the first question is that the milk a baby gets from his mother is sweeter than honey.

The answer to the second question is that the heart of a mother who sells her son is harder than steel or stone. The answer to the third question is a pregnant woman. In the beginning she is light, she then becomes heavy with child, and after the birth she is once again light.''

Hearing these answers from the wise boy, the king ordered that the agreement be carried out.

The adviser was killed and his blood spread all over the palace. After the ceremony, just as the king was about to go inside again, the old figure appeared at the opening and he said, ''Dear King, you may now enter this palace.''

And when he had finished speaking, he again disappeared.

The king entered the palace. The servants and workers also entered the palace, and all was well.

The king asked the wise boy to become his adviser, and he remained in the palace as the king's adviser always.

35

The Chasid's Good Deeds

n a small town there lived a chasid and his wife. They had no children. The couple had a small store, and the wife sat inside the store, and the chasid would sit near the doorway and study Torah. When someone came to buy something, the chasid would send the buyer to the store exactly opposite his, the store owned by a widow. And he would say to the buyer, "There, in that store, the goods are better and cheaper."

And one day, a farmer came to the chasid's store and wanted to buy herring. "Can I buy herring here?"

And the chasid answered him, "I don't have any herring."

"Then what can I buy in your store?" asked the farmer.

And the chasid answered, "I have flour and I have salt. But you should go to the store opposite me, because you will find the goods are better there and cheaper, too."

But the farmer insisted that he wanted to see the goods that were in the chasid's store. And so he went in and looked. Then he said, "Now I will go to the widow's store to see what she has."

And just as he left, the chasid saw a package the farmer had forgotten. Wanting to return it to its rightful owner, and fearing he would be accused of stealing it, he ran to catch him. He ran across

251

the road to the widow's store, but he didn't find the farmer there. The farmer had disappeared without a trace.

The chasid took the package, ran quickly to the town, and told the story to everybody. The rabbi heard the story and told the chasid, "The farmer was Elijah the Prophet himself. Elijah had heard about your good deeds, so he left this package as payment for your good deeds, your *mitzvot*. In essence you have really won a prize, because you always sent all your customers to the widow's store. And because of this, you guaranteed her and her children an income. It is a big *mitzvah*, since you worried about this widow and her children even before you worried about your wife and yourself."

Together the rabbi and the chasid opened the package, and in it they found a great deal of money. The chasid knew that he had received a great reward from Elijah the Prophet by helping the widow who had the store across the way.

In that case, he reasoned, the widow deserved part of this reward. So what did he do? He divided the money and gave half to the widow. And they all lived in plenty until the end of their days.

36

Elijah's Lullaby

 n a God-fearing voice, in a prayer-filled voice, my grandmother, Sarah, would sing this song. In a quiet and peaceful tone, she would sing this song when she wanted to calm the restless children before they fell asleep.

שלאָף, מײַן קינד, מײַן ליבער זון,
דײַן חלום זאָל זײַן אין דײַן שלאָף.
ציון, די הייליקע שטאָט ירושלים,
וווּ פּאַסטעכער און מלאָכים זײַנען געוועזן.

איבער דײַן וויגעלע שטייען מלאָכים,
זיי היטן דיך פֿון אַל דאָס שלעכטס.
מלאָכים צוויי שטייען לעבן דיר:
מלאך רפֿואל און מלאך גבריאל.

Schlof, Mayn Kind

Shlof, mayn kind, mayn li - ber zun, Dayn kho - lem zol zayn

in dayn shlof, Tsi - on, di hey - li - ke shtot Ye - ru - she - lay - im, Vu

fine

pas - te - kher un me - lo - khim zay - nen ge - ven.

I - ber dayn vi - ge - le shtey - en me - lo - khim, Zey

hi - tn dikh fun al dos shlekhts. Me - lo - khim tsvey

shtey - en le - bn dir: Ma - lakh Re - ful un ma - lakh Gav - ril.

Dayn vi - ge - le iz ge - boyt fun tse - der bey - mer, Di

bey - mer shta - men fun tsi - ons berg, Dayn vi - ge - le kumt

azh fun dort, Fun di hey - li - ke shtot Ye - ru - she - lay - im.

Shlof, mayn shvalb, shlof, mayn kroyn, Gu - te za - khn zay - nen do far

dir: Bok - ser, fay - gn, un vayn - troy - bn, Fun

dort vu day - ne o - ves zay - nen me - lo - khim ge - ven.

D.C. al fine

256

דײַן וויגעלע איז געבויט פֿון צעדערביימער,
די ביימער שטאַמען פֿון ציונס בערג,
דײַן וויגעלע קומט אַזש פֿון דאָרט,
פֿון די הייליקע שטאָט ירושלים.

שלאָף, מײַן שוואַלב, שלאָף, מײַן קרוין,
גוטע זאַכן זײַנען דאָ פֿאַר דיר:
באָקסער, פֿײַגן און ווײַנטרויבן,
פֿון דאָרט וווּ דײַנע אָבות זײַנען מלאָכים געווען.

Shlof, mayn kind, mayn liber zun,
Dayn kholem zol zayn in dayn shlof,
Tsion, di heylike shtot Yerushelayim,
Vu pastekher un melokhim zaynen geven.
Iber dayn vigele shteyen melokhim,
Zey hitn dikh fun al dos shlekhts.
Melokhim tsvey shteyen lebn dir:
Malakh Reful un malakh Gavril.

Dayn vigele iz geboyt fun tseder beymer,
Di beymer shtamen fun tsions berg,
Dayn vigele kumt azh fun dort,
Fun di heylike shtot Yerushelayim.

Shlof, mayn shvalb, shlof mayn kroyn,
Gute zakhn zaynen do far dir:
Bokser, faygn, un vayn-troybn,
Fun dort vu dayne oves zaynen melokhim geven.

Sleep my child, beloved son.
May your sleep be filled with dreams
Of Zion, holy land Jerusalem,
Where the shepherds kept their watch.
Angels now your cradle guard
And they keep you from all harm.
Two bright angels hover close—
Angels Raphael and Gabriel.

Your cradle's made of cedar wood
From trees that grew on Zion's hills,
Your cradle's from Jerusalem—
Jerusalem, the holy land.

Sleep my dove, sleep my jewel.
The gifts of earth are there for you.
Fruits and figs and sweet ripe grapes
Where our holy fathers
Among the angels dwell.

"Have you ever been to Jerusalem, Bubbe?" I asked one night when I couldn't sleep.

"In my dreams I go there often, my child," replied my grandmother. "Oh, how I would like to travel there, to live there. Maybe one day Elijah will take me with him on a visit." And she laughed a soft laugh as she hummed the lullaby.

Sitting next to my bed, she stroked my head gently, slightly swaying as if she was rocking a cradle, and continued singing.

"Bubbe, tell me a story before I go to sleep."

"With pleasure, my child. I will tell you the story of how I know this beautiful song."

* * *

There was once a poor Jew who supported his family—his wife and his child—working as a woodcutter. His wife also worked, as a washerwoman in rich people's houses. That was how they supported their family so they wouldn't have to borrow from anyone. The wife of the woodcutter became pregnant. But even while she was pregnant she worked, and this was the way she helped her husband support their household. In her seventh month she suddenly got labor pains and gave birth to a son. But after she gave birth, she died. After the mourning and the pain and sitting of *shivah,* the woodcutter went back to his work. He would leave the older son at home to take care of the baby in his crib. The baby was healthy, and he received milk from a neighbor who had nursed the baby from the time the mother had died.

One day, at a late night hour, the widower-father came back from his work. When he came into the house, he saw an old man standing next to the crib and rocking it and singing a song.

"Who are you, old man?" asked the father.

"I am Elijah the Prophet," answered the old man. And then he continued, "Don't worry. I'll come here every day to look after this poor baby."

And that's the way it was—day after day—in the house of the woodcutter. Elijah would come and bring the child all kinds of good things.

And then a rumor spread through the town that Elijah had come to the house of the woodcutter.

"And he sits next to the little poor orphan baby and sings," said one.

"And I hear he sings such a beautiful lullaby," said another.

"And I hear he sings with a voice of an angel," said a third person.

"And it is told that the angels sing the same tunes as Elijah sings," said another.

Everyone in the town was talking only about Elijah and his lullaby. Finally, with great excitement and anticipation, they decided to go to the woodcutter's house to see for themselves. When they all got to his house, they came close and peeked inside and saw Elijah the Prophet with their own eyes. They listened to the song. Then they were suddenly filled with fear and fright, and they left the house and ran away.

All the Jews in the city learned the beautiful lullaby that Elijah the Prophet sang to this baby.

* * *

"But Bubbe, how do you know the lullaby?" I asked.

"My great-grandmother lived in that town. She learned that lullaby and sang it to her children. Then my grandmother sang it to my mother when she was a child. My mother sang it to me. I sang it to your mother, and now I sing it also to you."

And then my grandmother would sing Elijah's Lullaby again as I closed my eyes, ready to sleep.

May you meet Elijah the Prophet!

Endnotes

he Israel Folktale Archives (IFA), founded in 1956 by Dov Noy, has collected over 17,000 folktales from storyteller informants in Israel. These tales can be found in the IFA Publication Series, with over thirty-five volumes published by the Haifa Municipality Ethnological Museum and Folklore Archives. Each tale is assigned an IFA number and is kept in the Archives. (For more about the IFA, see Noy [1961a,b].

Type refers to the Aarne-Thompson (A–T) classification system, as expanded in the IFA Type Index. A tale type or plot refers to a fixed sequence of specific motifs that are found in numerous existing tales. The basic list of tale types was made by Aarne and Thompson. An asterisk preceding a number or letter indicates an addition not included in the standard index but used in the IFA. Most of the additions are Jewish oicotypes. An oicotype is a local tale type extant in a specific ethnocultural area.

Motif refers to the Thompson Motif classification system, as expanded in the Neuman/Noy Motif. An asterisk preceding a number of a motif indicates an addition in the Neuman/Noy Motif to the standard motif index. A motif refers to "those details out of which full-fledged narratives are composed. It is these simple elements which can form a common basis for a systematic arrangement of the whole body of traditional literature" (Thompson 1966, p. 6). Some tales consist of a single motif and, therefore, the motifs are equivalent to the types.

Through these two kinds of classification schemes, tale type and motif index, which are internationally accepted, one can trace a tale from many different countries and with different titles. One can also identify other variants of that tale and realize that parallel stories are told among many peoples. For any comparative studies of folktales, these classifications are of major importance.

At present there are 575 Elijah the Prophet tales in the IFA. This testifies to the tremendous popularity of this folk hero among all the communities where Jews have lived in the world. Elijah the Prophet has been assigned V*295 as the motif in the IFA. Type *776 (Jason), "miscellaneous divine rewards, mostly through Elijah the Prophet [fertility, enrichment, etc.]" can be applied to most of these tales as well. The deeds that are rewarded include charity, hospitality, faith in God, study of Torah, keeping Shabbat, and reciting Psalms.

Several motifs appear frequently in Elijah tales and would apply to many of the stories in this collection: H1546 (test of hospitality); H1552 (test of generosity); K1811.3 (saint in disguise [Elijah] visits mortal); N810 (supernatural helper); Q1.1 (saint in disguise [Elijah] punishes inhospitality); Q42.3 (generosity to saint in disguise [Elijah] rewarded); V220 (saints); V221 (miraculous healing by saints); V246 (angel counsels mortal) and V410 (charity rewarded).

The stories in this book contain more motifs than I have actually listed in the commentary to the stories. I have indicated some key motifs only.

For additional readings about Elijah the Prophet and to understand more about his prominent role in Jewish folk literature, see Schwarzbaum's (1968) listings of books and articles, especially pages 317 and 391.

Introduction: When Will the Messiah Come?

Source: Sanhedrin 98a.

The Hebrew word for "today" is *ha-yom*, which has two meanings: "today" and "on this day," referring to the actual day of listening to God's voice. The latter reference is from Psalm 95:7, "Today if you will hear his voice." In other words, we must also be ready to work together with God toward bringing the Messiah, which will be a time when all the world will be filled with justice and righteousness and a knowledge of one God.

Introduction: Elijah and the Three Wishes

Source: As retold from the author's memory. Versions of this tale are known from Europe to China. There are at least six versions in IFA, from Morocco to Persia.

Tale type: Variation of type listed as AT 750A (the wishes).

Motifs: D1761.0.2 (limited number of wishes granted); G303.9.8.5 (gold causes man to become miser); H1564 (test of hospitality); K1811.3 (saint in disguise [Elijah] visits mortal); Q1.1 (saint in disguise [Elijah] rewards hospitality and punishes inhospitality).

The possible origin of this story may be found in *Baba Batra* 7b in this sentence: ". . . seeing that there was a certain pious man with whom Elijah used to converse until he made a porter's lodge, after which he did not converse with him any more."

Such brief enigmatic talmudic sentences have served as springboards for the rabbis to develop folktales which, in turn, are told and retold in more elaborate versions from generation to generation.

My earliest recollection of any story is this Elijah tale that my father used to tell me when I was a child. I had not been able to find a printed version, and so I retrieved it from my memory. Without even knowing it, this story had stayed in my memory as a special and powerful story. Because of this story I became especially fond of and fascinated with Elijah the Prophet as a folktale hero.

1. Elijah's Mysterious Ways

Sources: Ibn Shahin (1557); Hibbur Ma'asiyot (1647); Jellinek (1853–1877); Bin Gorion (1916–1921, 1976); Gaster (1924); Frankel (1989); Schram (1987).

Tale type: AT 750B (hospitality rewarded), AT 759 (God's justice vindicated).

Motifs: D1855.2 (death postponed if substitute can be found); K527.6; K528 (substitute in ordeal); Q141 (hospitality granted by poor man to saint).

This story is in the Hebrew collection of folktales, *Hibbur Yafe Mehayeshua,* dating from the eleventh century. Reb Nissim composed this book of stories for "Dunash, his son-in-law, to speak to his heart and to console him." Many of the tales found in this anthology are entertaining and humorous, but all are inspirational and deal with the theme of God as a righteous judge, no matter how mysterious His ways may seem. This genre of "tales of relief after adversity and stress" was widely used in Arabic folklore during the eleventh and twelfth centuries. No doubt the Arabic stories served as models for many Jewish writings and collections of tales. This "righteous judgment" legend was very popular in Arabic folklore. In fact, there is a similar story in Islamic literature about Khadir and Moses (Schwarzbaum 1962–1963, Wiener 1978).

The notion of a cow serving as redemption or substitute for the hospitable wife so that she is saved from her destined death is already extant in the eleventh century.

In other versions, Elijah repairs a broken stone wall in order to cover the hidden underground treasure. I have changed this element to an overturned tree that Elijah causes to turn upright.

In the classic versions of this story, it is Rabbi Joshua ben Levi who has the encounter with Elijah and who needs to understand the often confusing happenings in the world. Rabbi Joshua ben Levi was a third-century *amora* (scholar, teacher, and interpreter) who was well known as a great master of *aggadah.* He himself is the subject of many legends, especially involving Elijah the Prophet. This kind of intimate relationship, as between Rabbi Joshua ben Levi and Elijah, is not found with any other wise man. It seems that the folk imagination connected these two heroes as companions and friends. In my version of this story, however, I have changed the questioner into an "everyman" named Shmuel ben Yosef.

2. The Life-giving Flower

Source: TEM 1978, #2. IFA 11,547. Yoram Goren (Sha'ar ha-Amaqim) from Vicki Elimelekh (Morocco) in Bet-Shan.

Tale types: AT 930*E (IFA) (predestined marriage), AT 759C

(God's justice vindicated), and AT 301. Many versions, especially from Morocco (eight) and also from Tunisia and Yemen. Variant is AT 934*H (childless couple may choose between girl who will suffer and boy who will be poor all his life; boy is chosen; in spite of prophecy, he gets rich). Variants IFA 8903 and IFA 8812 (Palestine Sefardi).

Motifs: B542.1.1 (eagle carries off youth); D1500.1.4 (magic healing plant); D2161.3.11 (barrenness magically cured); E105 (resuscitation by herbs); E648 (reincarnation: man-object-man); F1041.1.4 (death from longing); F814 (extraordinary flower); F950 (marvelous cures); H94 (identification by ring); H1573.0.1 (angel helpers in religious test); K1955 (sham physician); V232 (angel as helper); V246 (angel counsels mortal); V246.2 (angel as mortal's teacher).

This story has some close parallels to the King Solomon legend found in *Midrash Tanhuma* and in Ginzberg. Instead of an eagle, the young man is carried by a *ziz* (a giant bird created on the fifth day of Creation and supposed to rule over all birds) and dropped in a high tower in the middle of the ocean. Solomon's daughter lives in this tower where Solomon hopes to protect her from the prophecy that she would marry a poor man. The daughter befriends the young man and they become betrothed. They manage to return to the palace by means of the same *ziz*. (See "The Princess and Her Beloved" in Schram [1987] and "The Princess in the Tower" in Schwartz [1983].)

There is an episode in "The Fisherman's Daughter's Story" (Schram 1987) that is also similar. In this story, the eagle swoops down to carry off a young man to a distant country. There, too, he finds his love, marries her, and they have two children. However, in this episode the eagle returns and brings the man back to his parents, and as a result he is still searching for his wife and children.

The story brings to mind the words of Agur, the son of Jakeh (one of Solomon's other names), in Proverbs 30:18–19:

There are three things which are too wonderful for me,
Yes, four which I know not:
The way of an eagle in the air;
The way of a serpent upon a rock;
The way of a ship in the midst of the sea;
And the way of a man with a young woman.

3. Welcome to Clothes

Sources: Segel (1904); Weinreich (1957), Tale 28 (with her permission); Weinreich (1988). IFA 3072 (Poland), IFA 1408 and 5870 (Persia), IFA 6645 (Europe Ashkinaze), IFA 6077 (Yemen), and IFA 6784 (Afghanistan).

Tale types: AT 1558 (welcome to clothes).

Motif: H1564 (test of hospitality); J1072 (man to be judged by his own qualities, not his clothes); J1561.3 (welcome to clothes); K1811.3 (saint in disguise [Elijah] visits mortal).

In Jewish folklore, some of the same humorous or trickster types of tales have been associated with different heroes "who have very often served conveniently as personality pegs on which to hang a popular story or jest" (Ausubel 1948, p. 286). This tale has been told with Elijah replaced by the Maggid of Dubno or Hershele Ostropolier or other folk heroes. These variants can be found in many other sources. See Schwarzbaum's (1968) extensive references, pp. 181–182.

In world folklore, the Syrian fool, Djuha, appears in the Syrian variant "Djuha's Sleeve," the Turkish fool Nasr-ed-Din Hodja in "A Guest for Halil," the Greek fool in "The Hodja Feeds His Sleeves," and the Italian fool Giufa in a Sicilian version, "Eat Your Fill, My Fine Clothes." One can readily tell from the titles that these are the same stories; they are widely popular among many Middle Eastern cultures as an important teaching tale regarding hospitality.

Perhaps all of these stories come from the talmudic statement in *Shabbat* 145b: "In my own city I am well known under my name, but in a foreign city I have to put on nice clothes."

4. Beroka and Elijah the Prophet

Sources: Bin Gorion (1976); Ibn Shahin (1557); *Ta'anit* 22a; Ben Yehezkel (1928–1929); Rotenberg (1911); Gaster (1924), #405; Isaacs (1893); Schwarzbaum (1968).

Motif: K1811.3 (saint in disguise [Elijah] visits mortal); Q177* (a share in future world as a reward).

The choice of jesters to inherit the world to come may puzzle some readers. However, humor and good cheer have played an important part in Jewish tradition throughout the ages, for good and healthy reasons. Talmudic scholar Bar Kappara, poet and author of many fables, apparently used various tricks and jests that are mentioned in aggadic literature. So, too, some chasidic leaders enjoyed humorous tales that, according to the Baal Shem Tov, "release[s] every mortal from narrow-mindedness, transferring him to wider spheres where he is taught how to cleave to the Almighty, and this is the reason why the Two Jesters mentioned in the Babylonian Talmud, *Taanit,* 22, are so much praised by the Prophet Elijah and rewarded with a seat in Paradise" (Schwarzbaum 1968, p. 88. n. 60). In fact, some chasidic leaders also employed jesters who would entertain them when they suffered from melancholia. One of these jesters was the legendary Hershele Ostropolier, who was a jester to Rabbi Borukh of Miedziboz in the eighteenth century.

5. The Wine of Paradise

Sources: Ben Yehezkel (1928–1929); *Sihot Hayim; Otzar ha-Massiyot B; Sihot Yekarot;* Klapholtz (1970–1979), vol. 2.

Motifs: H1564 (test of hospitality); K1811.3 (saint in disguise [Elijah] visits mortal); N810 (supernatural helper); Q42.3 (generosity of saint in disguise [Elijah] rewarded [wine multiplies]).

6. The Synagogue of Elijah the Prophet

Source: TEM 1976–1977, #16. IFA 10,990 written by Shmuel Cohen in Jerusalem from memory as he heard it in Yazad in Iran.

Motifs: K1811.3 (saint in disguise [Elijah] visits mortal); N810 (supernatural helper); V246 (angel counsels mortal).

Venerated throughout the ages, Jews in Israel and the entire Near East have honored Elijah by dedicating synagogues and caves in his name, especially in those places where Elijah is reputed to have appeared.

The initial conversation between Elijah and the weaver is based on a dialogue between Elijah and Rabbi Jose in *Barakot* 3a, which I inserted in the story.

7. Elijah's Three Gifts

Sources: Khalats (1558); Eisenstein (1915); Gaster (1924, #355; 1934); Cheichel (1968). IFA 5605. Also IFA 9188 (Morocco) and IFA 2112 (Tunisia).

Tale type: AT 750B (hospitality rewarded), AT 750D (three brothers each granted a wish by an angel visitor), Type *776 (Jason) (miscellaneous divine rewards, mostly through Elijah the Prophet).

Motifs: D1451 (inexhaustible purse); H1564 (test of hospitality); H1552 (test of generosity); K1811.3 (saint in disguise [Elijah] visits mortal); Q42.3 (generosity to saint in disguise [Elijah] rewarded).

This story is a variant of ''The Three Brothers'' (Schram 1987).

8. A Tale Retold at a Feast

Source: Farhi (1870); Klapholtz (1970–1979), vol. 3.

Tale types: AT 930 (the prophecy), AT 930A (predestined wife); AT 930–939 (boy reunited with parents), AT 750* (hospitality rewarded), AT *776 (miscellaneous divine rewards, mostly through Elijah the Prophet).

Motifs: D2161.3.11 (barrenness magically cured); K1811.3 (saint in disguise [Elijah] visits mortal); M371 (boy becomes great, returns unknown to his parents, and prophecy is fulfilled); T53.3 (saint as matchmaker); V246 (angel counsels mortal).

The verse the young boy repeats when he is lost on the island is from the opening of Psalm 23.

In this story, the scene when the young man meets his mother after many years but is not allowed by Elijah to disclose his identity reminds me of the biblical scene when Joseph's brothers come to buy grain in Egypt. But while Joseph knows who they are, they do not recognize him. For me, it is one of the most moving scenes in all of literature.

As in ''The Agunah, the Rabbi, and the 'Sheep,''' the son reveals his true identity to his parents by retelling the story of his life and experiences.

9. Things Could Be Far Worse

Sources: Legends of Elijah the Prophet; Klapholtz (1970–1979), vol. 2; Schwarzbaum (1968); Gross (1955).

Tale type: AT 947 (the man followed by bad luck).

Motif: H1558.7.2 (friends desert when man reports loss of his money); N251 (person pursued by misfortune); V146 (angel counsels mortal).

This story may remind readers of the folktale "It Can Always Be Worse" about the poor man whose house is too small and noisy and who is counseled by the rabbi to take the farm animals in, then to take them out. By comparison, then, the man discovers his house is roomy and quiet after all. As one discovers in this story, things could be far worse. But the Jewish philosophy, as presented by Elijah, is that one shouldn't complain too much but rather trust in the Almighty.

10. The Healing Fruit

Source: Ibn Shahin (1557).

Tale type: AT 610 (healing fruits), Type *776 (Jason) (miscellaneous divine rewards, mostly through Elijah the Prophet).

Motifs: K1811.3 (saint in disguise [Elijah] visits mortal); N810 (supernatural helper).

Healing fruit is a common motif in folktales. In "The Magic Pomegranate" (Schram 1987), the fruit that heals the princess is the pomegranate, although it is an apple in other variants, such as in "Who Cured the Princess?" (Noy 1961b). In "The Two Bridegrooms" (Schram 1987), the young man also heals the king, but with an apple coated with honey.

11. Her Wisdom Is Her Beauty

Sources: TEM 1962, #2, IFA 4510 (Morocco), Bin Gorion (1916–1921, 1976); Farhi (1870); Frankel (1989); Schram (1987). Eight parallels of this story in the IFA come from Yemen, Iraq, and Eastern Europe, including IFA 1338 (Eastern Europe), IFA 640 (Iraq), IFA 3811 (Yemen), and IFA 1014 (Palestine Oriental).

Tale type: AT 873 (king discovers unknown son), AT 873*A (the girl with the animal face)—this type leaves the loved one incognito.

Motifs: D1500.1.8 (magic healing bottle); D2161.3 (magic cure of physical defect); H81.1 (hero lies by sleeping girl and leaves identification token with her); H94 (identification by ring); H1381.2.2.1.1 (boy twitted with illegitimacy seeks unknown father); N731 (unexpected meeting of father and son); T645 (paramour leaves token with girl to give their son); T646 (illegitimate child taunted by playmates).

This transformation tale is not well known outside the area where it was collected by the volunteers of the IFA. However, in several Jewish stories it is usually a young man who takes the form of an animal, often a snake or a bear. See "The Agunah, the Rabbi, and the 'Sheep'" (no. 31, this volume) and "The Snake Son" and "The Fisherman's Daughter" (Schram 1987).

12. Elijah's Partnership

Source: Lehman (1933); Weinreich (1957), Tale 3 (with her permission).
Tale type: AT 759 (God's justice vindicated).
Motifs: N810 (supernatural helper); Q42.3 (generosity to saint in disguise [Elijah] rewarded); Q1.1 (saint in disguise [Elijah] punishes inhospitality).

Elijah serves as a traveling companion to a deserving person in some stories in order to demonstrate that miracles can happen as long as there is faith and hope. See "Elijah's Mysterious Ways" [tale no. 1, this volume; Schram (1987)].

13. Elijah the Prophet and the Son of a Wise Man

Source: TEM 1974–1975, #20. IFA 10,635. Collected by Tamar Fleishman (Nes Ziona) from Jacob Ben-Yishay (Algeria).
Tale types: AT 517 (the boy who learned many things), AT 517*A (IFA) (A child is promised to a barren couple in a dream or by Elijah the Prophet), AT 725 (the dream), AT 930 (the prophecy).
Motifs: D911.4 (fish swallows man); D1812.3.3 (future revealed in a dream); F911.4 (Jonah [or water monster] swallows a man); H51.1 (recognition by birthmark); L441 (boy refuses to tell his dream to his father . . .); M370 (the dream is fulfilled); M312 (boy dreams that his parents will serve him and that the king will pour water on his hands); M312.0.1 (dream of future greatness);

M312.2 (prophecy: parents will humble themselves before their son); M311.0.3.1 (prophecy: child to be born to childless couple); M371 (boy becomes great, returns unknown to his parents, and prophecy is fulfilled); N810 (supernatural helper); S11 (cruel father); V220 (saints); V246 (angel counsels mortal); X1723.1 (swallowed person is discovered in animal's stomach still alive).

There are many parallel versions from Yemen, Iraqi Kurdistan, Iraq, and Tunisia. A sixteenth-century variant from Persia, "A Plague of Ravens," can be found in Schwartz (1986).

In this story, as in "The Ignorant Beadle," the learned young woman makes a mistake in her *Torah* studies. This allows the seemingly ignorant young man to identify himself as her destined bridegroom. But Elijah has orchestrated this so that the young woman will know the young man's true qualifications before anyone else.

The motif of a lost son being recognized by his mother through a mark or sign on the body is often found in folktales and also in Shakespeare and other classic dramas. The boy being swallowed by a fish is reminiscent of the Jonah and the Whale story.

14. Looking for His Luck

Sources: This is a combined version of two stories: IFA 3947 (Kurdistan) in Baharav (1964) and IFA 9113 (Iraqi Kurdistan) written by Efrach Haviv according to the story by Menahem David. IFA 3947 does not have Elijah as a character in the story, but IFA 9113 does. Other variants include: IFA 5788 (Persia), IFA 6400, 1604, 2973 (Iraq); IFA 805 (Yemen), and IFA 425 (Afghanistan).

This is a world folktale found also in an Armenian version, "The Foolish Man."

Tale types: AT 460B (the journey in search of fortune), AT 460*C (poor and luckless man goes wandering to seek his fortune), AT 461 (stupid man's journey in search of fortune), AT 461 III (the questions), and AT 1693 (literal fool).

Motif: H1281 (wanders abroad to see fortune); H1291 (various questions are given to which the youth is asked to find answers); H1292.2 (question: why does a tree not flourish?); V246 (angel counsels mortal).

In some variants, other questions are asked of the foolish man as he searches for his luck, including:

1. Why is the brave king losing his battles?
2. Why is the hardworking man unsuccessful and his land barren?
3. Why is the lion sick?

The answers to these questions generally parallel those given in this story. However, traditionally the answer to the "brave king" dilemma, since "he" is a woman, is for the king-woman to marry a brave man who will be successful in the battles or strengthen the government. In this instance I changed the answer to make them *partners,* and then they will succeed. The idea of partners, inherent in *ish* (man) and *isha* (woman) as equals in the Creation Story, seems to me to be a more valid Jewish approach.

There are also a number of variants of this tale where a poor brother is told to "go to Azazel" ("go to the Devil") by his rich miserly brother. So the poor brother sets off on the journey to search for Azazel in the same way that the foolish man searches for his mazel in this story. However, the poor brother fares much better in IFA variants 3598, 8214, and 1161. The Moroccan version (3598) has been retold in Schwartz (1986) as "The Wise Old Woman of the Forest."

15. The Emissary of Elijah the Prophet

Sources: Ben Yehezkel (1928–1929); *Sippure Tsaddikim;* Schwartz (1977); *Otzar ha-Massiyot A,* Klapholtz (1970–1979).

The hidden saint or "secret righteous" who appears as a simpleton is a common theme in Jewish folktales. According to the Babylonian Talmud, there are thirty-six righteous individuals, or *lamed vav tzaddikim* (*lamed vav* are the Hebrew letters equivalent to the number 36) in every generation and upon whom the world depends for its continued existence (*Sanhedrin* 97a–b, *Sukkah* 45b).

Legends from a later period describe them as very humble Jews who make their living by working at lowly jobs. They are unaware of each other's existence, and they always deny their position as a *lamedvovnik* (Yiddish name) so that they are not accidentally discovered. (See Foreword to this volume.) When there are great dangers for the Jews, the *lamed vav tzaddikim* find a way to rescue the Jews, but then they immediately return to their unassuming lives and continue to live in anonymity.

Many kabbalistic and chasidic legends tell about the deeds of these thirty-six. The number 36 is a symbolic number with great significance. It is double *chai,* which is 18, the symbolic equivalence of "life."

16. The Man Whose Words Came True

Source: Cahan (1931); Weinreich (1957), Tale 52 (with her permission); Weinrich (1988). There are a number of variants: IFA 5605 (Morocco), IFA 5097 (Tunisia), IFA 6406 (Egypt), IFA 6098 (Europe Ashkinaze), IFA 6473 (Turkey), and IFA 5934 and 6086 (Iraqi Kurdistan).

Tale types: AT 675 (+) (the lazy boy), AT 750D (three brothers granted a wish by an angel visitor).

Motifs: D1790.3 (I. the hero's magic power: hero gets power of making all his wishes come true); D1600.13 (II. hero tries his powers); T512 (IIIa. princess laughs at him, and he wishes her pregnant); H481 (IIIb. princess has a child, and child picks hero out as father); S141 (IV. banishment: hero and princess abandoned in a glass box in the sea); D1131 (V. reinstatement: by wishing he makes a castle next to King's and takes his wife into it); H1130 (superhuman tasks); H1131 (task: building enormous bridge); K1811.3 (saint in disguise [Elijah] visits mortal); L10 (victorious youngest son); L101 (unpromising hero); L133 (unpromising son leaves his home); L160 (success of the unpromising hero); L161 (lowly hero marries princess); L215 (unpromising magic object chosen); N810 (supernatural helper).

The ending for this story—the last three lines—is one of the ritual closings that the storyteller uses to finish a tale. Through such a formal closing, the audience is returned to real time and the real world after hearing a story. Rhymed endings have been used in many cultures, including Jewish East European and Middle Eastern tales.

In Jewish tradition, words are viewed as equivalent to deeds or actions. Words are treated with great respect, and even an alphabet letter or part of a letter can be powerful. God created the world through His word. The name of the fifth book of the *Torah,* translated as "These Are the Words," is referred to as *Devarim,* "Words." It is through words that truth is spoken. The most respected persons in the society had always been the rabbi and the scholar, who study, and the scribe, who writes the words of *Torah* (which must be written without a single mistake).

One of the most important prayers we have was not composed by a committee of rabbis but rather, according to tradition, transcribed by the Men of the Great Assembly about 2,400 years ago from a script that fell from Heaven. It is the prayer recited daily just before the morning service:

בָּרוּךְ שֶׁאָמַר וְהָיָה הָעוֹלָם, בָּרוּךְ הוּא. בָּרוּךְ עוֹשֶׂה בְרֵאשִׁית, בָּרוּךְ אוֹמֵר וְעוֹשֶׂה.

Barukh she'amar v'haya ha'olam,
Barukh hu. Barukh oseh b'reishit,
Barukh omer v'oseh . . .

Blessed is He Who spoke, and the world came into being—
blessed is He. Blessed is He Who maintains creation;
blessed is He Who speaks and does . . .

In this prayer, we hear how God, as Creator, brought all of creation into being and maintains it with no more than His word.

It is interesting to note that this prayer is composed of eighty-seven words, a number equivalent to the numerical value of the Hebrew word *paz*, which means "refined gold."

Words are so important that there are thirteen hermeneutical principles of biblical exegesis of Rabbi Ishmael by which to interpret *Torah*. Words have such import that they can have world-shattering effects in their interpretation. The positioning and repetition of words have meaning beyond the plain sense of the text. Indeed, it is not farfetched that what is said has an effect in our lives as well as in biblical narrative.

According to *Gemara*, the interpretation of dreams could determine the outcome of the dreams. Thus we can conclude that words and their intent have powerful effects on actuality.

We humans are made in God's image. God breathed sacred breath into us, which is part of our makeup. According to *Sefer Tanya*, a book of chasidic theology, there is an actual part of God in us, and through the *Torah*, which connects us to God in a very real sense, we learn not only how to conduct our lives but also the principles on which our lives are based.

Many of the commandments that rule our lives deal with speech, such as "Guard my tongue from evil and my lips from speaking guile." Thus we see how, in Judaic thought, words and actions have an intimate relationship. (My thanks to Rabbi Aryeh Gold for speaking with me about words.)

17. Elijah the Prophet on the Seder Night

Source: Marcus (1966), #5. IFA 7000. Told by Sol Okonos (Greece) to her grandson, Shelomo Alaluf.

Tale type: AT 812 (the Devil's riddle). The Devil is replaced by the Angel of Death, and the supernatural helper is Elijah.

Motifs: K1811.3 (Elijah in disguise visits mortal); M211 (man sells soul to Devil); M218.1 (pacts with the Devil made ineffective by a saint); N810 (supernatural helper); V75* (first night of Passover).

At the beginning of a seder, there is a call to the poor and hungry to join the seder. *Ha lachma anya* is "a call to the street, to the ghetto, to the village, to the world that the poor need not despair. In the same spirit, the prophet Isaiah shouted to the world, 'Ho! All ye who thirst, come and drink from the living waters [of the *Torah*]' (Isaiah 55:1)" (*The Passover Haggadah,* with commentary by Rabbi Shlomo Riskin. Hoboken, NJ: Ktav, 1983).

18. The Neighbors

Source: TEM 1967, #8. IFA 7803. Collected by Aharon Yafe (Hayogev) from his mother Lea (Lebanon).

Tale type: AT 750 *J (IFA) (poor woman washes clothes in river and meets Elijah the Prophet but doesn't complain; Elijah blesses her home.) There are sixteen versions, also from Rumania and Tunisia, and in thirteen of these the old man is Elijah. Some of the variants include IFA 6101, 6844, 6863, and 6932 (Morocco), IFA 6840 (Tunisia), IFA 3484 (Egypt), and IFA 4740 (Turkey). Type *776 (Jason) (miscellaneous divine rewards, mostly through Elijah the Prophet [fertility, enrichment, etc.]).

Motifs: J2415 (foolish imitation of lucky man); K1811.3 (saint [Elijah] in disguise visits mortal); L300 (triumph of the weak); Q3 (moderate request rewarded: immoderate punished); Q4 (humble rewarded, haughty punished); V75* (poor provided with necessities on Passover; first night of Passover).

Passover stories often revolve around the conflict of the poor and the rich. After all, at Passover one needs more money than usual to prepare for the holiday properly. In these folktales there is the expected reversal of fortune, that is, the poor person becomes wealthy while the rich person becomes poor (or at least not rewarded). Passover stories also frequently take place near a river, a sea, or even a well, since water (the Red Sea) is part of the holiday, and a miracle happened with the splitting of the water.

19. The Modest Scholar

Sources: Hemdat ha-Yamim (1763); Farhi (1870); Bin Gorion (1916–1921), vol. 1; Klapholtz (1970–1979), vol. 3; Sadeh (1989); Ginzberg (1909–1938), vol. 6. Also IFA 8802 (Palestine Sefardi).

Tale type: AT 750* (hospitality rewarded), Type *776 (Jason) (miscellaneous divine rewards, mostly through Elijah the Prophet [fertility, enrichment, etc.]).

Motifs: H1564 (test of hospitality); K1811.3 (saint in disguise [Elijah] visits mortal); N810 (supernatural helper); Q42.3 (generosity to saint in disguise [Elijah] rewarded); V75* (first night of Passover).

20. A Blessing in Disguise

Sources: Suppurei Maasiot (1971); Klapholtz (1970–1979), vol. 4. Also IFA 8988 (Morocco) and IFA 998 (Iraq).

Tale type: AT 750* (hospitality rewarded), AT 517*A (a child is promised to a barren couple in a dream or by Elijah the Prophet).

Motifs: D2161.3.11 (barrenness magically cured); K1811.3 (saint in disguise [Elijah] visits mortal); Q42.3 (generosity to saint in disguise [Elijah] rewarded); Q45.1 (saint in disguise [Elijah] entertained unawares); V75* (first night of Passover).

Seder has two meanings: (1) the ceremony and meal on the first two nights of Passover and, (2) in Hebrew, "order." Thus the blessing for "disorder" at the Passover seder is a pun on the word "seder." Jews have always enjoyed stories that utilize a play on words. See commentary for "The Man Whose Words Came True" (tale no. 16, this volume).

Stories with such a play on words also allowed Jews to keep some control in their lives, especially when they usually had neither power nor political and economic control in the society at large. As a result, these kinds of stories, along with riddle stories, double-meaning phrases or signs, tall tales, and the like, served as powerful releases from the frustrations and feelings of powerlessness in Jewish lives.

21. The Ignorant Beadle

Source: TEM 1972, #7. IFA 9480. Collected by Galit Hasan-Rock (Jerusalem) from Avraham Logasi (Morocco).

Tale types: AT 873*A, (girl with animal face). There are eight parallels from Morocco, Yemen, Iraq, and Kurdistan; AT 934*G, (rescue of boy fated to die on his wedding night). There are thirteen parallels from Kurdistan-Persia and Iraq. AT 712 (magic healing power); AT 800–809 (journey to Heaven).

Motifs: D2161 (magic healing power); F11 (journey to Heaven); F111 (journey to earthly Paradise); F933.1 (miraculous spring [lake] bursts forth for holy person); F950 (marvelous cures); F1099.3 (words heard only and not uttered); F1033.1 (person lives on water [from holy well] for a year); L160 (success of the unpromising hero); N810 (supernatural helper); T53.3 (saint as matchmaker); V51.5 (man who does not know how to pray is so holy that he walks on water); V221 (miraculous healing by saints); V246 (angel counsels mortal); Z71.2 (formulistic number: four).

This story, "The Ignorant Beadle," is long enough to be a novella. While the first part of the story focuses on the prayer of a simpleton who brings about miracles, the second part centers on Elijah the Prophet drilling Torah into the simpleton's son, an even greater ignoramus. Fathers and sons are a recurrent theme in Elijah stories. Elijah is thought of as the one who will be a peacemaker between fathers and sons (Malachi 3:24), which can be interpreted as a symbolic reference to God as "father" and Israel as His "children." In *Seder Eliyahu Rabba* (Friedmann 1902) and *Seder Eliyahu Zutta* (Friedmann 1904), Elijah is often titled "father Elijah."

In this story, it is the father who gives himself the identity as the "Son of the Name." This appelation was translated into Hebrew as *Ben Hashem* or "Son of God." The teller actually told the story in Judeo-Arabic, the Moroccan dialect (called *Marokait* in Hebrew) and used the Arabic words *Walid Allah* for "Son of God." This phrase suggests Christological implications. But it should be noted that neither the heavenly (angelic) nor the earthly Elijah is regarded as a Divine figure. And indeed it is not clear what it means, because it no doubt has kabbalistic and mystical connotations and interpretations. I can only try to offer a few thoughts because I have not delved into the realm of mysticism.

Since "father" is symbolic of God and "son" of the Jewish people, the beadle might have used "Son of God" or "Son of the Name" simply to introduce himself as a follower of God rather than be mistaken for a heathen. The beadle may also be referring to "I will declare the decree: the Lord hath said unto me, Thou *art* my Son; this day have I begotten thee" (Psalm 2:7).

Dov Noy, Professor of Folklore at Hebrew University and founder of the Israel Folktale Archives, "raised the possibility of the connection to *Baal Shem,* Master of the Name, and exchanging *Shem* for the name of God, *HaShem,* and also as a shortening of a specific name or of *Shem Tov,* Good Name, or as it relates to Ecclesiastes 7:1" ["A good name is better than fragrant ointment . . ."] (Cheichel 1973). It is interesting to note in connection with this play on words that the Baal Shem Tov, Master of the Good Name, is a name usually associated with Rabbi Israel, the founder of Chasidism. However, while some interpret this "good name" as belonging to Rabbi Israel, the "Shem Tov" also refers to God.

The connection is not clear but echoed in this tale of the father and son. It is God's will that Elijah has the power to be an angel in Heaven and to be a person on earth. There is a biblical verse, "Who hath ascended up into heaven, and descended?" (Proverbs 30:4), which the *Zohar* explains as meaning that it is Elijah who has ascended and descended. "'Before he ascends he is Eliyahu, and when he descends as messenger and miracle worker he is Eliyahu.' . . . The identification of the name of the ascending Elijah with that of the descending Elijah called 'son' . . . means psychologically that the 'heavenly' Elijah as archetype is, as it were, the father of the earthly Elijah-figures appearing in the world from time to time"

(Wiener 1978). According, then, to mystical interpretations, it is as though the heavenly archetype is the father of the earthly figure, which is the son. For more on Elijah in Jewish mysticism and discussion about his names, see Wiener (1978).

Water plays an important and metaphoric role throughout the story, beginning with the beadle washing and cleaning the Beit Medrash and ending with the water, which transforms the son into a whole other person, namely a *talmud chakham*. The emphasis of water in this story reveals the world view of the storyteller (who is from Morocco) and of the culture in which the story is told. This story, like other long tales the storyteller Avraham Logasi told, belongs to a rich literary tradition that comes to the teller from his teacher Moshe Ohayun (Cheichel 1973).

In folklore, water is symbolic of life, birth, and a mother's womb. In Judaism, however, it is also symbolic of Torah. Many stories compare Torah to water (i.e., the famous parable of Akiva and the fish). In Jeremiah 2:13 and Jeremiah 17:13, God is referred to as "the fountain of living waters." In the story, Elijah says, "The more water you drink, the more you'll drink *Torah*." That water is *mayim hayim*, the water of life—in other words, *Torah*.

See note to "The Neighbors" regarding the relationship of water, miracles, and Passover. See note to "Elijah the Prophet and the Son of a Wise Man" regarding the young woman making a mistake in her *Torah* studies.

See note to "The Man Whose Words Came True" regarding performing miracles through words alone and the power of words in Judaism.

22. Laughter and Tears

Sources: This is a combined version of IFA 9068 (Kurdistan) and IFA 2554 (Morocco). IFA 9068 was collected by Ronite Bornstein Dotan from Zakhi Mou'aziz, who is from Kokhi, Iran. IFA 2554 was collected by Yakov Avitzuk from Avraham Elush. There are forty-five versions in IFA.

Tale types: AT 875 (the clever peasant girl) and AT 922*C (IFA).

Motifs: F1041.11 (laugh and cry at the same time); H1064 (task: coming laughing and crying at once); H500 (test of cleverness or ability).

Neither of these two IFA tales includes Elijah the Prophet. However, I have introduced Elijah into my version (for in many tales Elijah appears in a marketplace and offers various helpful items for "sale"). I have also introduced the resourceful young woman who is given the secret of producing laughter and tears at the same time. In one version, IFA 9068, it is the rabbi who makes the king laugh and cry together by telling a funny story while cutting an onion. In IFA 2554, the king threatens the Jewish community if it doesn't find a man who will cry and laugh at the same time. Here a clever Jew succeeds by cutting onions and making the king cry while laughing at his own tears.

There are such stories where there is a question (or series of questions) or other challenges made to the Jews, usually by a king, in order to have them meet the challenge on pain of death or expulsion. These tales sometimes include Elijah, in the disguise of the clever Jew, who then exposes the villain in the plot.

Laughter and tears seem to be synonymous with the Jewish people. Sholom Aleichem's writings perhaps best symbolize this Jewish characteristic of "laughter through tears." Somehow, in Jewish life, the two are omnipresent, often blending and allowing us to keep our balance, like a "fiddler on the roof" or a person walking a tightrope.

23. The Jewels of *Mitzvah*

Source: Ben Yehezkel (1928–1929); Horowitz (1967); Klapholtz (1970–1979), vol. 4.

Tale type: *776 (Jason) (miscellaneous divine rewards mostly through Elijah, such as enrichment).

Motifs: K1811.3 (saint in disguise [Elijah] visits mortal); V246 (angel counsels mortal); V410 (charity rewarded).

This story brings to mind a different story involving a jewel and Elijah. Rabbi Isaac owned a jewel worth thousands upon thousands of gold pieces. At that time, a similar jewel was lost from the emperor's idol. When the emperor heard that Rabbi Isaac had a jewel that would be a worthy replacement, he sent for him, willing to pay whatever sum he asked for this gem. On the ship, Rabbi Isaac thought of a plan by which this jewel would be "accidentally" dropped into the sea, because he would rather take this loss than contribute in any way to idolatry. Because the loss of the gem was due to an accident, the emperor did not accuse Rabbi Isaac of any treachery, and nobody in his court knew of Rabbi Isaac's real reason for "losing" the gem. As Rabbi Isaac was returning to the ship, Elijah met him and told him that because of his action in fulfilling God's will, his wife would bear a son who would be "a jewel beyond compare in the whole world." And so it happened. Rabbi Isaac's son was Solomon ben Isaac of Troyes (1040–1105), who became known as Rashi, one of the greatest of all sages and whose famed commentary on the *Torah* and the Babylonian Talmud continues to be quoted extensively.

There are also a number of stories about Elijah foretelling the birth of other great sages, such as the Baal Shem Tov, Rabbi Isaac Luria, and Rabbi Levi Yitzchok of Berdichev, as a reward for hospitality, sacrifice, and other *mitzvot*. In these stories Elijah often counsels the father that the *brit* should not be performed until he arrives.

24. The Inheritance

Source: Adapted from *Aggadah* in Talmud; Ausubel (1948); Isaacs (1893).

Motifs: L113 (hero of unpromising occupation); L133 (unpromising son leaves his home); L160 (success of the unpromising hero); V246 (angel counsels mortal).

The saying *Talmid al yoreh halakhah bimkom rabo* is from *Sanhedrin* 5b. This is an expression of respect and humility shown to one's teacher.

25. All Because of a Loaf of Bread

Source: Ben Yehezkel (1928–1929); *Marvels of Maharal;* Klapholtz (1970–1979), vol. 4.

Motifs: K1811.3 (saint in disguise [Elijah] visits mortal); N810 (supernatural helper); T53.3 (saint as matchmaker).

26. The Proper Response

Sources: Ginzberg (1909–1938), vol. 4; Steinschneider (1858); Plungian (1857); Klapholtz (1970–1979), vol. 2. IFA 1606 (Iraq).

Tale type: AT 830C (if God wills).

Motif: N385.1 (person has successive misfortunes while making plans because he forgets to say "If God wills.")

27. Rachel and Akiva: A Love Story

Sources: Nedarim 50a (Aggadah); *Gittin* 56a; Ginzberg (1909–1938), vol. 4; Bin Gorion (1976); Ausubel (1948); Klapholtz (1970–1979), vol. 2; Frankel (1989). IFA 3354 (Iraq) and IFA 5282 (Tunis).

Motifs: H1552 (test of generosity); J80 (wisdom/knowledge taught by parable); J883.1 ("man compelled to live on peas takes comfort when he sees a man once rich eating hulls"); J1011 (lazy woman resumes her work—"she sees how a little bird by persistence pecks a hole in a stone").

This is one of the most wonder-filled stories of love and faithfulness. While Akiva was studying, Rachel continued to live in poverty, even selling her long, beautiful hair to buy food. After twelve years, Akiva returned with 12,000 students. When a neighbor mocked his wife for being abandoned by her husband, Rachel replied that she would rather have Akiva study for another twelve years than return ignorant. Akiva, hearing this reply, returned to his studies for another twelve years. When he did come home for good, followed by twice as many students, some of them wanted to chase Rachel away from Akiva, thinking she was just any old woman. Akiva shouted out, giving *kavod* to his wife by saying, "All the *Torah* we know we owe to her." By this time, Kalba Savua, Rachel's father, regretted his action against his daughter and asked the great sage Akiva how to resolve this family separation. Akiva then identified himself as his son-in-law. Kalba Savua embraced his daughter and Akiva, asking forgiveness and giving them half his wealth. For another love story, see "The Bride's Wisdom" (tale no. 28, this volume; Schram [1987]).

28. A Beggar's Blessing

Sources: Ginzberg (1909–1938), vol. 4; Gaster (1924), #435; Midrash. Also in Weinreich (1957), Tale 38 (with her permission). There are also many versions recorded in IFA: 49 (Turkey), 195

(Samaritan), 384 (Tunis), 437 (Peki'in Village), 829 (Aleppo), 879 (Palestinian, Sephardi), 960 (Poland), 1038 (Eastern Europe), 1053 and 1065 (Morocco), 1229 and 1313 (Egypt), and 2922 (Eastern Europe).

Tale types: AT 750A (the wishes) and AT 565 (the magic mill).

Motifs: D1720.1 (man given power of wishing); D2100.1 (inexhaustible treasure); D2172.2 (magic gift: power to continue all day what one starts); H1564 (test of hospitality); J2071 (a limited number of wishes will be fulfilled); J2073.1 (wise and foolish wish: keep doing all day what you begin); J2415 (foolish imitation of lucky man); K1811.3 (saint in disguise [Elijah] visits mortal); Q1.1 (saint in disguise [Elijah] rewards hospitality); Q286.1 (uncharitableness to holy person—punished); Q42.3 (generosity to saint in disguise [Elijah] rewarded).

This legend was widespread among European nations, and then transformed into a Jewish version, which was especially popular among German Jews. However, as can be noted from the many versions of this story in the IFA, it is also a most popular story among Eastern European and Sephardi Jews. A very old version can be found in *Mishle Sinbad.* Another version can be found in *Kitve ha-Maggid mi-Dubno.* (In this version, a rabbi bestows the blessing upon a traveler to continue doing all day what he first does upon arriving home. When his wife refuses to get the money to count, they begin to quarrel. This is what they then keep doing all day.) In some versions, the result of what the couple continues to do is more earthy. Other sources for variants include Tendlau (1860); Benfey (1859); the fables of Aesop and Marie de France; *Sefer ha-Bdiha veha-Hiddud; Sihot Hayim; Rosinkes mit Mandlen;* Ben Yehezkel (1928–1929); Noy (1961b); Schwarzbaum (1968), extensive notes on pp. 241–245.

The source of "Foolish Wishes" may be 2 Kings 4:1–7, which is the story of Elisha, the disciple of Elijah, and the widow's oil. The blessing "May what you do be blessed until you say 'Enough!'" is illustrated in this message in Second Kings.

29. The Bride's Wisdom

Sources: Midrash Tanhuma; Haazinu 8; *Book of Tobit;* Ibn Zabara (1912); Gaster (1924, 1934); Bin Gorion (1975); Cohen (1721);

Ashkenazi (1687); Klapholtz (1970–1979), Vol. 3; Frankel (1989); Schram (1987).

Tale types: AT 934B (the youth to die on his wedding day), AT 934*F (charity rescues from death), AT 934*G (rescue of boy fated to die on his wedding night; Elijah annuls death decree)—13 parallels from Kurdistan Persia and Iraq.

Motifs: H1564 (test of hospitality); M341.1 (prophecy of death on wedding day); V246 (angel counsels mortal); V410 (one good deed wards off punishment, even if decreed); V152.

The Talmud and the Midrash have many stories with the same theme as this tale, and they have influenced the literature of many nations. The story of faithfulness and love that may have been the model for our story can be found in the legend about Rabbi Akiva's daughter (*Shabbat* 156b). The astrologers predicted that Akiva's daughter would die on her wedding day. However, just at the moment when the serpent was about to sting her, she rushed to the door to give charity to a beggar. Instead of the serpent killing her, she killed the serpent. Proverbs 10:2 states: "Charity delivers from death." Another bride who confronts the Angel of Death is the character of Miriam in I. L. Peretz's story *Messiras Nefesh* ("Devotion unto Death"). In folktales it is a common feature for the Angel of Death to engage in conversations with people while on his way to take a soul.

The Talmud (*Berakhot* 54b) and Rashi's commentaries stress that both bride and bridegroom should be carefully guarded at the wedding and on the wedding night. The evil eye lurks everywhere at such times of joy, and one must be careful so that the Angel of Death does not become jealous of their great happiness.

30. The Repentant Rabbi

Source: Ta'anit 20a; Gaster (1924, 1934); Isaacs (1893); Frankel (1989).

Although in Isaacs's version the dwarf is not identified as Elijah specifically, Elijah does appear in the other versions but in disguise as a tall black man. Thus I felt that Elijah could take on the disguise of a dwarf because, in all the versions, the lesson he teaches the rabbi is the same.

Greetings are important in Jewish life and so, too, the attitudes with which we approach one another. See "The Greeting" (tale no. 32, this volume).

31. The Agunah, the Rabbi, and the "Sheep"

Source: TEM 1970, #8, IFA 8903 (Iraq). Collected by Berakha Dalmatski (Haifa) from Samuel Hay of Iraq.

Tale types: AT 930–939 (boy reunited with parents), AT 400 (the man on a quest for his lost wife), AT 850 (the birthmarks of the princess), AT 517*A (a child is promised to a barren couple in a dream or by Elijah the prophet).

Motifs: D2161.3.11 (barrenness magically cured); D1500.1.16 (magic healing bottle); H50 (recognition by bodily marks or physical attributes); M311.0.3.1 (prophecy: child to be born to childless couple); V246 (angel counsels mortal).

The theme of metamorphosis appears to reflect deep-rooted fears and hopes, for it occurs repeatedly in the folklore of every nation and can be found as well in Jewish folktales. For another transformation story, see "The Fisherman's Daughter" (Schram 1987) in which a very common theme, that of a woman redeeming her animal lover, occurs. Also see "Her Wisdom Is Her Beauty" (no. 11, this volume; Schram [1987]).

As in "A Tale Retold at a Feast" (no. 8, this volume), the son reveals his identity to his parents by retelling the story of his life and journey.

32. The Greeting

Source: Adapted from *Sefer Gevurath Israel* (1924); Ausubel (1948); Frankel (1989).

Greetings are very important in Jewish life because of our emphasis on the concept of *chakhnosas orchim*, hospitality. The traditional Jewish greeting is *Sholom aleikhem*, which means "Peace be unto you." The response is to reverse these two words and say *Aleikhem sholom*. It is such an important opening that one of the greatest Yiddish writers, Shalom Rabinovitch, took the actual greeting as his *nom de plume;* and he became known worldwide as Shalom Aleichem. This greeting of *sholom* encompasses the entire Jewish worldview of hoping and praying for peace. (See "The

Repentant Rabbi" [tale no. 30, this volume] for a different kind of greeting between the rabbi and the dwarf.)

There are several stories in which various characters express a desire to meet Elijah, but when they do, they do not recognize him and therefore keep "waiting" for him. In one story, the students of the Baal Shem Tov, the founder of the chasidic movement and a performer of miracles, too, plead that he should show Elijah to them. The Baal Shem Tov finally agrees. However, when they meet a Polish nobleman on the field, the students ignore him while the Baal Shem Tov speaks with him. Later, when the students again ask to see Elijah, the Baal Shem Tov explains that the nobleman had indeed been Elijah but that the students hadn't bothered greeting him or inquiring as to who he was. In other words, it was not permitted for the Baal Shem Tov to have identified Elijah in the beginning, but only to have brought them all together.

There were two Rabbi Meirs of Peremyshlyany. The first one, known as "the First" or "the Great," lived in the early eighteenth century and was a disciple of the founder of Chasidism, Rabbi Israel ben Eliezer Baal Shem Tov. The second was his grandson, whose name was also Rabbi Meir of Peremyshlyany (1780?–1850), and he continued following the chasidic tradition. He became known as a great *tzaddik*. There were many stories of the miracles he performed, and these well-known stories were later printed and widely circulated.

Peremyshlyany, a town in Poland, became famous during the eighteenth and nineteenth centuries because of its dynasty of chasidic leaders, including the two Meirs.

33. A Choice of Years

Sources: Midrash Ruth Zutta; Yalkut Ruth; Halkut Shimoni; Ginzberg (1909–1938); Bin Gorion (1916–1921, 1976); Klapholtz (1970–1979), vol. 4; Weinreich (1988); Jellinek (1853–1877); Gaster (1924, 1934); Eisenstein (1915); Frankel (1989).

IFA 3482 (Egypt), IFA 6769, 3938, 4903 (Morocco), and IFA 5982 (Persian Kurdistan).

Tale types: AT types 938, 938A (misfortunes in youth) and 938B (better in youth) and AT 938 *C. Type *776 (Jason) (miscellaneous divine rewards, mostly through Elijah the Prophet).

Motifs: J214 ("When do you wish to hear your hardships: in youth or old age?"); K1811.3 (saint in disguise [Elijah] visits mortal); H1552 (test of generosity); N251 (person pursued by misfortune); V410 (charity rewarded).

The most famous version of this folktale was written by the great Yiddish writer Isaac Loeb Peretz. It is found in many anthologies under the title "The Seven Good Years." In some versions, Elijah appears in a disguise other than that of a handsome nobleman. His other disguises include a poor beggar and an Arab.

34. The King, the Adviser, and the Jewish Boy

Source: TEM 1965, #12. IFA 6552. Collected by Aliza Shenhar from Mordekhai Ben-Simhon (Morocco). Also in Gaster (1924).

Tale types: AT 839*C (IFA) (miraculous rescue of persecuted person) (52-plus versions from Morocco, Tunisia, Iraq, Iran, and Eastern Europe), AT *730 A (IFA) (miraculous rescue of a Jewish community), AT 922 (14 versions) (the shepherd substituting for the priest answers the king's questions), AT 922*C (king sets task to Jews on pain of death), AT 927 (outriddling the judge). Variants IFA 11,137 (Afghanistan) and IFA 8168 (Iraq). Also AT 756B (the Devil's contract) and AT 1528*D (contest in cleverness between Jew and Gentile; Jew wins).

The riddles of riddling contest are reminiscent of AT 875 (the clever peasant girl) and AT 921 (the king and the peasant's son) and their subtypes (47 and 25 versions, respectively).

Motifs: C931 (building falls because of breaking of taboo); H541.1 (riddle propounded on pain of death); H633.3 (What is sweetest? Mother's breast); H637.1 (What is hardest? Parent's heart—said by child being sacrificed); H671 (riddle: What is sweeter than honey?); H673 (riddle: What is harder than stone?); H691 (riddle of weight); J120 (wisdom learned from children); K1610 (deceiver falls into his own trap—miscellaneous incidents); K1010 (deception through false doctoring); K1955 (sham physician); N810 (supernatural helper); S12 (cruel mother); S221 (child sold for money); S261.1 (child as foundation sacrifice smiles and wins freedom); V246 (angel counsels mortal).

Some of the versions pose other questions to the Jews, which they must answer on pain of death, such as:

1. What preceded God? Answer: nothing.
2. What side does God face? Answer: all sides, like a candle.
3. Who is richer than a king? Answer: the man whose large size will need more space in the grave.

In these tales, it is usually a simpleton, a drunkard, or a child who volunteers to represent the Jews and succeeds.

35. The Chasid's Good Deeds

Sources: TEM 1972, #11. IFA 9484 collected by Amir Richt (Holon) from his father, David (Poland). Also IFA 9472 (charity rewarded) and IFA 9476 (riches through Elijah).

Tale type: AT *776: miscellaneous divine rewards (collective oikotype). Over sixty versions.

Motifs: H1552 (test of generosity); K1811.3 (saint in disguise [Elijah] visits mortal).

36. Elijah's Lullaby

Source: IFA 7637. This is an unclassified tale and collected from Pinchas Guterman from Poland.

A number of Jewish stories interweave text and tune, a genre called *cante fable*. Many of these stories explain how a secular melody becomes transformed into a sacred *nigun*, a Chasidic melody without words. Other kinds of *cante fables* explain the origin of a famous song or tune, tell how the hero bought or sold a song or tune, or illustrate the magic qualities of a song or tune. Many of these have been collected in the IFA (see Noy 1968; see also "The Melody" and three additional stories with music in Schram [1987]).

I have written a family story of how Mikl Gordon's lullaby (composed in 1868 in Lithuania) *"Az Ikh Volt Gehat Dem Keiser's Oitzres"* (If I could have had all the king's treasure) was handed down in my family through four generations. See introductory notes and story, "The Lullaby" (Schram 1987, pp. 472–476).

The lyrics and structure of the lullaby in this story do not seem to indicate that it is a true folksong. Since the IFA did not have any music recorded for this lullaby, I asked Chana Mlotek, the music archivist of the YIVO Institute for Jewish Research, to research the melody for the lyrics. A notice in the bi-weekly column on Yiddish poetry and song that she co-edits in the *Jewish Forward* did not succeed in finding anyone who knows this song. Then she sent me a letter with some music and wrote, "I felt that a lullaby, which seemed to me to have been translated from Hebrew, would sound nice if rendered with a Hebrew melody—and Joel Engel's *wig-lied* came to mind." (A *wig-lied* is Yiddish for a cradle song or lullaby.) Therefore she adapted the melody from Joel Engel's song *"Numi, Numi."* The English lyrics, written in a poetic, singable translation, are by Roslyn Bresnick-Perry.

Joel Engel (1868–1927) was one of the leading spirits in the movement for Jewish music in Russia and in Israel. He is regarded as the father of Jewish music and was instrumental in founding the Society for Jewish Folk Music in 1908. In 1912 Engel accompanied S. Anski on an ethnographic expedition to collect folk songs from the Jews living in South Russia. Fourteen years later he composed incidental music for Anski's famous play *The Dybbuk*. The Engel Prize for outstanding composers was established by the Tel Aviv municipality in his honor. Since Engel himself adapted Jewish folk songs and had such a great love of Eretz Yisrael, it seems to me to be even more appropriate to choose one of his composed lullabies as the music for the lyrics in this story.

Engel's *wig-lied*, *"Numi, Numi,"* was originally published in *Sechs Leichte Chöre* (Moscow: Musiksektion des Staatsverlages, 1930). It can be found in a more recent music anthology, *A Harvest of Jewish Song*, compiled and edited by Tzipora H. Jochsberger with Velvel Pasternak (Cedarhurst, NY: Tara Publications, 1980).

Glossary

Unless otherwise noted, the following expressions are Hebrew. Nearly all of them are used in Yiddish as well. Ashkenazic pronunciation is indicated by (A), Sefardic pronunciation by (S). The vowel combination ei *is pronounced* a *as in* cake; ai *is* i *as in* kite. Kh *and* ch *are as in the German,* ich.

Agunah A woman who cannot remarry (or marry) under Jewish law because her husband (or betrothed) has deserted her or because his death cannot be verified.

Aleph bet The first two letters of the Hebrew alphabet. The alphabet is referred to as the *aleph-bet*.

Am ha'aretz a foolish or ignorant man.

Bar mitzvah Son of the Commandment at 13 years of age. At this age the young man accepts the obligation to observe the precepts of Judaism. He becomes a responsible adult Jewish member of the congregation and the community.

Beadle The caretaker of a synagogue; also called a *shammash*. Sometimes the beadle would summon people to prayer or act as messenger.

Beit Din House of Judgment. A term that refers to a Jewish court of law. It exercises jurisdiction over personal matters that need to be decided according to Jewish law.

Beit Knesset The synagogue where formal prayer services are held.

Beit Midrash (S); **Beis Medrash** (A) House of Study; a part of every synagogue. In the talmudic age it was a school for higher rabbinic learning (study, discussion, and prayer). In post-talmudic times most synagogues had a Beit Midrash, or else the synagogue itself would be referred to as the Beit Midrash, since they were places of study. Also called *Beit HaMidrash*.

Ben Zakkai, Yochanan First-century C.E. *tanna* (a rabbi, scholar, and teacher from the period of Hillel to the compilation of the Mishnah, c. 20–200 C.E.). He was the leading sage in the period following the destruction of the Temple. In 68 C.E., he established the most important center of learning in Yavneh in the land of Israel, which became the seat of the Sanhedrin, the Supreme Court in Israel during the Roman period until 425 C.E., after the fall of Jerusalem. Ben Zakkai was the most respected and influential rabbi of his time; two of his pupils were Rabbi Akiva and Rabbi Joshua ben Hananiah.

Bikur cholim Visiting the sick in order to cheer them and relieve their suffering is regarded in Judaism as a religious duty. There were special *bikur cholim* societies for this purpose, called Chevrat Bikur Cholim.

Bimah An elevated place or platform in the synagogue where the rabbi and cantor stand and where the *Torah* is read.

Birkat hamazon Grace after meals. At the end of these blessings, this prayer is added: "May the Merciful One send us Elijah the Prophet—remembered for good—that he may bring us good tidings, salvation, and consolation."

Brit The ritual of circumcision performed on boy babies on the eighth day after birth. It is the religious act of entering into the covenant with God. A *mohel* performs the operation. The godfather, who holds the child on his lap/table, is the *sandak*. The chair on which the child is placed before the *brit* and on which the *sandak* sits is called the Chair of Elijah. Certain blessings are recited over a cup of wine while the child is given his name.

B'seder With order. (*See* seder.)

B'shalom With peace.

Bubbe Grandmother (Yiddish).

Chakham (**chakhomim,** pl.) A wise man. (*See* talmud chakham.)

Chakhnosas orchim The *mitzvah* of offering hospitality. Abraham was the basic prototype of hospitality.

Challah (Challeh in Yiddish) A braided white bread baked especially for the Shabbat and festivals.

Charoset A symbolic food served at the Passover seder made from a mixture of nuts, apples, cinnamon, and wine to resemble clay used by Jewish slaves in Egypt to make bricks.

Chasid A pious one. A follower of Chasidism.

Chatan A bridegroom.

Chevrah (Chavurah) A formal membership association formed for a religious or philanthropic purpose. (*See* bikur cholim and Chevrah Kadisha.)

Chevrah Kadisha Aramaic for holy brotherhood. This communal organization performs the holy commandment of caring for and washing the dead person, accompanying the body to the grave, and burial. It is considered a great honor to become a member of this society.

Chol hamoed Intermediate days of Passover and Sukkot festivals. During this period, essential work may be done, although marriages and mourning are not permitted.

Chuppah A Jewish wedding canopy.

Citron—etrog (S); esrog (A) A citrus fruit that resembles a large lemon and over which a benediction is said during Sukkot. It is one of the four species used on the festival of Sukkot. (*See* lulav and Sukkot.)

Davening Praying or chanting prayers in the synagogue.

Drash (drashim, pl.) ''Interpretation'' from *midrash*. Refers to the sermon given on a Shabbat in the synagogue, interpreting and elaborating on a portion of the Torah reading.

Eliyahu HaNavi Elijah the Prophet in Hebrew. In Yiddish his name is spelled Eliyohu HaNovi.

Eretz Yisrael The Land of Israel.

Erev The evening before the Shabbat or festival begins.

Eshet-chayil ''A woman of valor.'' These are the first words of Proverbs 31:10–31 describing the virtuous wife. The verses are chanted in the home on Friday evening (*erev* Shabbat).

Etrog (etrogim, pl.) *See* citron.

Gabai (gabaiim, pl.) The lay communal official of a synagogue; the word is part of the term *gabbai tzedakah* (charity warden).

Gabriel The angel whose function was to reveal the messenger from God, thus his association with Elijah. He is the only angel mentioned in the Bible (Daniel 8–10) and in apocryphal and rabbinic literature. Gabriel is described as a leader of the angelic host; an archangel.

Gan Eden Garden of Eden; Paradise.

Gut Shabbos In Yiddish, "good Sabbath."

Haggadah A recounting of the Exodus from Egypt and freedom from bondage. It includes poems, songs, psalms, and stories, and is recited at the Passover seder in the home.

HaKodosh Barukhu The Holy One Blessed be He.

Halakhah Jewish law; the legal part of Talmud or "letter" of the law, as distinct from *aggadah,* the nonlegal "spirit" of the law.

Hamotzi The blessing recited over bread or *challah.*

Hoshana Rabba A semifestival on the seventh day of Sukkot. During that early-morning service there are special processions seven times around the synagogue, and a number of chants beginning with the word "Hoshana!" (Save!), while carrying a bunch of willow branches along with the *lulav* and *etrog.* At the conclusion of the *Hoshanot,* everyone beats the willow on the floor five times as a symbolic act. It is a time to pray for rain to water next year's willow and our lives, both physically and spiritually. This is the last time for using the *lulav* and *etrog.* This is also a solemn time because it is an extension of Yom Kippur, the Day of Judgment. During this period of eleven days, the Heavens remained open. But on this twenty-first day of Tishri, the gates of judgment close.

Kaddish Aramaic prayer recited by mourners during the period of mourning and on the anniversary of the death. It is a prayer in praise of God, and there is no mention of death in the *Kaddish.*

Kallah A bride.

Kein Yehee Rotzon "May it be His Will." A response after a prayer, especially after the priestly blessing.

Kiddush Sanctification. A prayer recited over a cup of wine in the home and synagogue to consecrate the Sabbath and festivals. The Passover seder begins with *Kiddush.*

Kiddushin Betrothal. In Jewish law there are two stages in the marriage ceremony: betrothal and marriage. *Kiddushin* takes place in front of witnesses, and usually the young man gives a token or symbolic sum of money to his betrothed. This legal ceremony binds the woman as his wife so that she may not marry anyone else unless he dies or divorces her.

Kol Nidre Aramaic for "All Vows." This prayer for the annulment of vows made rashly to God by the worshiper is chanted by the cantor on the eve of Yom Kippur, the Day of Atonement. This prayer, chanted at the beginning of the service, is so important that the entire evening is referred to as *Kol Nidre*.

Kavod (Koved in Yiddish) Honor.

L'chaim "to life." It is used as a toast, especially at a wedding and on other happy occasions.

Lulav A bundle of branches and leaves of three species: willow, myrtle, and palm. It is used along with the *etrog* during Sukkot to symbolize the fruit and trees—the natural beauty of Israel. (*See* citron.)

Maharal Rabbi Judah Loew (c. 1525–1609), who was one of the outstanding leaders and scholars of Ashkenazi Jewry; chief rabbi of Prague and subject of legends, especially the tale of the Golem.

Maharshal Rabbi Solomon ben Jehiel Luria (c. 1510–1574). Rabbi and codifier, he officiated in several Lithuanian and Polish communities. Although many were critical of his views, primarily that the Talmud was the sole halakhic authority, the greatness of his learning was undisputed.

Matzah Unleavened bread eaten during the eight days of Passover to recall the haste with which the Jews left Egypt, since there was no time for the bread to rise.

Mazel Luck.

Mezuzah Doorpost. A parchment scroll with selected Torah verses placed in a container and affixed to the doorpost of a Jewish home.

Mikveh A collection, especially of water; a ritual bath.

Mishnah The code of basic Jewish law (*halakhah*) redacted and arranged into six orders and subdivided into tractates by Rabbi Yehuda Hanasi c. 200 C.E. Contains the Oral Law transmitted for generations.

Mitzvah (mitzvot, pl.) A good deed; a commandment or precept.

Mohel The one who performs the circumcision or *brit*. (*See* brit.)

Nar (naronim, pl.) A foolish or stupid person.

Nar groiser A big fool (Yiddish).

Nefesh A soul; a person; a creature. More often an innocent; a person of no consequence; someone who is weak and pathetic.

Neshamah Soul.

Nisan Hebrew month. The first month of the year, called in the *Torah* the "month of spring" (Aviv). The festival of Passover occurs on Nisan 15.

Nissim (**nes,** sing.) Miracles.

Nu An expression in Yiddish, usually a question meaning "So?"

Parsa'ot A measure of distance.

Parsim Those who belong to the Zoroastrian religion in Persia.

Pesach Passover, the festival of freedom that takes place in the spring on Nisan 15 and lasts for eight days (seven days in Israel). It commemorates the Exodus from Egypt. (*See* seder, matzah, charoset, Nisan.)

Rabbinut The authoritative teachers or rabbis of a town who supervise all religious communal and personal activities of the Jewish community, including lawsuits, divorces, ritual slaughter, ritual baths.

Raphael Archangel and divine messenger who is given the special function of healing, an area associated also with Elijah. Raphael is first mentioned in the apocryphal books of Enoch and Tobit. His name means "God will heal." Raphael was one of the three angels who visited Abraham. (*See* chakhnosas orchim.)

Ribono shel Olam "Creator of the Universe."

Sandak Godfather of a child at the *brit*; the one who holds the child on his knees during circumcision. (*See* brit.)

Seder Literally "order." It refers to the ceremony that follows an order or service (including the meal) that takes place in the home on the first two nights of Passover. (In Israel, only one seder is held.)

Seikhl Common sense in Yiddish.

Shabbat Sabbath. *Shabbos* in Yiddish.

Shacharit Daily morning prayer recited after daybreak.

Sholom Peace; also a greeting in Yiddish.

Sholom aleikhem "Peace be unto you," a greeting; the response is *Aleikhem sholom. Shalom aleikha* is singular.

Shavuot Weeks; this festival occurs on the fiftieth day after the first day of Passover, Sivan 6. Also called Pentecost as well as Feast of First Fruits and Harvest Feast. Traditionally, it is the anniversary of when the Torah was given on Mount Sinai; thus it is also known as Festival of the Giving of the Torah. The Ten Commandments and the Book of Ruth are read in the synagogue on Shavuot. (*See* Torah and Talmud.)

Sheva Brakhot Seven Benedictions. These blessings are recited as part of the marriage ceremony and at meals during the traditional seven days of wedding feasts.

Shma Yisrael "Hear O Israel." The Jewish credo.

Shul Synagogue in Yiddish.

Simchah Refers to a celebration or happy occasion, such as a *brit,* a *bar mitzvah,* or a wedding.

Sukkot Literally "booths." The harvest festival that begins on Tishri 15 and is known also as the Festival of Tabernacles. It commemorates the booths in which the Israelites lived as they crossed the desert after the Exodus from Egypt. It is also a harvest festival. The festival lasts seven days, of which the first two days are *yom tov* (sacred days when no work is permitted) and the others are *chol hamoed.* The last day of the festival is Hashana Rabba. (*See* chol hamoed and Hoshana Rabba.)

Tallit A four-cornered prayer shawl with fringes, worn in the synagogue during morning services.

Talmud The commentaries on the Torah and the Oral Law that were transmitted through the generations. There are two Talmuds: the Jerusalem Talmud and the Babylonian Talmud. The Babylonian Talmud has had the greatest influence on Jewish thought, study, and practice. It is a storehouse of Jewish history and customs containing both stories (*agaddah*) and law (*halakhah*). The Talmud is the most sacred Jewish text after the *Torah* and is comprised of the Mishnah and the Gemara. (*See* Torah and Mishnah.)

Talmud chakham (talmidei chakhamim, pl.) Someone who is wise in the learning of *Torah;* a scholar.

Tefillin Phylacteries. They consist of two black leather boxes containing parchment inscribed with Bible verses and connected to leather straps. One is worn on the left arm and the other on the forehead during morning prayers, except on Shabbat and festivals.

Torah The first five books of the Old Testament, the Pentateuch. The Torah is read aloud in the synagogue on Mondays,

Thursdays, Sabbaths, and festivals as long as a *minyan,* a quorum of ten people, is present. (In an Orthodox service the quorum must be ten men.)

Tzaddik A righteous person. This title is given to a person known for deep faith and piety. The concept of the *tzaddik* became especially important in the chasidic movement of the eighteenth century, when the *tzaddik* was regarded as possessing extraordinary powers and could serve as an intermediary between God and man. (*See* commentary notes for "The Emissary of Elijah the Prophet" regarding the *lamed vav tzaddikim.*)

Tzedakah Justice; charity.

Vortzoger A speaker of words in Yiddish. It refers to a spokesman or leader whose opinion matters and who shapes ideas of others.

Yom Kippur The Day of Atonement. It is a day of fasting and atonement, occurring on Tishri 10. It is the most important holy day of the religious year. The day is spent in the synagogue praying to be inscribed for a year of life. Yom Kippur begins on the eve before, with *Kol Nidre.* (*See* Kol Nidre.)

Yom tov A festival or holy day.

Zakhur latov "Remembered for good"; this is often added after mentioning the Prophet Elijah's name.

Zikhrono livrakhah "May his name be remembered"; said after mentioning the name of someone who has died. The words *alav hashalom* ("may peace be unto him," "may he rest in peace") are sometimes added.

Bibliography

Aarne, A., and Thompson, S. (1964). *The Types of the Folktale: A Classification and Bibliography.* 2nd rev. ed. Helsinki: Academia Scientarum Fennica.

Ashkenazi, S. (1687). *Yalkut Shim'oni.* Frankfurt.

Ausubel, N. (1948). *A Treasury of Jewish Folklore.* New York: Crown.

Baharav, Z. (1964). *Sixty Folktales* (Hebrew). Haifa: IFA Publication Society.

Ben Yehezkel, M. (1928–1929). *Sefer Ha-Ma'assiyot* (Hebrew). 4 vols. Tel Aviv: Dvir, 1925–1929; 2nd enlarged ed., 6 vols. Tel Aviv: Dvir, Leipzig. 1960.

Benfey, T., ed. (1859). *Panchatantra.* 2 vols. Leipzig.

Bin Gorion, M. J. (1916–1921). *Der Born Judas.* 2 vols. Leipzig and Frankfurt, 1966–1973.

_____ (1976). *Mimekor Yisrael.* 3 vols. Bloomington, IN: Indiana University Press.

Buber, S., ed. (1885). *Midrash Tanhuma* (Hebrew). Vilna.

Cahan, J. L., ed. (1931). *Yidishe Folksmayses* (Yiddish). New York and Vilna: Yidishe Folklor Bilyotek. 2nd ed., Vilna: 1940.

Cheichel. E., ed. (1966). *Never Despair* (Hebrew). Collected by Yifrah Haviv. Haifa: IFA Publication Society.

_____ (1968). *A Tale for Each Month 1967* (Hebrew). Haifa: IFA Publication Society.

_____ (1973). *A Tale for Each Month 1972* (Hebrew). Haifa: IFA Publication Society.

Cohen, E. (1721). *Me'il Tzedaka.* Smyrna and Lemberg: 1856.

299

Eisenstein, J. D., ed. (1915). *Otzar Midrashim (Treasury of Midrashim)* (Hebrew). 2 vols. New York.

Farhi, Y. S. (1870). *Ose Pele* (Hebrew). 3 vols. Livorno and Leghorn: 1902.

Frankel, E. (1989). *The Classic Tales: 4,000 Years of Jewish Lore.* Northvale, NJ: Jason Aronson.

Friedmann (Ish-Shalom), ed. (1902). *Seder Eliyahu Rabba* (Hebrew). Vienna; 2nd ed., Jerusalem: Bamberger and Wahrman, 1960.

———— (1904). *Seder Eliyahu Zutta* (Hebrew). Vienna; 2nd ed., Jerusalem: Bamberger and Wahrman, 1960.

Gaster, M. (1924). *The Exempla of the Rabbis.* New York: Ktav, 1968.

———— (1934). *The Maaseh Book of Jewish Tales and Legends.* 2 vols. Philadelphia: Jewish Publication Society.

Ginzberg, L. (1909–1938). *The Legends of the Jews.* 7 vols. Philadelphia: Jewish Publication Society.

Gross, N. (1955). *Ma'aselech un Mesholim* (Yiddish). New York: Distributed by the *The Forward.*

Hemdat ha-Yamim. Leghorn, 1763.

Hibbur Ma'asiyot (1647). Verona.

Horowitz, I. J. (1967). *Be'er Yitzhak* (Hebrew). Jerusalem: Kiryah Naamana.

Ibn Shahin, N. (1557). *Hibbur Yafe Mihayeshua.* Ferrara. Also Amsterdam, 1745; trans. by H. Z. Hirschberg, Jerusalem, 1953.

———— (1977). *An Elegant Composition Concerning Relief After Adversity.* Trans. W. M. Brinner. New Haven, CT: Yale University Press.

Ibn Zabara, J. (1912). *The Book of Delight (Sefer Hasha'ashuim).* Trans. I. Abrahams. Philadelphia: Jewish Publication Society.

Isaacs, A. S. (1893). *Stories from the Rabbis.* New York: Charles L. Webster.

Jason, H. (1965). Types of Jewish-Oriental oral tales. *Fabula: Journal of Folktale Studies* 7:115–224. Berlin: Walter de Gruyter.

———— (1975). *Types of Oral Tales in Israel,* Part 2. Jerusalem: Israel Ethnographic Society.

Jellinek, A., ed. (1853–1877). *Beit HaMidrash* (Hebrew). 6 vols. Leipzig and Vienna; 2nd ed., Jerusalem: Bamberger and Wahrmann, 1938.

Khalats, Y. (1558). *Sefer ha-Mussar.* Mantova.

Klapholtz, Y. Y. (1970–1979). *Stories of Elijah the Prophet.* 4 vols. Vol. 1, Jerusalem: Feldheim. Vols. 2–4, Bnei Brak, Israel: Pe'er Hasefer.

Legends of Elijah the Prophet.

Lehman, S. (1933). *The Prophet Elijah in Folk Imagination.* Warsaw.

Marcus, E., ed. (1966). *Min Ha-Mabua (From the Fountainhead)* (Hebrew). Haifa: IFA Publication Society.

Marvels of Maharal.

Nahman of Bratislaw (1881). *Sippure Ma'assiyot.* Warsaw. Also Lemberg: 1902.

Neuman (Noy), Dov. (1954). *Motif-Index of Talmudic-Midrashic Literature,* dissertation. Bloomington, IN: Indiana University Press.

Noy, Dov (1960). "Elijah the Prophet on the Seder Night" (Hebrew). Haifa: Museum of Ethnology and Folklore.

_____ (1961a). The first thousand folktales in the Israel Folklore Archives. *Fabula* 4:99–110.

_____ (1961b). *Folktales of Israel.* Chicago: University of Chicago Press.

_____ , ed. (1963). *A Tale for Each Month 1962* (Hebrew). Collected by A. Elbaz and S. Elbaz. Haifa: IFA Publication Society.

_____ , ed. (1966). *A Tale for Each Month 1965* (Hebrew). Haifa: IFA Publication Society.

_____ , ed. (1971). *A Tale for Each Month 1970* (Hebrew). Haifa: IFA Publication Society.

_____ , ed. (1976). *Faithful Guardians* (Hebrew). Collected by Zvi Moshe Haimovits. Haifa: IFA Publication Society.

_____ (1978). *A Tale for Each Month 1974–1975* (Hebrew). Jerusalem: IFA Publication Society.

_____ (1979a). *A Tale for Each Month 1976–1977 (Hebrew). Haifa: IFA Publication Society.*

_____ , ed. (1979b). *A Tale for Each Month 1978* (Hebrew). Haifa: IFA Publication Society.

Noy, M. (1968). *East European Jewish Cante Fables* (Hebrew). Haifa: IFA Publication Society.

Otzar ha-Massiyot.

Patai, R., Utley, F. L., and Noy, D., eds. (1973). *Studies in Biblical and Jewish Folklore.* New York: Haskell House.

Plungian, Z. (1857). *Sefer Zekhirah.* Warsaw.

Rotenberg, Y. I. (1911). *Eliyahu ha-Navi.* Podgorze.

Sadeh, P. (1989). *Jewish Folktales.* Trans. H. Halkin. New York: Doubleday.

Schram, P. (1987). *Jewish Stories One Generation Tells Another.* Northvale, NJ: Jason Aronson.

Schwartz, H. (1983). *Elijah's Violin & Other Jewish Fairy Tales.* New York: Harper & Row.

———— (1986). *Miriam's Tambourine: Jewish Folktales from around the World.* New York: The Free Press.

Schwartz, Z. (1977). *Temimei Derech.* Brooklyn, NY: Hevra Mafitzay Torah M'Mishpachat Kol Aryeh.

Schwarzbaum, H. (1962–1963). "The Prophet Elijah and Rabbi Joshua ben Levi" (Hebrew). *Yeda-Am,* VII. 22–31 (Journal of the Israel Folklore Society). Tel Aviv. 12 vols (1948–1967).

———— (1968). *Studies in Jewish and World Folklore.* Berlin: Walter De Gruyter.

Sefer Gevurath Israel (1924) (Hebrew). Warsaw.

Sefer ha-Bdiha Veha-Hiddud.

Segel, Bar Ami (1904). Elijah der Prophet; eine Studie zur judischen Volks—und Sagenkunde. *Ost und West* (German). Berlin.

Sihot Hayim (chapbook). Piotrkov, s.a.

Sihot Yekarot.

Sippurei Massiot (1971). Jerusalem: Mosad Harav Kook.

Sippurei Tsaddikim (1886). Cracow.

Steinschneider, M., ed. (1858). *The Alphabet of Ben Sira.* Berlin.

Tendlau, A. (1860). *Spruchworter und Redensarten deutsch-judischer Vorzeit* (German). Frankfurt am Main.

Thompson, S. (1966). *Motif-Index of Folk Literature.* 6 vols. Rev. ed. Bloomington, IN: Indiana University Press.

Weinreich, B. S. (1957). *The Prophet Elijah in Modern Yiddish Folktales* (unpublished M.A. thesis). New York: Columbia University.

———— (1965). Genres and types of Yiddish folktales about the Prophet Elijah. In *The Field of Yiddish: Studies in Language, Folklore, and Literature,* ed. U. Weinreich, pp. 202–231. London: Mouton.

———— (1988). *Yiddish Folktales.* Trans. L. Wolf. New York: Pantheon.

Wiener, Aharon (1978). *The Prophet Elijah in the Development of Judaism: A Depth-Psychological Study.* London: Routledge & Kegan Paul.

Yalkut Sippurim Umidrashim (Hebrew). (1923). Warsaw.

Index

ABOUT THE AUTHOR

Peninnah Schram is internationally known as a professional storyteller and recording artist. A native of New London, Connecticut, she graduated from the University of Connecticut and Columbia University. She is an Associate Professor of Speech and Drama at Stern College of Yeshiva University in New York City.

Ms. Schram is the founding director of the Jewish Storytelling Center at the 92nd Street YM-YWHA in New York City. She has written several books, including *The Big Sukkah*, an illustrated children's book, and *Jewish Stories One Generation Tells Another*, a volume that features sixty-four stories from the Jewish oral tradition. She is also the co-author, with Steven M. Rosman, of *Eight Tales for Eight Nights: Stories for Chanukah*.